Michael Pye

Strategies in the Study of Religions

Religion and Reason

Founded by Jacques Waardenburg

Edited by
Gustavo Benavides and Michael Stausberg

Volume 51

De Gruyter

Michael Pye

Strategies in the Study of Religions

Volume One: Exploring Methods and Positions

De Gruyter

ISBN 978-1-5015-1300-8
e-ISBN 978-1-61451-189-2
ISSN 0080-0848

Library of Congress Cataloging-in-Publication Data

A CIP catalog record for this book has been applied for at the Library of Congress.

Bibliographic information published by the Deutsche Nationalbibliothek

The Deutsche Nationalbibliothek lists this publication in the Deutsche Nationalbibliografie; detailed bibliographic data are available in the Internet at http://dnb.dnb.de.

Printing: Hubert & Co. GmbH & Co. KG, Göttingen
∞ Printed on acid-free paper

Printed in Germany

www.degruyter.com

Dedication

This work is dedicated to
Christine Pye
who has accompanied my comings and goings for so many years and supported my endeavours with endlessly faithful criticism and good-will

Preface

The idea for this collection was first proposed by Jacques Waardenburg, the former editor of the series Religion and Reason, with whom I have been privileged to be acquainted for nearly half a century. Our approach to the study of religions is in many ways similar and we have both sought to ensure the stability and long-term welfare of this discipline in our writings and other work in the academic world. My thanks are gratefully extended to him. In addition, my sincere thanks are due to Albrecht Döhnert, Alissa Jones Nelson, and Michael Stausberg, on the publishing and editorial sides respectively, who have shown both patience and persistence in helping this work forward to the stage of its *de facto* appearance. I would also like to acknowledge the support of various academic institutions, notably the universities of Lancaster and Leeds in England, the University of Marburg in Germany (formally known as the Philipps-Universität Marburg after the landgrave who supported the protestant Reformation), and most recently the Buddhist-oriented Ōtani University in Kyōto, Japan.

There are many individual persons throughout the world who have helped me in my work over the years, whether with critical commentary, linguistic expertise, practical research arrangements, contextual conferences, and in some cases co-publication. This is noted at the various relevant places below, but my heartfelt thanks go also to many others who have helped me in indirect ways but who are not personally named in any particular papers selected for inclusion. I am extremely grateful to all those understanding colleagues and advanced students who have both listened and responded to my efforts in various contexts. I hope that I have sometimes given something back. One sometimes experiences the loneliness of the long-distance runner in training, and yet when it comes to the real marathon there seem to be more and more of us who follow the great route, and not necessarily in competition. My hope is that, if only in small ways, the papers collected here will encourage others to follow through some of the strategies which are outlined below, and which require much more than the efforts of a mere individual.

Michael Pye
Marburg, April 2012

Editorial Note

The papers selected for inclusion in these volumes have arisen over the course of many years and have appeared in extremely varied places, often not readily accessible. The central intention here is to present each paper as it was conceived at the time, while setting it in the context of a wider pattern of thought. In most cases therefore hardly any changes have been made during the compilation and editing process. Typological errors have been corrected and the orthography of non-English terms and names has in some cases been up-dated. Sometimes a sentence has been polished for greater clarity without changing the sense. Where an article has been abbreviated to avoid undue overlap with others, this is signaled. In the original articles references were sometimes made to earlier publications, and these have been left in place; new here is a certain amount of cross-referencing between the articles, using the numeration shown in the contents pages.

Each article is provided with a brief indication of its original context, at the head, and the details of its earlier publication, if any, at the end. In quite a few cases (as academics often experience) a paper was "presented" at a conference in one year only to have a much later first publication date. In a few places, a clearly marked "retrospective footnote" may also be found which gives some relevant updated information or signposting.

Bibliographical streamlining using the "author-date" system has been undertaken throughout, and this has reduced the number and length of the original footnotes. In some cases bibliographical details could be improved or completed. References to writings of the present author are differentiated alphabetically within any one year, as required; but to avoid clashes between the reference lists of different articles, the alphabetic designation follows a systematic list which is given at the end of each volume.

This editorial process means that the individual articles no longer look quite like photocopies of the originals. Nevertheless, no significant revisions of content have been undertaken. Consequently, thought sequences across the forty years from 1972 up until 2012 will be readily discernible for any readers who are interested in that aspect. In sum, any one article can be read in its own right, as originally intended; yet the coordinated arrangement over seven well-defined parts maps out the author's understanding of various options, strategies and opportunities in the study of religions.

Contents

Volume I: Exploring Methods and Positions

Volume II: Exploring Religions in Motion

General Introduction

The papers drawn together in these two volumes reflect many years of work in the study of religions and have been selected in particular to illustrate methodological and theoretical aspects of this academic discipline. The strategies documented below have found particular application, in the course of the writer's own research, in the field of Japanese religions and Mahāyāna Buddhism. For reasons of space however the number of detailed papers on such subjects has been kept to a minimum. It is hoped, nevertheless, that even with restraint in detail a certain picture will emerge of what it is like to study any religions at all. Various questions are high-lighted which arise in similar ways whichever religious traditions and systems are being studied. Indeed, as will be seen below, the approaches taken have in fact been tested with respect to a wider range of religions throughout the world. If at various points a certain amount of detail is allowed to show through, this is because it is considered inappropriate to expatiate on matters of method and theory without ever studying religions in the historical or contemporary field.

While there is no normative orthodoxy in the study of religions, certain perspectives have gradually been establishing themselves over the years. There are general ways of going about things, or "strategies" as we call them here, which in spite of variations are nowadays widely understood by researchers in this field. The papers selected below reflect several such strategies, illustrating the manner of their emergence, some of the ways in which they are applied, and how they hold together. It is believed that this broad coherence in the discipline here called "the study of religions" will be more important in the long run than the inevitable disputes and indeed interesting debates over particular initiatives taken from time to time.

Since these papers are drawn from a long period of activity, some of the older ones may seem old-fashioned – depending on the reader's academic formation. The writer is well aware of this. However the more recent papers may not seem particularly fashionable either! In some cases a certain development may be seen, a strengthening of perceptions and a widening of the range of reference points. Any readers interested in such developments should also take account of other writings not included here, for this is by no means a comprehensive collection. At the same time there is an overall consistency. This arises not least because the field – the phenomenon of "religions" – has not gone away during recent decades. Indeed this writer, against the trend of some older sociology, and thanks to numerous impressions gained in Asia and in Eastern Europe during times of presumed secularization, never expected it to do so.

Consistency will also be remarked because now, as before and indeed perhaps more than ever, it is necessary to study religions as they are, as far as possible without prejudice or distortion. It is often claimed that this cannot be done, that "we" all have our childhood assumptions, prejudices arising from religious indoctrination, massive training in western philosophy of the Greek variety, or other distorting assumptions, which we bring to bear on religious systems of innocently unsuspecting peoples. This problem is usually exaggerated and often functions as an excuse for not even trying to study phenomena as they arise before us. Of course there are procedural difficulties. Of course there are also failures. However, the many years of work reflected here, mainly research-related but also institutional and organisational, has been dedicated to precisely such an objective. Whatever an individual's long-term or changing personal judgements about particular religions may be, the corporate achievement of reliable knowledge and analytical perceptions about the religious systems in the world cannot but be a worthwhile matter.

We distinguish here between an academic field and an academic discipline. The study of religions, or to use the convenient single German term, *Religionswissenschaft*, is understood here to be an integrated academic *discipline*. There is of course also the *field* with which this discipline is concerned, which is, quite precisely, religions, i. e. religious systems in all their complexity. Note that the plural "religions" is used to designate this field. By "field" is meant, in this context, the whole of the history of religions together with the contemporary range of religions in today's world. This field is studied by people with varying expertise in a range of disciplines, especially in the social sciences and in history, who focus with greater or lesser clarity on religious systems as such, and show considerable interest in contextual and often quite extraneous matters. However, a vague multi-disciplinary approach not infrequently leads to analytical confusion. By contrast it is contended here that the study of religions can be understood and carried out in practice as a coherent discipline in its own right, and that it should be. Of course it is fructified by other disciplines, and quite rightly so. However it is a discipline which arises in relation to the academic, or more precisely the scientific study[1] of its own particular field. This discipline can be learned and, of course, improved.

In general, the clarification of what is required methodologically, and what is necessary or feasible theoretically, is best carried out in the context of specific studies. Supposedly pure theory or pure methodology can easily be out of touch with the field itself. By contrast it is characteristic of most of the essays below that there are various references to the on-going study of particular cases or examples, even though such studies are not themselves presented in extensive detail.

The seven parts of this work in two volumes will each be introduced specifically as we come to them, and so only a few words will be said about them here. We begin with a number of "methodological orientations" in Part One. As explained in the first essay, entitled "Methodological integration in the study of religions" (1.2), delicate correlations are required between the various methods which can be drawn upon for working out the study of religions as an integrated discipline. Some of these are more relevant to contemporary studies of religion, and some are more relevant to the study of religions in history. For example, the contemporary field of religions may be studied partly, and not least, by means of field-work. Yet this does not imply that the whole field of religions is restricted to that which is accessible by means of "field-work" in the style of anthropology. The latter discipline does not always reach the relevant parts of what may be called *deep tradition.* Another methodologically sensitive matter is the problem of the relations between the work of those who specialize in the study of religions and the frequently powerful religious traditions and systems themselves, with their often articulate representatives. These relations, sometimes summed up as the insider/outsider problem, are often perfectly harmonious but can also be quite tricky. They can be best understood by methodologically alert specialists who have actively pursued their own

1 It would not be wrong to refer to this discipline as "the scientific study of religions" if the notion of "science" is taken to include historical and related research as well as social-scientific and other approaches such as cognitive studies. However the simpler expression "study of religions" is marginally preferred for the sake of its simplicity. It should always be taken as understood that we are referring to an academic discipline which is ruled by the appropriate scientific methodology and is not some kind of religious "study" intended to support a particular religious program of some kind.

work in real situations. It is only those who in fact study religions who will experience "getting into trouble with the believers" –the subject of the concluding paper in Part One.

Part Two is about the international character of the study of religions in an intellectual sense. As hinted already the study of religions is usually somehow rooted in deep-seated assumptions about what "religion" might be, varying in different cultural regions. These assumptions therefore have to be brought out and reflected upon if the discipline is to have any kind of world-wide coherence. But difference is not everything. One of the major assertions in this work, as in the previous publications drawn upon, is that the study of religions is not and should not be thought of as entirely culture-bound. Part Two therefore, entitled "East Asian starting points," is devoted to an exploration of ways in which this is not so, with special though not exclusive reference to the case of Japan. While this matter has often been overlooked, in spite of a longer sequence of papers than can be reproduced here, there should no longer be any excuse for that.

In Part Three, entitled "Structures and Strategies," we turn to the international character of the study of religions in an organizational and institutional sense. If the study of religions may be thought of as a discipline in its own right, then it needs its international organizational and institutional bases, just as it needs its lectureships and professorships in various countries. As a relatively underprivileged discipline there is always the danger of its being taken over and subsumed by larger interests such as (in some countries) theology or by one of the social or behavioural sciences such as sociology, in which the canons of such an institutionally stronger discipline are regarded as the norm, with distorting effects for the study of religions. These problems have often been debated in the relevant organs, journals and electronic lists, and the writer's own positions regarding them have remained quite stable over the years. In part, the papers relating to this reflect my active participation in the work of the International Association for the History of Religions (IAHR) and its various affiliated national and regional associations.

It might be thought that "comparing and contrasting," the theme of Part Four, is also an aspect of methodological orientation, and so indeed it is. Methodological orientations continue to be unfolded as strategies are worked out. As is often noted, the phrase "comparative religion" has had a chequered history, and while it was once used in some quarters as the name of the subject itself (without differentiation between field and discipline), it has since become deeply unfashionable. The writer is not in favour of its re-introduction as the name of an academic discipline, for in fact it can only be a part of a discipline. Religions or elements of religions can only be compared if those religions are first, or at the same time, studied in their own right. The question of balance in this regard often comes jumping out as a problem in the delineation of dissertation topics. Students may wish to "compare" things which they have not studied, or they may wish to study particular cases without well-considered reference to more broadly, and hence comparatively based terminology. In fact, the process of comparing and contrasting is unavoidable if a serious analysis of religions is to be attempted. While illustrating these matters in Part Four the process of methodological reflection will be continued.

Indeed, acts of comparison continue to inform Parts Five and Six. If throughout the years there has been one set of features of religious systems which has been of particular interest to this writer, it may be summed up as the "dynamics of religion." The expression refers to the operating patterns of religious systems in motion, which in some way or other they always are. While somewhat distinctive understandings of terms such as "tradition" and "syncretism" are documented here, these understandings have, as usual, been worked out in a variety of specific contexts, and are broadly based. While much of the writer's work has been centred on Japanese religions and on Buddhism in wider Asian contexts, he has carried with him a grounded knowledge and a continued interest in various branches of the Christian tradition. Moreover, the task of teaching about a variety of religions has quite appropriately been accompanied and underpinned by wide-ranging, though otherwise unpublished personal observations of Islam, Sikhism, Cao Dai, Chinese religions and others. The concepts discussed in Part Five and Part Six have therefore been carefully considered with regard to their viability and heuristic value in various contexts, even though the presentation of case studies is limited here for practical reasons.

Finally, while it is asserted again and again that "the study of religions" should maintain a clear profile as an academic (or as some might say, a "scientific") enterprise, it is not inappropriate to take a look at the borderlands of this discipline. The present writer takes what will probably seem to be a relatively hard line in the identification of the discipline as such and seeks to avoid the woolly approach which often characterises "religious studies" in the popular mind. Nevertheless, the essays in Part Seven take up a number of contextual matters: "identity, plurality, dialogue, education, peace", which are understandably matters of great concern to many in the contemporary world. Such themes, or variations upon them, go beyond "the study of religions" more precisely conceived, and yet, unsurprisingly, are often highlighted in particular conferences around the world. It is hoped that, with all due attention to the varied substance addressed here, readers will also appreciate how "the study of religions" can maintain its own disciplinary integrity in such a complex world, contributing to our understanding of it and even, if only by extension, to its better management. At the same time, several of the previous, more analytical topics will be found to resurface in the papers in Part Seven. This is because responsible discussion of such further questions should presuppose serious study of the field in the first place.

Coming full circle, the overall aim of the seven parts of these two volumes is to present a view of certain working academic orientations, procedures and strategies in a world-wide perspective. It is hoped that by assembling these hitherto rather far-flung papers under one title, a contribution will be made to the conceptual strengthening and further development of "the study of religions" as an academic discipline which can find widespread assent and bear fruit in future generations.

Part One
Methodological Strategies

1.1 Introduction to Part One

The study of religions as an academic discipline has attracted at least its fair share of methodological debate, especially in the western world, during the process of its extraction and crystallization from within the wider range of scholarly endeavour. It is quite natural therefore that here in Part One some articles should first be assembled which set out the way in which the study of religions is to be understood. This discipline has emerged over many years in the context of universities all over the world in a process which has required continual critical reflection. A major feature of this process of "discipline identification" (as it is referred to in 1.2 and 3.2 below) has been the drawing of distinctions with regard to other academic perspectives, while at the same time the study of religions draws perforce on many of these for methodological and theoretical stimuli.

In the western world, a major distinction which should be noted immediately is that between the normative, partly normative, or would-be normative perspective of Christian theology, and the observational, exploratory, comparative, analytical and explanatory undertakings of "the study of religions" or, to use the convenient German term, *Religionswissenschaft*. Unfortunately, in Britain and in North America the use of the expression "religious studies" has often had the effect, either deliberately, or just vaguely misleadingly, to slur over such a difference. Institutional and organizational complications of this necessary distinction will be further considered in Part Three below. It may be gladly admitted that Christian theology in its various academic forms has itself included, at least in modern times, certain forms of study which are non-normative, or largely non-normative, especially in the areas of historical, textual, contextual, and philosophical enquiry. Obviously, the specifics vary greatly across the world, and to some extent in accordance with denominational orientation.

In terms of academic history, this relationship is complicated by two further features. First, the study of religions arose in the west not only in the context of Christian theology, but has also been derived quite massively both from philologically grounded oriental studies addressing major world civilizations and from various social sciences such as social anthropology. Professionally speaking, academics continue to enter the discipline of the study of religions from these very diverse directions and consequently, whether they recognise it or not, they need to redirect or re-acquire their academic orientation to take account of the field with which they newly concern themselves. This process may be spoken of as discipline identification.

For the comprehension of what follows, a few autobiographical elements will be mentioned here to illustrate the writer's own appropriation of the study of religions as a sustained academic task. Having benefited at Cambridge University (England) from the Modern and Mediaeval Languages syllabus which contained not only literature but also "history of ideas" elements, I turned to a range of subjects in a Theology syllabus which was not (and today also is not) denominationally defined. These studies were undertaken as a humanistic exercise without any related professional intentions. A far-sighted supervisor in theology also directed me to a decidedly non-theological course on the historical development of social anthropology, which was running at the same time. Following these studies came an extended sojourn in Japan (1961–6) which led to an encounter with, and observations of the plurality of religions in that land. Some years later a further personal process of discipline identification was induced and clarified because of new teaching duties at Lancaster University in England, under the leadership of Ninian Smart. Autobiography is not the intention here, but it may be helpful for the reader to know that, in effect, the writer experienced, through individual discovery, a kind of recapitulation of the wider development and crystallization of the study of religions as an emergent discipline in its own right.

In the early days, that is, in the 1960 s and 1970 s, it was still necessary to work out a positioning *vis-à-vis* the phenomenological school of religion, partly rejecting it and partly respecting it. It was partly rejected precisely because its representatives often failed to separate the normative from the descriptive, the programmatic from the comparative and analytical. It was partly accepted, on the other hand, because its representatives sought to understand matters lying outside the regular thought patterns of the investigator, but within the thought patterns of those being investigated. The idea of empathy was similar to the readiness of anthropologists to respect emic viewpoints. But the further baggage of philosophical phenomenology had inhibited the necessary clarifications and seemed to have little methodological relevance. The basic argument over this will be found in the introductory chapter of my early work *Comparative Religion. An Introduction through Source Materials* (1972a).[1]

The very idea of "comparative religion" has often been presumed to be inherently value-laden, but this does not have to be so. Rather, the act of comparison itself is a perfectly normal feature of any kind of investigative research, a point which will be further developed in Part Four. On the other hand, it has for long been common to refer to "religion" in the singular, as if we automatically know what that is, even though various religions have increasingly been held in view. It is therefore quite appropriate that more recently the plural form "religions" has come to be preferred, as far as grammatically convenient. In fact the plurality of religions has always been recognized by the present writer and is presupposed in the essays presented here, even where the singular form may sometimes be found. Indeed, it was the recognition of religions in their plurality at the time of the European Enlightenment which provided one of the first important motivations for a different, non-theological kind of investigation, a modern, relativized, non-normative one. However, there are Asian parallels to this, as will be seen later in Part Two. It is in general significant that comparative and historical studies belong naturally together in the study of religions.

It is argued at many places below that the study of religions can and should be understood as an independently functioning academic discipline, and not just something which can be subsumed according to taste under theological, sociological or other discourses. This need was the subject of "The study of religion as an autonomous discipline" (1982a), published (appropriately) in the journal *Religion*. The title of this article has sometimes been carelessly misread as suggesting that "religion" is some kind of autonomous item in a semi-platonic universe, leading even to accusations of "essentialism". This is a gross misunderstanding. There is no intention here, or anywhere else, to turn the study of religions (*Religionswissenschaft*) into a search for some unifying "essence" of religion, making it a kind of surrogate theological endeavour, as some associated with the phenomenological school did. The idea that there is a common "essence" of religion is itself no more than an interesting datum in the history of religions. It is fascinating that people have tried to search for it! It should also be clearly understood that the idea of an "essence of religion" (*Wesen der Religion*) is not at all the same as the

1 Cf. also the short article from the same period entitled "Problems of method in the interpretation of religion" (Pye 1974).

idea of "the essence" (also *Wesen*) of a particular religious tradition such as Christianity; the latter simply summarizes a task of interpretation which raises itself again and again for those involved in particular traditions, i. e. above all for its theologians. Since this question, in some form or other, does not go away for the religious persons themselves, it needs to be followed with interest by those who study the processes of religious tradition (cf. Part Five below).

If the study of religions is to be "autonomous," and refers to a specific field, what is the field? The reader will find that normative definitions of religion are consistently eschewed here. They would simply bring all the problems back in again. Nevertheless the field of study can be adumbrated in various ways, so that an investigator can begin to attend to it. The verb "to adumbrate" appears to be not widely understood; according to *Chambers English Dictionary* (Schwarz 1990) it means "to give a faint shadow of" or "to shadow forth" and so I use it to imply a tentatively sketching out. The question of whether or not particular "cases" of religion[2] or similar phenomena are to be included in such a preliminary sketch should be considered pragmatically on the basis of the concept of family resemblances. The field has fuzzy edges. Nevertheless, strict attention should be paid to a consistent morphology. Moreover working definitions of sub-concepts (such as syncretism, on which see further in Part Six) can be profitably used. The various distinctions touched on here were also summed up, it may be hoped conveniently, and a little combatively, in "Religion: shape and shadow" (Pye 1994b, not included in these volumes).

The question of the relations between the study of religions and other disciplines may seem to remain. The discussion is sometimes haunted by the supposition that if there is a particular field to be studied, there must be a particular, special method with which to study it. However the answer to this is simply that there simply is no special or unique method which is somehow peculiar to the study of religions. The older espousal of the so-called "phenomenological method" may have been an attempt to find one, suggesting that special knowledge could be gained by researchers who disposed not only of widely based information but also had special personal insights. In spite of that red herring, or

2 The former Cambridge philosopher of religion Donald MacKinnon once chuckled at length over the idea that one could speak of "a case of religion," which however seemed to me then as now to be a completely natural expression if one is studying phenomena which are tentatively designated as religions.

distraction, it is certainly necessary to cluster the available scientific methods in an appropriate manner, as explained below in "Methodological integration in the study of religions" (1.2). It is this selection and clustering of methods which is specific to the study of religions. Every field of study requires its appropriate methods, but this does not usually mean that they are unique. It is the particular combination of otherwise known and available methods which is special to any one academic discipline. The further significance of this is set out in the second essay below, entitled "Field and theory in the study of religions" (1.3).

On this basis, more practicalities are worked out in the further papers selected for Part One. The writer's exposure to Japan led progressively to the prosecution of field observations, over many years as occasion permitted, and hence to methodological reflection on the relation of fieldwork on contemporary religion to historical perspectives, the theory of tradition and so on. Fieldwork itself gave rise to an interest in particular concepts such as primal religion or civil religion, and to the rejection of some worn-out but ill-defined phrases such as "folk religion." In field-based studies it is also necessary to consider the nature of various kinds of source material, and the value of ephemera is highlighted in this regard, particularly but not only for Japanese situations. Ephemera provide a particularly helpful way of resolving certain problems of access, a matter discussed below in "Philology, fieldwork and ephemera in the study of Japanese religions" (1.4, dating from 1990 in an earlier version). The two concluding papers in Part One offer more widely ranging discussion of the opportunities and sensitive areas of field work: "Participation, observation and reflection: an endless method" (1.5, from 2000) and "Getting into trouble with the believers. Intimacy and distance in the study of religions" (1.6, from 2004, but previously unpublished). Themes such as insider/outsider relations have frequently been discussed on an "armchair" basis, but the discussions presented here arise substantially out of the practice of the discipline itself.

Bibliographical references

Pye, Michael 1972a. *Comparative Religion: An Introduction through Source Materials.* Newton Abbot (David and Charles) and) and New York (Harper and Row).

– 1974. "Problems of method in the interpretation of religion" in: *Japanese Journal of Religious Studies* 1 (2–3): 107–123.
– 1982a. "The study of religion as an autonomous discipline" in: *Religion* 12: 67–76.
– 1994b. "Religion: shape and shadow" in: *Numen. International Review for the History of Religions* 41 (1): 51–75.
Schwarz, Catherine et al. (eds.) 1990. *Chambers English Dictionary*. Edinburgh (W. & R. Chambers).

N.B. Publication details of articles cross-referenced within these volumes will be found at the end of the article in question and in the list at the end of each volume.

1.2 Methodological Integration in the Study of Religions

The following was first advanced at a symposium on methodology in the study of religions at the Donner Institute in Åbo (Turku), Finland, in 1997 and published in its proceedings in 1999.

Methodological clustering

These pages present a call for an integrated approach to the academic study of religions which does justice to its specificity, but without separating it artificially from other related avenues of research. For a discipline to reflect upon its methods is a normal part of academic endeavour, and this applies to the study of religions (or *Religionswissenschaft*[1]) as much as to any other scientific research. This statement implies, and is intended to imply, that the study of religions may be regarded as a "discipline". "Religions" constitute a field of study and accordingly "the study of religion (or religions)" is a discipline. What is a discipline, that is, in the scientific sense? It is no more, and no less, than a methodically ordered approach to the study of a field. The field "religion(s)", no less than any other fields, requires a methodically ordered approach for its study. The methodically ordered approach, the discipline, takes on particular characteristics as required for the best study of the field. Consequently, the discipline of the study of religion(s) is not necessarily quite the same as the discipline required for the study of other fields, though it may be rather similar to the discipline required for the study of closely related fields.

1 The German term (like its equivalent in various languages) has the advantage of including the element "science" in it, but the disadvantage of referring to religion in the singular. Care should be taken to avoid the term which puts the sciences into the plural, namely *Religionswissenschaften*, for this suggests on the one hand that "religion" is one, idealised entity, while on the other hand avoiding the strenuous task of being clear about what the appropriate science for its investigation is.

The view of the field and the understanding of the discipline interact with each other. A stable methodological perspective corresponds to a stable view of the field. The destabilisation of either leads to the destabilisation of the other. However, an advance in methodology may lead to a correction in the view of the field, and on the other hand, newly perceived or newly emergent features in the field may lead to pressures on currently held understandings of method. While openness to the recasting of perspectives is desirable, one may hope nevertheless for a certain, relative stability in the understanding of both field and discipline, for otherwise the critical interaction between individual investigators typical of a "science" cannot function at all. It is to be hoped that conferences on the subject of methodology in the study of religions, as famously held in Turku, contribute to the stabilisation process.[2] When there is relative stability, the discipline can be learned, practised, taught, corrected and developed.

The understanding that there is, and indeed must be such a process of methodological development and reflection does not imply that the study of religions has some one special method, unique to itself. At the same time the discipline of the study of religions requires its own particular gathering, or as we might better say, clustering, of methods. Though the methods at our disposal are in themselves known in the context of other disciplines, they are brought together in a particular way in order to facilitate the study of the precise field in question, namely religions. The resultant discipline is not quite the same as the disciplines required for the study of other fields, or of fields differently defined.

It is desirable to clarify, at this point in the argument, the nature of the specificity which the discipline requires and the reasons for which it should be affirmed. It arises firstly for the simple reason that there does not seem to be any other one, single discipline which could plausibly claim to be, alone and precisely, the discipline required for the study of religions. For example, "history" does not quite fit the requirements, because it does not usually include the methodological niceties of carrying out fieldwork among living people. Nor however does "sociology",

2 I am referring to the IAHR conferences on methodology in 1973 (cf. Honko 1979) and in 1997 (cf. Ahlbäck 1999). On the whole I believe that these conferences have in fact tended to stabilise methodology, even though in each case some contributions might provide illustrations for some of the difficulties discussed in the next section of this paper.

because in general, quite correctly in its own terms, it subordinates the study of religious ideas and behaviour to wider questions about the nature and functioning of society. Such questions are of course valuable, but there are other questions of interest concerning religious idea-complexes, for example questions about their internal structure and dynamics, which are not necessarily "sociological" in nature. For analogous reasons the disciplines of anthropology, art history, archaeology, political science, and so on, also do not amount to just that discipline which is required, overall, for the study of religions. Unfortunately the use of the words "autonomy" or "autonomous" have sometimes been subject to misunderstanding or to misuse in this connection. This is because they have frequently been associated with an "essentialist" or "sui generis" view of religion as a unitary phenomenon, that is, with the idea that behind all the various religions there is some unifying essence which only specialists in religion can understand and which makes their study different in kind from the study of anything else. This position is by no means adopted here. Nor shall it even be discussed at this point, since such a view of religions is not relevant to the argument being advanced.[3] It is quite a different matter to point out that none of the other disciplines currently practiced in the human and social sciences specifically and adequately relate to the field of "religions". In some way or other they fail adequately to explore or elucidate the subject matter. Some do too little, and some, it might be said, do too much. This does not mean that the study of religions requires a special method which is unique to itself. What it does mean is that the right selection of available methods must be made and that these must be clustered together in a manner appropriate to the subject matter.

While it is necessary to realise that a specific clustering of methods is necessary to maintain and develop the discipline of the study of religions, it is not necessarily important to achieve complete agreement about what this clustering of methods should look like. Consequently there is no intention to offer a dogmatic statement about it here. Nevertheless, after clearing the way with some notes on present difficulties and the reasons for them, the following presentation will seek to

3 To avoid any misunderstanding it may be added that the intention behind the usage in the phrase "The study of religion as an autonomous discipline" (Pye 1982a) is consistent with the approach being taken here. Unfortunately the word "autonomous" may have too many misleading associations and so should perhaps be avoided.

show what such a clustering of methods might reasonably be expected to look like. The statement is formulated in what may appear to some to be disappointingly uncomplicated terms. However, this is intentional and is regarded here as an advantage. Simplicity is a strength, not a weakness. It is anticipated that those who are themselves engaged in the study of religions, in practice, will find it relatively easy to reach broad agreement along these lines. And indeed it is important, while continuing the methodological discussion within the discipline, that there should be a widely recognisable tradition of study which can be identified as "the study of religions" (or whatever formulation is preferred). Indeed, it may be maintained that to some extent there is already such a recognisable tradition of study, even if it is in need of greater crystallization.

Reasons for some present difficulties

Unfortunately, in spite of much attention to methodological questions in the study of religion there continues to be uncertainty, vagueness, and even irresponsibility in not a few quarters. Why is the methodological identity of the study of religion so widely misunderstood? There are various reasons.

First, it is deplorable that basic distinctions which ought to be easily understood continue to be slurred over or dismissed as trivial. A classic example of this is the difference between studying religious statements and making religious statements. It is remarkable, but true, that even today, after decades of methodological clarification, it is still necessary to make this distinction clear. Again and again, theologians appear who confidently assert that they are making statements which pertain to *Religionswissenschaft*, when they are in fact giving a *religious* analysis of some cultural situation. It is not surprising that other members of the public, even of academe, cannot take the trouble of making this distinction. However, as most real specialists in the study of religions would agree today, it is quite significant for the study of religion that it should not be identified with the making of religious statements. That would be a matter for theologians, Buddhist apologists, neo-shamans, and many others.

Second, there is a certain amount of intellectually obstinate compartmentalization furthered by the use of conventional phrases such as "comparative religion", "phenomenology of religion", "anthropology of religion", "psychology of religion" and so on. Though these are usually recognised to have a certain history, which is rehearsed from time to time, it is not so common to see them assessed conspectually and critically, with a view to their correlation, integration or abandonment as might be required. More commonly they are just listed as options which people may take up as they please. However if the field is regarded as coherent, then a greater degree of methodological coordination, or even integration, is intellectually desirable and ought therefore to be sought. For example "comparative religion" or "comparative study of religions" cannot really exist by itself. Nor can "ethnology of religion", in spite of the immensely valuable contributions of those working at the interface between ethnology and the study of religions.[4]

Third, persons coming freshly to the subject often bring with them methodological perspectives which have been strongly formed in other disciplinary contexts. This is often enriching, but can also perpetuate mistaken assumptions and misunderstandings about the study of religions. Thus it sometimes happens that a person who has been trained as an anthropologist or ethnologist, and who goes on to specialise in religion, simply does not go to the trouble of acquiring a methodological orientation in the discipline of the study of religions. Humanly speaking, this may be acceptable in itself, depending on the case and the situation, but it becomes irresponsible when younger students, new to the subject, are told that the study of religions as such has no particular method. In such cases it appears that the researchers in question feel a professional need to continue to be identified above all as whatever they were before. Anthropologists, for example, once they have undergone their double initiation through field work and first publication, are sometimes a bit like boy scouts who have the saying "Once a scout, always a scout". The result is a failure to achieve "discipline identification"[5] or integration with respect to specialised, or new fields of study such as "religions".

A fourth reason for a certain amount of confusion is the development of serious methodological divergence as the result of an interest

4 Phrases built on the pattern "ethnology of x" and equivalents in other languages such as "X-ethnologie" are easily framed but usually very imprecise in their meaning.

5 Although it may sound somewhat forbidding, this phrase (Pye 1991b, see 3.2 below) refers to a normal and appropriate process in any discipline which is enriched by recruits from varied quarters.

in new lines of thought which seem to make their own methodological claims. Sometimes new insights in a particular direction seem to demand to take over the methodological discussion entirely, while earlier gains are despised or forgotten. For example, because it is interesting to consider religion as a pattern of brain operations, we are tempted to regard cognitive science as *the* appropriate method for studying religions. If we are not careful, the need for fieldwork, for textual studies, and for disciplined comparison may then be forgotten. Putting it more generally, it is not infrequent for interesting figures such as Claude Lévi-Strauss or Michel Foucault to make the running, creating a bandwagon effect which disregards some of the everyday methodological requirements of the study of religions. The impact of various intellectual currents must surely be taken up keenly by specialists in religion, as in the case of other disciplines, but at the same time it is necessary to work out carefully where the possibilities of integration lie. Otherwise tested and worthwhile methods will simply be scorned or forgotten in favour of a series of fashions.

Fifth, in recent years there has been an increasing recognition that the "history of religions" is not, and indeed never really was quite the same as "history" in a looser or more general sense. The adumbration within the field of history implied by the adjunct "of religions" implies an incipient theoretical horizon. It has therefore been asserted not infrequently that "history of religions" somehow brings along with it the systematic, comparative or typological study of religions. However, this is not enough. Simply to make this connection does not provide the methodological integration which we require. Moreover this stance deflects attention from the possibility of extremely valuable field research among the numerous religions open to direct study today. It is adopted, typically, by those who prefer to reject out of hand the methodological contributions of the various social sciences in favour of "the historico-philological" method. The approach also obscures the important point that "comparison" may be carried out both with respect to the internal characteristics of religion (leading to the typologies typical of the phenomenological school) and also with respect to functionalist explanations over the much wider range of sociological and psychological research. One cannot simply say that it is the "comparative" part of research which somehow makes the study of religions systematic and therefore scientific, or that this feature in itself makes it a distinctive discipline.

Sixth, the argument has moved forward in recent years. It has become widely accepted, contrary to the last mentioned trend, that "history of religions" can only stand in a full sense for the "study of religions" if the latter itself is also understood to be located within the overall range of the social and/or cultural sciences. Nevertheless these two major wings, the historico-philological (often with an emphasis on the study of texts) and the social-scientific, are still sometimes contrasted, as if inimical to each other. The recent debate over the name of the International Association for the History of Religions (IAHR), conducted during the years 1990–95, reflected these tensions, although it also had pragmatic aspects. In general it may be said that, because of their varying academic formation throughout the world, representatives of various trends in this discussion did not always find it easy to understand one another. This was the case even when some important positions were in fact shared, as in the contributions by Ugo Bianchi and Donald Wiebe.[6]

For all of these reasons uncertainty and lack of direction is often sensed by students and younger researchers. Nevertheless, it is argued here, considerable agreement can be perceived in the experience of specialists about how to go about studying religions. We will now turn, therefore, to strategic considerations for the development of an integrated methodology for the study of religions.

Strategic considerations

It is no longer sufficient simply to set out in a miscellaneous list, as has often been done, the apparently varied tasks of history, comparison, phenomenology, hermeneutics, sociology, psychology, philosophy and so on. What is needed is to make the necessary effort to correlate and integrate clearly those features of academic (or in some languages "scientific") method which are particularly necessary in the study of religions. This will make truly inter-disciplinary discussions with specialists in other disciplines far more fruitful. What, then, are the key strands in a methodologically integrated study of religions? Without claiming finality, this paper will now continue by giving a broadly conceived answer to this question. Three focal points in the articulation of an inte-

6 Their statements, and other related contributions, are preserved in the informal IAHR bulletins between 1990 and 1995, when the discussion was taking place.

grated methodology for the disciplined study of religions will be first briefly mentioned and then treated in more detail below.

First is the relation between subject-matter and method. Certain methodological orientations arise out of the simplest available morphology of the subject-matter, namely in terms of four elementary aspects of religion. This amounts to an adumbration of the field to be studied rather than a pointed definition of the object of study. The four aspects to which attention is drawn are: the behavioural, the conceptual, the subjective and the social. This enumeration is reduced here to a form which is as simple as possible without gross omission, and further details and argumentation thereon may be found elsewhere (Pye 1972a; Pye 1994b). It will also be noticed that these four elementary aspects are enumerated at such a level of abstraction that they can also be discerned in other subject-matters, e.g. sport or politics. However as soon as the pattern is filled out with an example (or "a case") of religion, certain methodological requirements emerge quite clearly which may not be applicable in quite the same way to all other fields of research. These will be explained below.

The second focus is the relation between sources and method. Sources are not the same as subject-matter. The subject-matter is a complex set of socio-cultural data for which sources provide evidence. The methodological question here is, therefore, how the sources in question should be studied. Thus the focus on sources gives rise to secondary methodological orientations arising out of the threefold nature of the primary sources available for study, namely written, oral and material sources. There is no unique method here which is particularly characteristic of the study of the religions. However there is a characteristic clustering of methods which arises out of the particular grouping of the sources which are relevant. As will be seen, one of the most important requirements in this regard is to achieve a coherent correlation between the "historico-philological" method and the methods typical of fieldwork in "living" and "oral" situations.

The third focal point lies in the methodological requirements of theory formation. It is necessary to distinguish between "theory" and "method", because an interest in new theories has often been mistaken for methodological advance. For example, a theory on gender relations in religion, or an interest in semiotics or cybernetics, does not necessarily imply an advance or a change in methodology as such. Admittedly, new theoretical positions may lead to *some* methodological adjustment. However there are two major aspects of method which contribute in particular degree to the development of categories and theories in the study of religions, namely: comparison and contextualisation. Since these are not exciting, like new theoretical approaches learned from elsewhere, they are sometimes neglected and scorned. Sometimes, too, they are over-emphasised. The main problem here, as a third step, is to correlate them appropriately with the requirements which emerge from the subject-matter and from the sources available.

Subject matter and method

These three focal points will now be explained in a little more detail. As indicated above, the enumeration of the conceptual, behavioural, social and subjective aspects of religion is regarded here as being the briefest possible indication of the subject matter which maintains a holistic view of it. That is, the enumeration enables us to think of the subject matter at once aspectually and conspectually. It may be that the same enumeration could be applied to other subject-matters, but the picture takes on colour in the study of religions when a particular religion or religions are regarded in this way. Any further delineation leads into increasingly complex questions of morphology and typology, about which differences of view might increasingly arise. However, the disagreements would be theoretical, not methodological. At the level of methodological reflection currently entertained it does not matter if views differ about the way in which morphological theories might be developed in greater detail, e. g. by listing more "dimensions", as done by Ninian Smart for example (Smart 1996). It should be noted therefore that, at this point, I am concerned only with the elementary methodological principles which arise from the simplest possible delineation of the subject matter.

The first requirement is that as far as possible, that is, as far as the available sources and research facilities permit, all four of these four elementary aspects should be considered in their integral relation to each other. Stating it negatively, for example, religious ideas should not be studied as if they had no relation whatever to religious behaviour. If this is done the researcher is likely to end by simply contributing to the further development of the religious tradition in question (as many pursuing "religious studies" in fact do). Similarly, the subjective aspects of religion cannot be completely separated from their conceptual accompaniment, a point which it has still seemed necessary to argue quite recently, and widely, in connection with mysticism.[7] Or again, the social forms of religion should not be studied as if it does not really matter what the people involved think, feel or do. That is to say, the conceptual, subjective and behavioural aspects should be taken into account at the same time. For practical purposes a partial study may be undertaken, concentrating on one aspect by itself, but at least it should be recognised that the other aspects are latently relevant. In other words religion should be studied both aspectually and conspectually.

The second methodological requirement arising at this same level of analysis is that the poly-aspectual subject-matter should be studied, in the first instance, in terms of its integral meaning for the believers or participants in question. That is to say, it should be studied without reference to the value orientation or possible explanatory hypotheses of the researcher. If this is not attempted, the emergent characterization is very likely to be misleading in some significant respect. Naturally, it is perfectly legitimate, and indeed desirable, to proceed at a later point to questions of explanatory theory, and indeed later still into questions of truth and value which go beyond the task of the study of religions (*Religionswissenschaft*) as such. But in the first instance the study of religions should be recognitional, that is, the integral meaning of the subject-matter for the believers or participants in question should be recognised in its own right. It is this which requires to be elucidated and characterised in the first instance. Otherwise mistakes will surely be made which will vitiate any other forms of enquiry or debate. The word "recognitional" is newly coined to express this because of problems with other previously used terminology, as will be illustrated in the next paragraph. This feature of the necessary method includes a) elucidation and b) characterization, two steps for which the wider discussion of hermeneutics is relevant.

This second methodological requirement has in fact been a commonplace in the study of religions since the emergence of the phenomenological tradition (in the study of religions), the term "bracketing" having become popular to express it. Unfortunately the point has often been obscured because it has been found necessary to reject other emphases found in the work of those who supposedly espoused it. In particular, it has been shown many times that leading representatives of the "phenomenological" school did not in fact proceed phe-

7 See *Mysticism and Religious Traditions* (Katz 1983), a multi-authored work in which all contributors take this view.

nomenologically in this sense, or at least not consistently. Rather, they pushed and pulled their materials into more or less theological categories derived from or characteristic of Christianity. Gerardus Van der Leeuw and Friedrich Heiler are prime examples of this.[8] In spite of this deficit it is very important that specialists in the study of religions should continue to attempt to study them as systems which have meaning for their believers or participants. Previously I have tried to preserve at least the adverb "phenomenologically" to indicate this important methodological requirement. In view of the dense forest of potential misunderstandings, however, I have now decided to abandon it altogether. That is the reason for the introduction of the word "recognitional". Earlier, like others, I have usually stressed the importance of the "self-understanding" of the believers, and I believe that Jacques Waardenburg has been making a similar point by referring to their "intentionality" (Waardenburg 1986: 241 ff.). However both of these terms focus a little too heavily on the conceptual aspect of religion. The term "recognitional" means that the researcher gives full recognition to the complex of experience covered by all four main aspects of religion for those who are involved in it.

This argument includes the idea that "specialists in the study of religions should continue to attempt to study them as systems which have meaning for their believers or participants", to repeat the phrasing already used. The word "attempt" is used deliberately here, for it is commonly held today that total objectivity or non-subjectivity simply cannot be achieved. This is not the place for a general discussion about the viability of a "value-free" science. However I firmly reject the oversimplified view that, because it is difficult to study religious systems in their own terms, this should not, and may not be attempted. To accept such a view would lead away from science into mere arbitrariness, and simply allow old prejudices to be replaced by new ones. However sophisticated the epistemological discussion becomes, there remains a difference between achieving a good elucidation and characterization of the religion of a specified group of people, or getting it all wrong because one's own beliefs and values continually get in the way.

The third methodological requirement arising out of the subject-matter as delineated above is that, even while proceeding on the one hand recognitionally, attention should also be given to the potential

8 It is hardly necessary to go into this in detail, but attention may be drawn to recent assessments of Van der Leeuw (by Jacques Waardenburg) and of Heiler (by myself, 1997d) in Axel Michaels' *Klassiker der Religionswissenschaft* (1997).

emergence of questions or insights which stand in tension to, or cut across, the self-understanding of the believers or participants. This tension (or "tension with believers factor," see further in 1.6 below) increases with the move from elucidation towards characterization and into explanation. As a result the tension arises for the following three reasons, which may amount to a particular characteristic of the methodology appropriate to the study of religion as a complex, but integrated enterprise.

a) Within any one example studied, a structure may appear which is not apparent, or only partially apparent, to the believers or participants in question. The researcher's perception of this structure may therefore be more "correct" than that of the believers or participants (in so far as they are interested in the matter at all). At this point therefore the first degree of tension arises over against the idea (which used to be designated as "phenomenological") that the believers are "completely right" (Kristensen 1960: 14).
b) The structure of any one religion may be rendered more visible as the result of comparative studies, that is, the as yet continuing, recognitional study of further cases. Though any one study in itself will continue to be recognitional, the theoretical perspective resulting from comparative knowledge may not be visible to the believers or participants, and if it becomes visible it may not be acceptable. This is the second degree of tension.
c) Finally, the intersections of any one of the four aspects set out above with related historical or socio-cultural contexts are likely to give rise to correlational reflections which require, and suggest, explanation in the stronger sense of the word. This is the normal task of those wider disciplines such as sociology or psychology which have a strongly explanational orientation. However it also applies to other contextual studies such as intellectual history, in so far as it includes the history of religious ideas as part of a much wider whole, or to contextual behavioural studies of different kinds such as research into the operations of the brain.

Sources and methods

The enumeration of the four basic aspects of religion has allowed and required us to make the first steps in the definition of the necessary methodology for their study. As noted earlier, further delineation of the subject matter in detail leads into questions of morphology and typology, and only secondarily into methodological questions. The next major step in the identification of a correct methodology lies elsewhere, namely in a general view of the sources. Again, the simplest possible view which does justice to the whole is preferred. This is as follows. The sources for the study of religions fall into three major groups: written sources, oral sources, material sources. "Material sources" here includes artefacts, buildings, non-verbal symbols, bodily positions and movements, etc. The order "written, oral, material" reflects nothing more than the order in which they have, historically, come to be perceived as relevant. It could be reversed or jumbled. However the perception of the importance of all three is important, and does not always occur. For example it seems to be rather neglected in the collected essays of Kurt Rudolph (1992). While each of the three major classes of source has attracted its own methodological debates in the past (hermeneutics, problems of access, and so on), it is important today to correlate them in an integrated fashion. Successful correlation at this level will help to stabilise the discipline of the study of religions.

Each of these three main kinds of source has leading characteristics which overlap with those of the others. Taken severally, the leading characteristics of the sources are as follows. (a) Written sources are linguistic, mainly historical, and only to a lesser extent field-based. (b) Oral sources are linguistic, mainly field-based, and only to a lesser extent historical. (c) Material sources are above all field-based and historical, and only in a derived or contextual sense linguistic. Thus, it will be seen that each of the three main types of source shares a leading characteristic with one of the other two, the common leading characteristics being as follows. Written and oral sources are preeminently linguistic, when compared with material sources. Oral and material sources are preeminently field-based, when compared with written sources. Material and written sources are preeminently historical, when compared with oral sources. That there can be a natural integration of these methodological perspectives in the service of the study of religions can be illustrated in an easily conceived diagram.

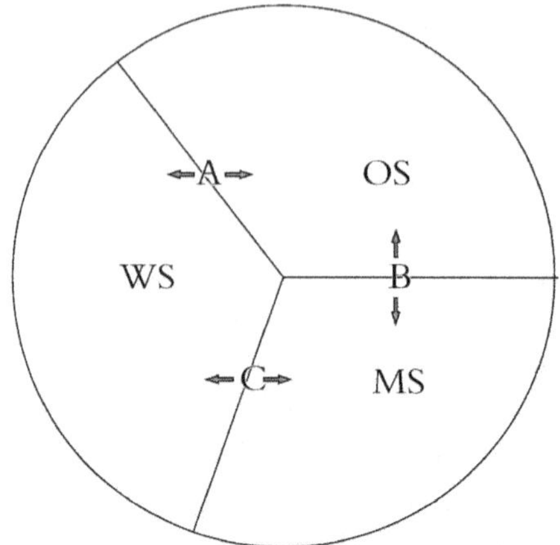

OS Oral Source — A Linguistic knowledge required
WS Written Source — B Fieldwork required
MS Material Source — C participants / believers often not available

Some of these relations will seem immediately obvious, but others may be less so. Oral sources are primarily field-based, and in further detail attract the modes of enquiry developed largely in social anthropology and sociology.[9] They are only "historical" in cases where they have been gathered and elucidated in the past. In a weaker sense oral sources are also part of recent history. Material sources (buildings, ritual objects, bodily positions and movements, etc.) may be rather new, but most commonly they are part of a continuous history and may even be very old. Moreover, material sources are not themselves linguistic in character. (This aspect may be accentuated by referring to them negatively as "non-verbal sources".) Although they take on their meaning from contexts which have a linguistic aspect, which may be at least partly recoverable, it is methodologically important to draw in the appropriate methods of archaeology, numismatics, art history, and so on. It would be desirable to develop this sub-field of methodology further to take particular account of objects used mainly or only in religious contexts. There does not, as yet, seem to be any comprehensive name for this. Traditional terms like "iconography" only refer to a part of

9 As an exemplification of this see the chapter entitled "Eine qualitative Befragung" in Pye and Triplett 2007:169–206, in which the concept of limited qualitative questionnaires is introduced methodologically and followed with particular examples from the field of Japanese religions.

it. As to written sources, care is needed to perceive their full range. Written sources include well-known texts, little known but formally impressive texts, inscriptions of many kinds and from many periods, and ephemeral texts. Such texts may be wholly, partly, or only indirectly religious in intention, a point which also applies to artefacts.

The most important point which arises out of an integrated grasp of methodology at this level is as follows. It is evident that the "historical" or the "historical-philological" method is not enough by itself to meet the methodological requirements of the study of religions. It should be realised however, that the "extra" which is required does not arise simply because of the tradition of associating "comparative" studies with the history of religions. The "systematic" requirements of *Religionswissenschaft* are more far-reaching and strenuous than this. Such a view does not do justice to the requirements arising from the main groups of sources. In particular, it fails to integrate the methods drawn from history on the one hand and social anthropology on the other hand, even though both of these are widely recognised to be of great relevance to the study of religions. When the methods are appropriately clustered and integrated the study of religions is much the stronger.

Methodology and theory formation

This section of the argument will be stated with particular brevity because it is really a different subject and there is no intention here of moving into theory as such. The detailed development of typologies, for example, belongs to the realm of theoretical reflection rather than to methodology as such. It was noted earlier that it is necessary to distinguish between "theory" and "method", for the simple reason that an interest in new theories is often confused with methodological advance. However there are two aspects of method, or strands in the clustered methods which make up the discipline of the study of religions, which contribute in particular to the development of theoretical categories and models in the study of religion. These are, above all, comparison and contextualisation. Where do these methods, or aspects of method, belong in an integrated discipline for the study of religions?

In certain ways, comparison and contextualisation overlap with each other. A comparison may be developed on the basis of two or more cases of religion which are being studied recognitionally. That is to say, several religions or aspects of religions which have been effectively characterised can thereupon be compared. This will lead into the construction of thematic elucidatory categories (such as pilgrimage, tradition, mysticism) or of explanatory categories (such as syncretism) which are internal to religious systems. However, comparison may also be of great interest in the elaboration of explanatory hypotheses which correlate religious data with other social or psychological factors. This was massively exemplified by Max Weber, for example, whose work, while contextual, was also comparative. In summary, comparison is required both in the recognitional phase and in the explanatory phase of the study of religion. Contextualisation means, as may readily be understood, considering one or more of the aspects of a given case of religion in the setting of its historical, socio-cultural and even biological context. While this may have an instructive value in the recognitional phase, it becomes much more prominent and is indeed indispensable in the fully explanatory phase. Contextualisation is ambiguous in the recognitional phase of study. It may be necessary for the elucidation of what believers mean. Incorrectly handled, however, it may lead imperceptibly but mercilessly away from the self-understanding of the believers or participants. Explanatory theories, on the other hand, quite correctly, *only* make sense in context.

Conclusion

The purpose of this argument was to illustrate in brief that methodological integration in the disciplined study of religions can be achieved with relative simplicity. Of course there is a continuous need for clarification and discussion at specific points. Strategically however, what is needed at the present time is not so much discussion of the detail as a clear focus on those features of academic or "scientific" method which are necessary and fruitful in the disciplined study of religions. This will make it easier to carry on worthwhile methodological and theoretical discussions with specialists in other fields which themselves require distinctive methodological orientations. If the detail is left aside, some important clarifications have emerged. It has been seen that there is a need for coordination and clustering of the various methods corresponding to the sources which are in fact available for scrutiny. The undogmatic perception of these sources leads in particular to the correlation of fieldwork methods with historical methods, and relativises the latter considerably. It has also been seen that the special character of the discipline does not lie merely in a cross-fertilisation between historical and comparative method. This popular correlation is a mis-match which does justice neither to the appropriate clustering of methods as related to sources, nor to the ways in which comparison is related to both recognitional and explanatory research.

Finally, it is important to insist that, at the level of greatest generalisation, the procedures for the study of religions, though open to refinement, are not arbitrary or optional. Elucidation and characterization are not optional. In the academic study of religions they should precede explanation. Moreover elucidation and characterization must also be "recognitional", as explained above. Neither religious ingression, for example in the form of theological debate, nor premature explanatory reductionism are acceptable in this phase of research. Again, the broad classification of sources is not really optional. The available sources cannot be pushed around on the basis of personal whim or university politics. There really are oral sources and material sources in the field as well as the well-known and less well-known written sources.

Methodological integration is envisaged here. The disciplined study of religion cannot be split down the middle, for example between history and ethnology, just because some people prefer to work with a certain kind of source material or prefer a certain kind of professional badge. It is an unduly easy alibi to say that the study of religion is "interdisciplinary", even if this is helpful in a preliminary way.[10] All too often an emphasis on "interdisciplinarity" seems to suggest an openness to a variety of methods, while it in fact allows the challenge of methodological reflection to be avoided. By contrast, as has been seen above, the discipline of the study of religions both requires and can find its own specific methodological integration.

Bibliographical references

Ahlbäck, Tore (ed.) 1999. *Approaching Religion, Scripta Instituti Donneriani Aboensis XVII (1)*, Åbo/Turku, Finland (Donner Institute for Research in Religious and Cultural History).

10 Cf. Donald Wiebe's criticism of "polymethodism" advanced during the 1997 Åbo (Turku) conference on methodology in the study of religions. (Wiebe 1999).

Honko, Lauri (ed.) 1979. *Science of Religion: Studies in Methodology. Proceedings of the Study Conference of the International Association for the History of Religions, held in Turku, Finland, August 27–31*, 1973. The Hague (Mouton).
Katz, Steven T. (ed.) 1983. *Mysticism and Religious Traditions*. Oxford (Oxford University Press).
Kristensen, W. Brede 1960. *The Meaning of Religion: Lectures in the Phenomenology of Religion*. The Hague (Martinus Nijhoff).
Michaels, Axel (ed.) 1997. *Klassiker der Religionswissenschaft: Von Friedrich Schleiermacher bis Mircea Eliade*. München (Beck).
Pye, Michael 1972a. *Comparative Religion: An Introduction through Source Materials*. Newton Abbot (David and Charles) and New York (Harper and Row).
– 1982a. "The study of religion as an autonomous discipline" in: *Religion* 12: 67–76.
– 1991b. "Religious studies in Europe: structures and desiderata" in: Klaus K. Klostermaier and Larry W. Hurtado (eds.), *Religious Studies: Issues, Prospects, and Proposals* (University of Manitoba Studies in Religion, 2). Atlanta (Scholars Press): 39–55.
– 1994b. "Religion: Shape and Shadow" in: *Numen* 41 (1): 51–75.
– 1997d. "Friedrich Heiler (1892–1967)" in Michaels 1997: 277–289 and 399–400.
Pye, Michael and Triplett, Katja 2007. *Streben nach Glück. Schicksalsdeutung und Lebensgestaltung in japanischen Religionen* (Mit Beiträgen von Monika Schrimpf) Berlin (LIT-Verlag).
Rudolph, Kurt 1992. *Geschichte und Probleme der Religionswissenschaft*. Leiden (Brill).
Smart, Ninian 1996. *Dimensions of the Sacred: An Anatomy of the World's Beliefs*. London (HarperCollins).
Waardenburg, Jacques 1986. *Religionen und Religion: Systematische Einführung in die Religionswissenschaft* (Sammlung Göschen 2228). Berlin (de Gruyter).
Wiebe, Donald 1999. "Appropriating religion. Understanding religion as an object of science" in: Ahlbäck, Tore (ed.) *Approaching Religion, Scripta Instituti Donneriani Aboensis XVII (1)*, Åbo/Turku, Finland (Donner Institute for Research in Religious and Cultural History): 253–272.

First published as "Methodological Integration in the Study of Religions" in: Tore Ahlbäck (ed.) 1999. *Approaching Religion, Scripta Instituti Donneriani Aboensis XVII (1)*, Åbo/Turku, Finland (Donner Institute for Research in Religious and Cultural History): 188–205.

1.3 Field and Theory in the Study of Religions

The following consists of edited sections of an article entitled "Westernism unmasked" which was first published in 2000 following a conference held in Copenhagen. In particular a section carrying the same title has been omitted because the subject is taken up in Part Two of the present volume. Here we focus more generally on the relationship between field and theory, while presupposing that scientific procedures are universally accessible and that the study of religions is not to be understood as a purely "western" enterprise.

Introduction

The position expressed in this article is that it is intellectually viable, worthwhile and interesting to work out theories of religion which not based on norms or viewpoints which are themselves religious. Such theories relate to phenomena or systems which can be identified in the wider context of human history, culture and society, and which can sensibly be designated as religion(s) for the purpose of investigation. This will be illustrated under the heading "adumbrating the field" immediately below. The adumbration of a field, i. e. its provisional circumscription, provides a starting point for the identification of sources which provide evidence for the phenomena in question and the selection of appropriate methods for their study, and for the engendering of theories to elucidate and explain them. Though the relation between method and theory is close and subtle, methodology will only be touched on in passing, since it is discussed in more detail in other papers in Part One of the present volume. Here we shall proceed rapidly to a consideration of the nature and place of theory in the study of religion(s). Theories of religion may be described as scientific in so far as they are rational, empirically grounded, explanatory and testable. Though common to all science, these features will be commented on with particular reference to the field in question, namely what we refer to as "religions."

Naturally, theories of religion are themselves developed in particular intellectual and social contexts, and have their own history. While there is an increasing recognition of the importance of this among specialists, it is argued below that several dominant conditions affecting recent and present work are among those least clearly seen. Accordingly a number of currently significant, but widely ignored conditioning factors will be pointed out under the heading "historical locations". In particular, there is a widespread view that scientific theories of religion are a product of "the western world" and are somehow reduced intellectually by being limited to such a world. Arguments are adduced against this view in the interest of promoting a more stable, interculturally recognisable understanding of the study of religions. Towards the end of the article, various questions which should be regarded as extraneous to the development of scientific theories of religion are briefly adduced under the heading "questions to be set aside". Though interesting in themselves, these questions have to be set to one side when proceeding scientifically, and they are considered here in order to indicate where the necessary distinctions between different kinds of reflection are thought to lie.

Adumbrating the field

Contrary to much vague discussion, it is not at all difficult to provide a tentative, open-ended adumbration of the field addressed in the scientific study of religions. This will be demonstrated by the following definition which is intended to be understood in terms of the well-known idea of family resemblances. The term religion may be used to refer to patterns of (i) various inter-related behaviours including, for example, ritual practices and the design and use of special sites and buildings, (ii) more or less normative beliefs, symbols, images and other representations, (iii) a variety of social forms such as mass movements, local gatherings, churches, special interest groups and the specialised roles of individuals, and (iv) a subjective focusing in an awareness of power, otherness, holiness, depth, security, healing, release, and so on. The order in which these four aspects are delineated is immaterial, and no one of them determines the others exclusively. Moreover the relations between them (six simple relations, not to mention complex ones) are as significant as the aspects viewed severally. These patterns can be distinctively documented in various cultures and can be seen to have developed and declined, to have been transmitted, to have been politically espoused or suppressed, and so on. They display signs both of mutual influence and of other similarities apparently related to the recurrent features of human experience. It pertains to this adumbration of the field to provide examples, and the reader shall not be left without them. Prominent examples of religion are the great cosmo-political systems of the ancient world, many of which persist in some form today or have successor examples such as Islam or the religions of specific peoples such as traditional forms of Hinduism, Judaism or Shintō. Many others are systems of salvation, release and guidance such as Buddhism, Christianity and smaller religious groups with their own specific teaching. Innumerable further examples could be named without difficulty, although their names may not be equally well known in all quarters (e.g. Byakkō Shinkōkai, Cao Dai, Umbanda) Many derivative and marginal cases have fewer of the common characteristics of religions but are nonetheless relevant for systematic observation and analysis. Also relevant to the field of investigation are less clearly organised religious spectra which have been designated as civil religion, invisible religion, implicit religion, common religiosity, etc. Given that there is such a field including a wide range of such phenomena, though not exhaustively delimited above, and that the field can be investigated, the question of the development of appropriate theory or theories arises.

This delineation of the object of study is an alternative version of one advanced quite a long time ago (Pye 1982a: 70), where it was termed a heuristic or operational definition. This terminology diverges from that of Robert Baird who, unadvisedly following the usage of logician Richard Robinson, uses "functional definition" in an analogous way (Baird 1971: 6ff). In the present connection "functional" is a very unsatisfactory term, for it commonly implies an explanation (as in "functionalism") which goes beyond the heuristic. It should therefore be avoided in the initial adumbration of the field of investigation. In seeking what he intended to be a heuristic definition, Baird landed on a spot very close to Paul Tillich's definition of religion as "ultimate concern." However, this too should be avoided, for while seeming to be generally formulated it in fact implies a normative, participant's view as to what should count as valid or significant religion. It was of course worth considering whether Tillich's definition *might* be taken over as an operational one for the general study of religions, and at that time it was widely current. However I distanced myself from it precisely in the interests of distinguishing an operational definition from a normative one (Pye 1972a, 10–12). As I pointed out then, there is much religion which is not really about "ultimate concern". Rather, it is about proximate concerns. Many examples of this could be drawn from all over the world, and it is strikingly the case in the countries of East Asia and Latin America. Thus we have a clear example of an idea which had penetrative theological force for its author, Tillich, but for this very reason, i. e. because of its one-sided, normative-definitive interest, was not in fact appropriate as an operational definition for the study of religions. The one-pointedness of such definitions always betrays their real import, as can easily be seen in the precursor definitions advanced by Schleiermacher (absolute dependence) or Otto (sense of the numinous), both of which are theologically derived and motivated. Compared with all these, the open-endedness of a (non-theological) "family-resemblance" operational definition of religion(s) and its appropriateness for the study of religions should be very obvious by now.

Relating method and theory

When people point out that the study of religions does not have any one single method which is unique to itself, this is often thought to imply that there can be no such discipline as the study of religions at all. Studying religions is just a part of history, or a part of sociology. What is overlooked thereby is that the study of religions does require a particular *clustering* of methods in order to do justice to its subject matter. This clustering of methods arises in part because of the nature of the sources which are, variously, written, oral and material. The need for an integrative clustering of methods arises in connection with attention being paid to these various kinds of source with regard to their relevance for the delineated subject matter, namely religion(s). As a result, the study of religions cannot be locked one-sidedly into the "historico-philological" method, if indeed any such investigatory method can still be purely maintained. Nor can it be located restrictively in social-scientific methods, as if the vast quantity of historical sources, both textual and material, could be relegated to the cellars. The main general steps in the method required for the study of religions are elucidation (of data), characterization, comparison, and explanation. The first two of these may further be defined as *recognitional* in that their primary purpose lies in taking cognisance of a particular unit of data. Comparison and explanation, being more complex, can only take place on the basis of prior recognitional study.[1]

There is a complex relationship between sources, method and theory in the study of religions, not least because the scientific study of religions is already in progress, so that new steps taken within the discipline make use of, and test, previous theoretical advances. On the one hand the development of particular theoretical constructs is itself part of the overall method required for studying religions. On the other hand particular aspects of method may be specified in accordance with the steps taken in research and theory development, as in the sequence: elucidation, characterization, comparison, and explanation. At the same time there are other features of method which, though not in themselves theoretical, are necessary if elementary steps in the investigation of the subject matter. An example of this would be the act of comparison, which is not in itself a "theory", although some theory might arise out of an act of comparison. As noted already, the study of religion(s) does not have any methods unique to itself, but it does have a typical *clustering* of methods which is particularly appropriate to its subject. The specific clustering of methods is devised not only to take account of the appropriate sources but also to mediate between the relevant data and theory development. As to theory, the main forms are general theory, morphology, typology, thematic analyses, and explanatory theory. The purpose of this paper is not to develop such theories in detail, which would take up far too much space, but to attempt to situate such theory development correctly. Suffice it to say that the argument does not take place in a vacuum, but in the context of my own attempts to contribute to theory development especially in the areas of morphology, tradition, syncretism and religious innovation.

Rational, empirical, explanatory, testable

The elementary features of any theory of religion(s) which could be regarded as "scientific" in the manner intended here are that it should be rational, empirically grounded, explanatory and testable. Each of these features is necessary for a theory of religion(s) but only taken together

1 On these matters see further my paper "Methodological integration in the study of religions" (1.2 above).

do they become sufficient. They are commonplace features of modern scientific enquiry which do not require any particular justification by specialists in the study of religion(s). A few additional comments on each one is necessary, however, in order to exclude some common misunderstandings and to make the general position clear.

While the relations between religion and reason and/or rationality have been the subject of debate in endless variations throughout western intellectual history, these debates have usually been concerned with the evaluation of religious truth claims. In other words, they have mirrored the question of the relations between revelation and reason or faith and reason, as reflected upon in all the western theistic traditions. Interestingly these debates have not been paralleled closely in other cultures, in spite of the intimate relations between Indian logic and both Buddhist and Hindu thought. In some cultural contexts it is even difficult to explain what the debates have been about. However that may be, such debates are not directly relevant to theories of religion(s). The extensive book series entitled *Religion and Reason* founded by its first editor Jacques Waardenburg lives partly on the borrowed capital of this chapter of intellectual history while some of its titles move away from it into the scientific study of religions. The same may be said of Ninian Smart's *Reasons and Faiths* which is partly about traditional questions in the western philosophy of religion concerning the correlation of reason with faith, and partly, and perhaps more importantly, lays a foundation for a substantial comparative theory of religions (Smart 1958). On the relation between science of religion as a rational enterprise and other questions pertaining to religion and rationality see further in the section entitled "Questions to set aside".

More recent times have also seen specialised debates about the relations between apparently conflicting systems of thought which claim to be rational, or appear to sophisticated observers to imply such a claim. Thus there is the question of the relation between "magic" as a ritual system which is rational in its own right, and "observer rationality" (Winch, Evans-Pritchard). Whatever the interest of these debates, it should be clearly recognised that it is not for specialists in the study of religions to mount their own particular view of "rationality". Nor is it possible to pretend that there are various optional "rationalities" which could all be operationalised in the scientific study of religions. Specialists in the study of religions as a scientific enterprise can do no other than presuppose, and maintain, the rationality of the enterprise itself. As human beings, they can of course, if they wish, simply give up studying religions and pursue whatever other interests they may have. That is another matter. During the scientific study of religions the internal coherence of any one of the systems under study should be respected, at least at the recognitional stages of elucidation and characterization (c.f. previous remarks on method). The manner of its plausibility for those who religiously entertain it or practice it is one of the features to be studied.

The second most important feature of any theory of religion(s) which could be regarded as "scientific" in the sense indicated above is that its reference is empirical. That is, it relates to historically or socio-scientifically documentable phenomena. Specifically, it relates to those which fall within the adumbration of the field. In this regard it is easy to be misled by the idea that "religion" is somehow in the mind. All religious systems exist at least in part in the minds of the believers or participants. But these believers are socially observable. They behave in various ways, and leave traces of activity and thought which become sources for the study of religions. Even more pernicious is the one-sided assertion that the object of study is located in the mind of the observer. In some sense, this is of course true. However it is not only located there. The study of religions refers to a field which is, in the common phrase, "out there". By contrast, if it is held that religious systems are "only" in the mind of the observer, or in some such sense "only" subjectively accessible by an observer, the theories produced will be scientifically ungrounded. For this reason "post-modernist" accounts of religion are often worthless. To put it another way, it is hard to find a post-modernist account of religion which is in fact about the field. By contrast the view is taken here that there are in fact data in the field which can be documented on the basis of sources open to more than one investigator and consequently studied in a publicly accessible manner. In this sense the reference of the scientific study of religions is empirical.

The third feature of a theory of religion(s) is its explanatory character. This means that the theory perceives and reports something which was not previously obvious to the casual observer or to the participant or actor in the religious system or situation. "Explanation" can be provided in two stages. Initially there is the stage of internal explanation, that is to say, the explication or clarification of coherences or structures within the system under study, viewed under its four main aspects (c.f. remarks under "adumbrating the field" above). It pertains to the rationality of theory that such coherences or structures are likely to be discernible in a series of separate cases or situations. Second, there is the stage of explanation in terms of historical, social, cultural or psychological factors other than the religious system or situation itself. This may be called functional explanation. It means that the religious and non-religious factors are correlated with each other in a manner which explains their mutual functions. It is desirable for this mode of explanation to be preceded by the first, since it is then less likely to be mistaken. For example, mistaken applications of Weberian explanation to Japanese religions have been based on a misunderstanding of the internal structuring of certain forms of Buddhism with regard to "this-worldly" and "otherworldly". In fact, both Pure Land Buddhism and even more markedly Shin-Buddhism, though entertaining the notion of rebirth in a "pure land" after death, display a this-worldly orientation as a result of a response to experienced grace, as in Lutheranism and Calvinism.

The fourth feature is testability. Though test-tubes can hardly be used in this regard the principle of testability is important in all scientific theory, for otherwise it languishes in the realm of speculation. In so far as theories of religion(s) display the three features already delineated, they are also in principle testable by other investigators attending to the same field. This may be difficult, for the field is changing, and disappearing, all the time. Usually it will be too late for another observer to study exactly the same phenomena. However, it should be possible in some sense to follow through the process of investigation and reflective analysis, once again, to such an extent that assent, or dissent, can be given by others to the results previously presented. To use a convenient German term, research should in principle be *nachvollziehbar.* This may be done by follow-up research in a given field, taking note of intervening social changes, or it may be done by a reworking of the accumulated data, taking new information and theoretical adjustments into account. Corrections do not necessarily invalidate the previous research. They adjust it and develop it.

Historical locations of theories of religion(s)

These elementary features of modern non-religious theories of religion (s) do not in themselves amount to a specific theory or theories, of which there have been very many. It is important to understand however that a theory of religion(s) can hardly arise as a complete abstraction. On the contrary, it can only be developed in the context of other intellectual movements. A theory of religion(s) may be the clear product of a particular, wider intellectual movement, it may be indirectly dependent on particular developments, or it may resist the general tide in some way.

It is not yet clear, for example, whether "post-modernism" as an intellectual movement will itself (or itselves) produce new theories of religion, simply destroy some previously current ones, or eventually turn out to have been largely irrelevant. Specialists in religion must be watchful in this regard. It is not self-evident that any one, rather recent intellectual movement is more likely to produce theoretical advances in the study of religion than those of previous intellectual movements which are now scorned. How much does it really help to designate particular theories of religion(s) as premodern, modern or postmodern, colonial or postcolonial? Sometimes one gets the impression that a theory of religion should be, above all, post-everything, and then it would be all right. I recently received an e-mail message with the structure: "Is there still anybody out there who thinks...if so I would like to hear from them!" The word "still" may sound rather plaintive, but often it is used as a term of abuse.

Nevertheless it has been evident for a long time, and at least for most of the twentieth century, that theories of religion(s) are themselves historically located, as clearly argued by Ernst Troeltsch. Typical of the twentieth century are influential works on the history of the study of religion(s), or historical appraisals of theory of religion(s), by writers such as de Vries (1961/1967), Evans-Pritchard (1965), Sharpe (1975), Waardenburg (1973, via source extracts), Preus (1987), Strenski (1987) and, more recently, McCutcheon (1997). There has been a parallel literature in adjacent disciplines such as social anthropology (Kuper 1973) and of course in the wider discussion of "orientalism". There has also been increasing interest in the historical characteristics of western studies of East Asian religions (Pye 1978b, Girardot 1999, Urban 1999) and in particular of Buddhism (Almond 1998, Amstutz 1997).

However there remain very considerable problems with the available presentations of the history of the study and theory of religion(s). In particular there is remarkably little agreement about the pivotal role, for the western world, of the European Enlightenment. Sharpe emphasised nineteenth century evolutionism as the matrix for the comparative study of religions, while recently Preus has quite rightly been looking back to the seventeenth century for the emergence of particular constituents of such study (Preus 1998). Relevant features of the European intellectual movements prior to the Enlightenment are usually identified very tentatively by reference to authors of classical antiquity (for example, Euhemeros or Cicero). But what happened in between? Moreover there is no balanced account even of the modern European development of the study of religion(s) which takes account of the various national traditions involved. A number of contributions have sought to redress the balance with regard to the francophone tradition (see especially Despland 1991). The matter can also be pursued in articles relating to Scandinavia, Poland, Spain, and elsewhere, as abstracted in the bibliographical journal *Science of Religion* under the heading "history of subject". But the resultant picture has not been drawn together. Much of it goes ignored in English-language writing.

Some of the above mentioned works are very up-to-date, and appear to have gained a vantage-point which is "post-" everything so far thought of. Yet it is not at all clear that all the components in the history of the study of religions have yet been identified, or that they have been well correlated with each other. Some of the important phases are very obvious by now, for example: the Enlightenment, Romanticism, colonialism, the missionary movement, evolutionism, historicism, and orientalism. However other important contextualisers are not recognised. Their importance remains underestimated. Four may be named: neo-colonialism, cold-war-ism, oil wealth, and intercultural exoticism. Attention has been drawn to these before (Pye 1997a) but the precise correlation of these with movements in the study of religion(s) has not even begun to be considered in detail. Thus while colonialism can be seen with relative retrospective clarity, leading to the use of the term "post-colonial", neo-colonialism appears to go largely unnoticed. The same applies to cold-war-ism. The history of theories of religion during the cold war, which covered half a century, will eventually have to be written with an adequate correlation of both sides. "Half a century" is approximate, but the Cold War did not immediately come to an end on the western side simply with the opening of the political frontiers. In fact, by many, it is still being waged, as I have argued in a paper entitled: "Political correctness in the study of religions: Is the Cold War really over"[2]. Similarly oil wealth has led to a special brisance

2 Presented at a special conference of the IAHR held in Brno, Czech Republic, in August 1999. This most interesting conference was devoted to an exploration of the history of the study of religions, east and west, during the Cold War period. For this paper see 3.5 below.

between the economic haves and have-nots and their diverse relations to the United States and its allies. Consequently quite special, and often misleading perceptions of Islam have become dominant, even while Islam-related studies are funded in part by the oil-rich. As a result the word "fundamentalism" has passed into widespread media use and has largely lost its value for theoretical analyses of religion. Finally, intercultural exoticism, in religious terms "New Age", has been the starting point for many students of the subject in recent decades and has to be understood both in relation to the home culture and to those used as exotic reference points. In short, if the history of the study of religion(s) is now being reconsidered under many aspects, these factors too need to be taken into account seriously.

But just how are theories of religion(s) related to a historical context? While it is important to appraise theories of religion in their intellectual and social context, it is not adequate to think that theories of religion are no more than the products of other things which are going on in "history". A scientific theory can be better or worse than others, and while its features can themselves be explained in terms of intellectual history the question of its appropriateness or validity remains to be answered. Moreover the force of any theory as related to knowable data, that is, its scientific plausibility, is likely to have some influence on its durability.

Finally, as regards historical locations of theories of religion, it is notable that most accounts of the history of theories of religion(s) are restricted to western intellectual history. That this should be prominent is indisputable, and yet it is not the whole story. It is mistaken to think, as is widely assumed, that the study of religions, and the development of theory about religions, is by its very nature a western "product" or "project". Such an attitude of "westernism" is criticised in Part Two below, and therefore will not be pursued at this point, as it was in an earlier form of the present article.

Questions to be set aside

It has now become a commonplace in the study of religions to recognise the separation between theories of religion and religious views of the world.[3] However, it is not essential for a theory of religion which is not itself religious to be described as "secular", for this term implies an opposition between "secular" and "religious" which might or might not be warranted. Indeed, a scientifically coherent theory of religions might conceivably be consistent with one or more religious orientations. On the other hand it might and probably must conflict with a number of religious orientations or with statements arising out of them. There is therefore a question regarding the consistency of a general theory of religions with the intellectual content of particular religions. As an appendix to the other matters discussed above it may be helpful to lay bare in utmost brevity my own understanding of this question.

Stated most generally, all possible and non-mistaken knowledge must be consistent because all known thought processes take place within the single universe within which we find ourselves. Even with respect to other conceivable universes we are only able to project the possibilities known to us in the known universe. This projection might include, in general, the possibility of difference, but it cannot include any specific denotation of difference. This view is consistent with modern cosmology and physics, and yet, interestingly, ancient Indian cosmologies also conceived of an indefinite number of universes which are essentially similar. Ancient Buddhist cosmology is a fine example of this. Thus the consistency of universes is presupposed, even though people differ about their precise description.

Non-mistaken knowledge could include some knowledge which we might for some reason wish to describe as religious. Many religious statements on the other hand are evidently false. Some are false because they can be demonstrated to be inconsistent with other knowledge. Others, even though they somehow claim to avoid the challenge of correlation with other knowledge, are mutually exclusive. In so far as religious statements are overtly not in agreement, they cannot all overtly be true. Thus the possibility of framing statements which are both incontrovertibly true and in some sense "religious" must be regarded as being, at best, minimal. In other words, the possibility of a holistic view of knowledge is kept open, but at the same time it is recognised, indeed asserted, that many if not most religious statements cannot be regarded, in the last analysis, as correct knowledge.

---

3 For the present writer's extended statement of this fundamental point see "Religion: shape and shadow" (Pye 1994b).

Yet this state of affairs is not at all surprising if we take into account that "inexpressibility" is itself a widepread reference point in religious consciousnesses. The implication of this is that statements which seek to convey "expressional truth" (Robinson 1967, 49) in relation to that which is deemed to be "inexpressibly" valuable or significant cannot be otherwise than "worldly" or "conventional", and hence in some respect self-avowedly false. This relationship has been articulated in the Buddhist tradition, among other ways, in terms of the concept of "skilful means" (see Pye 1978a). Verbal statements (and other forms of expression) which are imperfect to the extent of being false are the only means at our disposal to point towards a greater "truth" or value. Thus they have to be both articulated and deconstructed. Understanding this process and taking part in it is itself a religious path. In such a perspective all religious discourse may be understood as a provisional construct which will eventually disappear. At the same time it is necessary for it to be continually appraised with respect to its viability and value. While this orientation is itself thought, at least by the writer, to be consistent with a scientific theory of religion, it is possible that other religious orientations also are. That is a matter for independent perusal.

This position leaves open the question about what the traditional discipline of "philosophy of religion" should be concerned with today, if anything. The development of a theory of religion(s) is not to be equated with "philosophy", which has various tasks of which the study of religions is not one. Theorists of religion(s) do not need to solve general problems of epistemology, for example, which are the task of philosophers. They should not be side-tracked by questions such as "How does anybody know anything?" or about the general possibility of knowledge of other minds.

Even less is it the task of theories of religion(s) to introduce the notion of some special kind of "irrationality" just for religion. While there is still a tendency to hagiographise Rudolf Otto in some quarters, his work on "the holy" (rather than "the idea of the holy", as the title of his work *Das Heilige* was translated into English) may be regarded as a last desperate attempt to find a theoretical focus for the study of religion(s) which could plausibly coordinate the irrationality of some religion with Kantian modernity. Whatever their historical interest, those days really have passed now. Indeed they had already passed at the time, as can be seen in the very worthwhile essay by Ernst Troeltsch entitled "Das Wesen der Religion und der Religionswissenschaft", first published in 1906.[4] The above statement by no means ignores that irrationality may be important for religious people in their systems. Rudolf Otto was himself a religious person and irrationality was significant for him. Irrationality is important not only in the specialised experience of mystics but also in quite different religious attitudes such as fundamentalism. The fundamentalist believer lives partly by his or her disjunction from reason. So did Pascal. On the other hand a presumed consistency with general rationality is also important for a large number of religious people. Ernst Troeltsch, regarded by religious critics as a dangerous relativist, was in fact a rational and religious person. By contrast with all these options within the range of religious systems, the rationality of a scientific theory of religion(s) is itself independent of the rationality or the irrationality of any religious system.

A theory of religion(s), at the most elementary level, merely needs to be rational in the general sense that it can be expressed in words and/or numbers, and that it is itself internally coherent. That is, when stated it should not collapse into a sea of disorganised ink or jumbled bytes as in: "saltion a shiwith speciereferceando spectacles, saunan seura". A typical statement might, on the other hand, be: religious innovation takes place both in the context of existing traditions and, independently of these, in the form of new religious movements. If further investigation showed that this theoretical generalisation could not be maintained then it would have to be abandoned as inadequate. However it would have been rational. Attempts to remove the aspect of rationality from scientific studies and in particular from scientific theories of religion are simply doomed to self-destruction.

In this a scientific theory of religion is different from religious theories of religions, of which a significant number can be documented. Religious theories of religions are linked to whatever view of "reason" is held within whatever religious system advances the "theory". It is possible to conceive of a religious theory of religions which is consistent with a scientific theory of religion(s), but these are rare, and it is not the task of a scientific theory of religion to produce this consistency. This is not so much a question of academic territories, though institutional positions are important for the well-being of any discipline; rather, it is a question of achieving the necessary intellectual independence and clarity

4 English translation under the title "Religion and the science of religion" (Morgan and Pye 1977). C.f. also my article of appraisal entitled "Troeltsch and the science of religion" in the same volume (234–252).

for theories of religion to be plausible, and instructive in the preparation of future investigations.

General conclusions

While any of the detailed formulations used above could no doubt be improved upon, it has been shown that it is not much more difficult to delineate the field, the appropriate methods and the procedure of theory development with respect to the scientific study of religions than it is in other areas of scientific endeavour. Naturally, nobody is compelled to engage in this discipline, and if they prefer to pursue problems in philosophy, theology, politics, ethics, or any other contexts where interesting and in some cases urgent matters seem to require attention, then they may do so. At the same time it is not at all helpful if these contexts are simply confused with the field of religions as an area for scientific research in its own right.

At the same time the general story or history of the development of theories of religion needs to be retold in various respects, in relation to Europe and North America, in relation to East Asia, and in relation to the interculturality of today's world. This will help to clarify further the main features of thought which have contributed to the development of the discipline. However we already know enough to be able to assert that the general features of theory formation with respect to religion are only in an extremely limited sense culture-bound. "Westernism" should be unmasked for what it is, namely an illusion. The main intellectual features necessary for the development of the scientific study of religions can be documented in the intellectual history of more than one major cultural area, and they continue to be relevant world-wide.

Bibliographical references

Almond, Philip C. 1988. *The British Discovery of Buddhism*. Cambridge (Cambridge University Press).

Amstutz, Galen 1997. *Interpreting Amida. History and Orientalism in the Study of Pure Land Buddhism*. New York (State University of New York Press).

Baird, Robert D. 1971, 1991. *Category Formation and the History of Religions*. The Hague (2nd edition Berlin, New York) (Mouton de Gruyter).

Brear, Douglas 1975. "Early assumptions in western Buddhist studies." *Religion* 5: 136–159.

de Vries, Jan 1961. *Godsdienstgeschiedenis in Vogelvlucht*. Utrecht (Het Spectrum).
– 1967. *The Study of Religion. A Historical Approach*. New York (Harcourt Brace and World, Inc.)
Despland, Michel (ed.) 1991. *La Tradition Française en Sciences Religieuses. Pages d'Histoire*. Les Cahiers de recherche en sciences de la religion Volume 10. Québec (Université Laval).
Evans-Pritchard, E. E. 1965. *Theories of Primitive Religion*. Oxford (Clarendon Press).
Girardot, N. J. 1999. "'Finding the way': James Legge and the Victorian Invention of Taoism." *Religion* 29 (2): 107–121.
Kuper, Adam 1973. *Anthropologists and Anthropology. The British School 1922–1972*. Harmondsworth (Penguin Books).
McCutcheon, Russell T. 1997. *Manufacturing Religion. The Discourse on Sui Generis Religion and the Politics of Nostalgia*. New York, Oxford (Oxford University Press).
Morgan, Robert and **Pye, Michael** (eds.) 1977. *Ernst Troeltsch: Writings on Theology and Religion*. London (Duckworth) and Atlanta (John Knox).
Preus, J. Samuel 1987. *Explaining Religion: Criticism and Theory from Bodin to Freud*. New Haven (Yale University Press).
– 1998. "The Bible and religion in the century of genius. Part I: Religion on the Margins: Conversos and collegiants." *Religion* 28 (1): 3–14.
Pye, Michael 1972a. *Comparative Religion. An Introduction through Source Materials*. Newton Abbot, England (David and Charles) and New York (Harper and Row).
– 1976. "The end of the problem about other religions" in: Clayton, John P. (ed.), *Ernst Troeltsch and the Future of Theology*. Cambridge (Cambridge University Press): 172–95.
– 1977. "Troeltsch and the science of religion" in: Morgan and Pye 1977: 234–252.
– 1978a. *Skilful Means. A Concept in Mahāyāna Buddhism*. London (Duckworth) and (Routledge – 2nd edition 2003).
– 1978b. "Diversions in the interpretation of Shintō" in: Anthony, D.W. (ed.), *Proceedings of the British Association for Japanese Studies 1977 (Volume Two,Part Two: Social Sciences)*, Sheffield (University of Sheffield: Centre of Japanese Studies): 77–92. (Republished Pye 1982.)
– 1982a. "The study of religion as an autonomous discipline" in: *Religion*. 12: 67–76.
– 1982b. "Diversions in the interpretation of Shintō" in: *Religion*. 11: 61–74. (Republication of Pye 1978).
– (trans.) 1990a. *Emerging from Meditation (Tominaga Nakamoto)*. London (Duckworth) and Honolulu (University of Hawaii Press).
– 1994b. "Religion: shape and shadow" in: *Numen* 41 (1): 51–75.
– 1997a. "Reflecting on the plurality of religions (full text)" in: *Marburg Journal of Religion*. 2: virtual pages.

– 1999a. "Methodological integration in the study of religions" in: *Approaching Religion 1.* Ahlbäck, Tore (ed.) Åbo Finland (Donner Institute for Research in Religious and Cultural History): 188–205.

Robinson, Richard H. 1967. *Early Madhyamika in India and China.* Madison Milwaukee and London (University of Wisconsin Press).

Sharpe, Eric 1975. *Comparative Religion. A History.* London (Duckworth).

Smart, Ninian 1958. *Reasons and Faiths.* London (Routledge and Kegan Paul).

Strenski, Ivan 1987. *Four Theories of Myth in Twentieth Century History.* Iowa City (University of Iowa Press).

Urban, Hugh B. 1999. "The extreme Orient: The construction of 'Tantrism' as a category in the Orientalist imagination" in: *Religion* 29 (2): 123–146.

Waardenburg, Jacques 1973. *Classical Approaches to the Study of Religions: Aims, Methods and Theories of Research.* The Hague (Mouton).

The article entitled "Westernism unmasked" on which the above is based was first published in: Tim Jensen and Mikael Rothstein (eds.) *Secular Theories on Religion. Current Perspectives.* Copenhagen (Museum Tusculanum Press) 2000, 211–230.

1.4 Philology, Fieldwork and Ephemera in the Study of Japanese Religions

The concept for this paper goes back to a conference on methodology in the study of religions held in Warsaw in 1989 under the auspices of the Polish Society for the Science of Religions. The original paper (published 1990) was redesigned and updated for a very different conference at the International Research Center for Japanese Studies (Nichibunken), in Kyōto, in 2008 (published 2009). The present paper integrates and extends these two versions.

Philology and fieldwork

In the complex story of the development of the study of religions as a modern discipline two particularly important strands have been (a) the historical or philological approach and (b) approaches from the social sciences. The historical approach has taken on a certain profile through the activities of the International Association for the History of Religions (IAHR), while approaches from the social sciences have also been a most significant cradle for the study of religions in many countries. This is not in itself controversial for "historians of religion," for the IAHR according to its constitution, "...has as its object the promotion of the academic study of the history of religions through the international collaboration of all scholars whose work has a bearing on the subject." (Article 1) It should be remembered that the "history of religions" as a discipline is usually taken to include those aspects of comparative study which are necessary for the achievement of a balanced view in any one field. This means that the perspective of the IAHR is not restricted to the promotion of purely historical studies. Even more relevant for the topic treated here is that, insofar as the "history" of religions has continued right up to the present moment, this can only mean that contemporary social-scientific work is extremely relevant. We are concerned here with a particularly interesting overlap of a methodological kind.

In many cases it is not easy to draw clear distinctions between these academic disciplines when it comes to the description, analysis and explanation of recent religious movements or situations. At the same time, academic institutions and traditions do frequently lead to the relative isolation of differing disciplines and not everybody can be trained in all fields and in all methods of research. Nevertheless there have been academic contexts in which the two have been held together. As recorded above, the present paper, which proposes a close symbiosis of historical-philological and social-scientific studies was first devised for a conference organized by the Polish Society for the Science of Religions. For that society, the overlap between historical and social-scientific studies was regarded as normal over many decades, as may be seen from the contributions to its journal *Euhemer.*[1] When it comes to "Buddhist Studies" on the other hand, social-scientific approaches are generally less prominent than historical and textual studies. This may seem natural given the intellectual interest in the thought of the Buddhist tradition and the decidedly philological orientation of traditional European and modern Japanese Indology. Nevertheless it was striking that at the later conference for which a second version of this paper was devised (see note above) all other contributions were exclusively historical or textual in nature. So in spite of a frequently met theoretical welcome for interdisciplinary work there continue to be substantial firewalls between the methodological models of various disciplines. However the study of religions requires its own clustering of methods and here we present an integrative solution to a methodological problem which arises with particular persistence in the study of contemporary Japanese religions, namely the problem of access.

The matter is of interest from the point of view of interdisciplinary reflection because both of the two main disciplinary strands referred to above are important to the researcher into Japanese religions. On the one hand Japan has been an intensely literate society for centuries, so that the study of Japanese religion is laid open to all the complexities of historical and philological research. On the other hand there are few formal obstacles in the way of a field researcher going about his work in any area of the country, now, in our own time, and studying

1 It is no accident that the Polish Society for the Study of Religions, founded in 1958, was affiliated to the IAHR long before the collapse of the Soviet Union. The conference in question took place in September 1989, just at the time when the first non-Communist was in process of formation in Warsaw, but there had been various significant interactions with specialists in the study of religions over a period of many years. See also article 3.5 below.

Japanese religions in their present form. The researcher who chooses to do the latter can hardly avoid the literary heritage of religion in some form or other. The researcher who prefers to do historical research is also unwise to close his eyes to contemporary forms, for the country remains a veritable living museum of its own religious past. Needless to say, this can be deceptive; but probably less deceptive than when the historian tries to close his eyes to the present in the interests of a purer understanding of the past.

Example: ephemera at Shintō shrines

It would verge on eccentricity to write on the history of Shintō without paying some attention to the layout and architecture of shrines, which are documented not least by their present form. Admittedly the ambience of a Shintō shrine has changed a great deal and the present-day transport arrangements which surround it, the innumerable small indications in the appearance of the people who visit it, their clothing, their gadgets, their cameras and bags, not to speak of telegraph wires, concrete walls and pillars in various places, and so on, all add up to a total impact which must be in some degree different to what it was in the past. Thus the historian who is stimulated by present phenomena has to be very sensitive to the disturbing effects of his own observations on his view of the past. Nevertheless it would be unwise for the historian of Shintō to exclude its currently observable forms from his consideration. Yet the social scientist who is studying some aspect of Shintō today, for example, a village festival, will surely experience features which cannot be understood without reference to the literary tradition, whether formal or informal.

A clear case in point would be the interpretation of the *norito* (ceremonial prayer) recited by the Shintō priest at the shrine during a village festival, which at least in part must be understood as a variation on a centuries-old pattern. The priest recites the *norito* from a large sheet of white paper folded many times. He needs this because although most of the formulations are in themselves traditional, the specific version for the ceremony in question cannot be learned by heart. The form used will be a variation of innumerable others which have been constantly revised over decades and even centuries, and which are distantly, but not so divergently, related to well-known ancient models which have been preserved in the literary tradition.[2] It will usually be impossible, in the field situation, to see directly what the Shintō priest has been reciting, and hence it will be equally impossible to use it as a source. The *norito* are not discarded but kept in manuscript form, for example in a large box, The priest can then simply pull one out and revise it to suit the situation, either by adding in a phrase, crossing something out, or sticking a piece of paper over part of the original. It is of course not easy to acquire such *norito* as artefacts, but from the few which have come into my possession on particular occasions I have learned that they are always variations on a set style, geared to the particular occasion, and kept ready for use with various amendments by the performing priests. In the figure shown below, we see an example of this in the case of a *norito* used for a wedding (but only a detail is shown in order to avoid printing a complete name of one of the persons involved). Clearly such documents are ephemera in the full sense of the word. Under normal circumstances they are most unlikely to survive in a precisely fixed form.

Also interesting in the Shintō shrine context is documentation of the relative amounts of money given as a contribution by different individuals or families. At the festivals of Shintō shrines such information may be displayed on sheets of paper before the shrine. This material is of interest because it indicates not so much the relative generosity of individuals and families as their relative status in the town or village. It would be difficult to get oral information about this, yet here it is in written form for all to see, for a short while only. If such ephemera are to be analysed, they must of course first of all be read! This requires relevant philological expertise, however elementary. Once read and analysed, the postings amount to a source which escapes the glosses or the surreptitious distortion characteristic of oral information. The slight paper sheets are usually left hanging for some time, until rain and wind make it necessary to tidy up. In some cases slivers of wood are used and these of course last longer, perhaps even till the next festival. A typical donation announcement is also illustrated below.

From these examples of ephemera at Shintō shrines, we can see that the historian, who in the traditions of scholarship is supposed to apply the historico-philological method, and the social scientist, who is supposed to *observe* society before giving his description and explanation of it, cannot avoid each other in the study of Japanese religions. A spe-

2 For an English translation see Philippi 1959.

cialist in the study of religions must be the historian-philologist and the social scientist at one and the same time.

The problem of access in the study of Japanese religions

The question of "access" is one which poses itself for any contemporary research into religions. Some of these are quite general, such as the problem of how to enter into religious situations for observational purposes, when one is not oneself a believer, how to correlate observation and participation in ritual events, and so on. Such questions will not be considered in detail here (but cf. "Getting into trouble with the believers" at 1.6 below). There are also "problems" of access which can only be resolved by sustained hard work, such as learning how to read written Japanese, or how to negotiate Japanese train systems in order to be in the right place at the right time; but these are not problematic in a methodological sense.

In the study of Japanese religions the question of access is dominated by two fundamental considerations for the non-Japanese researcher. The first is the non-Japanese-ness, or foreignness of the observer. The second is the general attitude among Japanese people towards the divulgence of information. Neither of these make work on contemporary Japanese religions impossible, or even particularly difficult; but both have to be understood and dealt with in appropriate ways.

Access: foreignness and language

Except for Chinese or Koreans who have grown up in Japan, gone through the Japanese educational system (perhaps even adopting a Japanese name), it is not possible for a non-Japanese person not to be almost immediately recognisable as such. In most cases this will be evident from the facial and other features, although there are occasionally situations where the presence of a non-Japanese person with unobtrusive characteristics may be temporarily overlooked. Rather tall researchers are likely to be more obvious and hence have greater difficulties. Nowadays hair colour has become less of a problem because of the wide incidence of dyed hair in the population, among both genders. Anybody might have copper-coloured or yellow hair, so that a blond foreigner is not necessarily immediately identifiable from behind.

Non-native use of the Japanese language is also a factor, but naturally this varies greatly depending on the ability of the researcher. In country areas well away from Tokyo it may occur that persons interviewed regard the Japanese spoken by the questioner as standard, compared with their own dialect form of the language. If the questioner is known to come from a leading university in Tokyo or another major city the distance between such an established institution and the local village consciousness, that is, the internal Japanese distance, will be greater than any strain set up by the foreigner's Japanese language in itself. The question of language represents a specific difficulty therefore only in so far as the written language is particularly complex and the spoken language relatively fast. When spoken fluently, the informant is usually satisfied and does not modify his language. That is, he or she simply speaks polite Japanese, either in standard or dialect form.

Perhaps surprisingly, the foreign enquirer may even be assisted by certain characteristics of spoken Japanese. For one thing conversation usually consists of relatively short syntactical units which are strung together without necessarily being rounded off or adding up to a completed, lengthy sentence. This arises because Japanese speech habits are highly interactive; a conversation is felt to be a joint enterprise which should reach a satisfactory conclusion for both parties. Thus the conversation partners tend to help each other along with short speech units. Moreover Japanese conversation has a high level of explanatory content to assist communication. This is partly because of the complexity of arrangements in general but in particular because things which would be clear in print are not clear merely from sound. For example, because of the large number of Chinese-derived characters in use, the variety of ways in which they can be pronounced and the large number of homophones which also arise through various combinations of characters, it is often necessary to explain which particular word is meant, especially in the case of special terminology, not to mention names. Once a certain threshold has been reached, therefore, some of the normal features of spoken Japanese assist the enquirer in his or her work.

The problem of foreignness really lies elsewhere, namely in the psychological distance which the informant assumes to exist between himself or herself as a Japanese person and any foreign person. The Japanese person tends to adopt the role of representing the country of Japan, and expects the foreign researcher to be doing research in his capacity as a foreigner. Moreover the Japanese person tends to fit the researcher into the generalised image which he has of foreigners and often seeks to use the conversation to adjust, or to confirm this image. Thus, by the use of a few deft phrases the informant quickly becomes the researcher, and the researcher is transformed into an object of study. This can be quite aggravating for the inexperienced. The foreign researcher therefore has to display great patience, indeed obstinacy, as well as some skill, in order not to spend the whole of the interview simply giving information about him- or herself. In sum, the assumed distance between Japanese and foreigners does not necessarily have a linguistic effect, as explained above (though the language is not easy), but it can of course have a serious effect on the selection of content or the image which the informant seeks to convey. This aspect of the problem is not in principle different from the situation in other countries. However, in the case of Japan it is always present, because the foreigner researcher is usually very visible and hence regarded in the first instance as a foreigner.

Access: general attitudes towards information in Japan

In Japanese society a very high value is placed on information. It is commonly sought and accumulated, also bought, sold, preserved, protected and hidden. As a result there is often a strong interest in acquiring information, but not necessarily an interest in divulging it. Indeed, in general information is rarely divulged unnecessarily. For example, if someone is going to be late for a meeting or cannot attend it, he or she may indicate that this is so but provide an excuse in a manner which avoids giving the actual reason. When things go wrong, reasons are frequently not given because there are no acceptable reasons. So there are no reasons. If nothing can be said, as far as possible nothing will be said. It is quite natural that industrial and economic information should be carefully guarded, but this is more carefully done than in some countries. On the other hand, since information is regarded as important, many Japanese are professionally involved in gathering it. Almost all Japanese studying, researching or working abroad are in some way or other collecting information which will find its way back into the total Japanese store of information in published or unpublished form. For this reason the foreign researcher active in Japan is easily understood as someone who has a role to perform. He needs no further reason for being there. The question is, however, how much and what kind of information should be vouchsafed. Thus, the extent to which information should be divulged, or what kind of information should be divulged, are questions which exercise the mind of the informant as much as of the researcher!

Access: factionalism as a hurdle for the researcher

It is, furthermore, of the greatest importance to realise that the potential corpus of information in Japan is not at all monolithic. On the contrary much information reflects the markedly factional nature of Japanese society. This is true both generally and of religion in particular. Not only religion, but politics, industry and commerce, education, the media, and even such diverse sectors as health, transport or the arts are organised in such a way that the vertical patterns of authority exclude horizontal communication between different and often competing organisations to a really significant extent. Of course there are many cross-references as a result of family or other loyalties. However, worthwhile access from an informational point of view is most acceptably achieved by means of a long-term relationship which accepts the vertical perspective of a particular organisation. Only in this way can trust be established and the channels of communication be opened in a worthwhile manner. Precisely because many of the organisations in question are in competition with each other it is not easy to establish such relations with several at once.

Fortunately, in the case of the religions of Japan there is a relatively high degree of tolerance for the diversities of religion. Indeed the common believer may easily move from one religious context to another without feeling any particular strain. As soon as it is a question of the more coherent patterns of religion however, that is, of systems of belief and behaviour, social organisation and long-term emotional involvement, personal loyalty plays a significant role. It is also expected of a researcher who wishes to be taken seriously. Thus there is a natural tendency for researchers to concentrate on particular religions, even though one of the fascinating aspects of the religious situation in Japan is its very diversity. As a result, scholar A studies Ōmotokyō (also Oomotokyō), scholar B studies Gedatsu-kai, scholar C studies Shingon Buddhism, scholar D studies Jōdoshū (Pure Land Buddhism) and scholar E studies Jōdo Shinshū (a special form of Pure Land Buddhism). This applies no less to Japanese researchers than to foreigners, indeed perhaps even more. When the name of a certain Japanese sociologist of religion occurred recently, in conversation with an eminent religious leader of one Buddhist movement (Risshō Kōseikai) the name of the religion which he studied, namely Konkōkyō, was instantly supplied. In other words, official representatives of religious groups are likely to know not only who their own favoured researchers are but also which researchers have assigned themselves, so to speak, to rival religions.

Specialism in the study of a specific religion can lead to a lifelong association with that religion. Attention to other religions, on the other hand, especially similar but competing ones, such as the various competing lay Buddhist movements, Reiyūkai, Risshō Kōseikai and Sōka Gakkai, could be regarded as a slightly disappointing form of disloyalty. Apparent lack of interest over a period of months or years, because of the pressure of other work, but particularly if caused by research on different religions in Japan, may be taken as an indication that one's interest is only lukewarm, or at any rate transitory. These reflections are not meant to imply that the religious groups expect the researcher to take up membership, though this would in most cases be welcomed. The sincere statement that membership is not possible for the researcher is usually accepted with praiseworthy understanding. The point is however that in order to gain access to worthwhile information one is inevitably drawn, over a longer period, into a relationship with the particular religious group which involves, to some extent, an acceptance of the vertical compartmentalisation of Japanese organisations. Sometimes the problem is evaded through conspectual or thematic studies relating to several religious organisations at once, but with a corresponding loss of detail in depth.

The social definition of the scope of information which arises as explained above is further delimited by the conscious information or public relations policies espoused by not a few highly organised religions. The relatively new religions, Tenrikyō, Ōmotokyō and Risshō Kōseikai, for example, have extremely effective foreign relations and publications departments, to which the foreign enquirer will normally be directed in the first instance. In such cases clear ideas are held about what the observer should be encouraged to see, and what is "not very important." Unlike a traditional Buddhist temple, the Great Sacred Hall of the Risshō Kōseikai has an entrance which is under constant, if friendly observation, so that it is not easy for a foreign researcher to simply mingle with the believers, without himself being under observation. The believers themselves belong to recognisable groups, so that outsiders are noticeable even if they are Japanese. In the case of the Sōka Gakkai any visit to central buildings will be organised from start to finish by the public relations department, with guides to explain things in the right way; natural conversation with ordinary believers is not possible under such circumstances. When the massive head temple was still standing at Taisekiji (before the schism with the Nichiren Shōshū) the believers were organised in groups, so that even if the grounds could be entered unobserved it would be impossible simply to move around with the believers as at traditional temples.

In the case of branch temples or churches of the newer religious organisations the enquirer will usually be referred back to the headquarters for information, since the local leadership may not be confident of giving the right impression. While photography is a widely acceptable activity in Japan, and often encouraged, taking photographs of the building of a local branch may be firmly prohibited in case the results are not sufficiently impressive. These features have been experienced, for example, at a branch of PL Kyōdan.

Thus there are many situations where direct, informal contact with religious believers is limited in one way or another by the religious organisations. At the same time access to printed sources is to a significant extent conditioned by the perception on the part of the official representatives of any particular religion, denomination or movement, as to what kind of information is appropriate. The publicity department of the Sōka Gakkai, for example, is generous with its donations of books presenting the current position of the teaching and recent activities of the leaders; but it is not easy to assess precisely the impact which these have on the millions of ordinary believers. The exclusive use of such sources tends to push the enquirer back on to the application of the historico-philological method. It may be that he or she can supplement the sources so made available by further researches in library holdings of earlier materials. However these are not easy to find in libraries where the materials in question were not regarded as being "serious" sources at the time. The latest issues of religious magazines are easily available from the religious organisations themselves (though foreigners may sometimes be held at a distance with foreign language editions, which do not have exactly the same value for research). Issues from previous years or decades however are very hard to come by, for they are thought not to present the religion in the light which is preferred for the present day. Thus the holdings of public, secular libraries, in so far as they have been encouraged or allowed to collect such "non-scientific" materials, can take on an unexpected and unplanned importance.

Ephemeral sources in fieldwork situations

Within this overall situation there is a significant conclusion to be drawn, with practical implications, about the value of sources which can be derived from fieldwork situations. It was noted in the introductory example given above that research into the simplest village festival based on a Shintō shrine will naturally involve paying attention to documentary evidence of a temporary character. Such documents, which in themselves can only be studied in a "philological" manner, should complement any oral statements of those interviewed on the spot or notes based on observation and participant observation. They provide a means of circumventing the access obstacles which may otherwise hold up the researcher, and allow him or her to gather much complementary and statistically valuable information, thus providing a more stable picture of what is taking place.

There are many other types of ephemeral documents which may be viewed in the field situation, but which cannot usually be preserved without doing violence to the customs of the people. Very popular among visitors to shrines and temples are the votive tablets known as *ema,* which, bearing the hand-written prayers of devotees, are left in the shrine or temple compound. Also important are the *o-fuda* (paper or wooden amulets) acquired each year at the shrine or temple and then returned to be disposed of by a formal burning.

Such items can of course be bought and simply kept as documents without being used. In addition there are innumerable information leaflets and brochures which carry information about the religious institution, building or grounds. Without being overtly religious documents in themselves, such ephemera are also very significant sources for the researcher into religion in the field. The simple comparison of lists of annual events provided in such miscellaneous ways can, for example, be extremely instructive. Even in the case of the very highly organised religions which seek more or less consciously to control the flow of information there are usually additional ephemera, such as programs for particular occasions, or advertisements for ancillary services such as the sale of religious objects, which complement the officially promoted sources.

The main types of ephemera for Japanese religion in general may be listed as follows: *o-fuda* (paper or wooden amulets), *ema* (votive tablets), *mikuji* (fortune-telling slips), calendars, hanging scrolls, devotional booklets, travel guides, notice boards with maps of temple or shrine grounds, posters, announcements, *chirashi* (flyers delivered with newspapers). Others will no doubt mentally add further types of ephemera to those mentioned here, and in any case many ephemera are hard to classify, being little more than miscellaneous scraps of paper or impermanent religious accessories. To which genre belong, for example, tiny paper flags bearing the phrase Namu Amida Butsu, planted near the path to the top of Mount Hiko in Kyūshū? Some ephemera have a more transitory nature than others. In most walks of life, the normal way for ephemera to be lost, or to remain true to their "ephemeral" nature, is that they are thrown away or decay to the point of non-recognition. Newspapers may be used as wrapping paper and then be torn or discarded. Symbol-bearing railway cards are increasingly recycled. It should also not be forgotten that every year there is a burning of millions of amulets and other religious paraphernalia from the previous year. This is done, usually with an appropriate ritual (but interestingly not always), after all the stuff has been collected at shrines and temples. Even while everything is on its way to the fire, the various materials can be informative. A careful look at what has been deposited at the collection point will be rewarding, for it may often be observed that at major shrines and temples the materials "brought back" were not in fact acquired there, but somewhere else. When *o-fuda* from Meiji Shrine turn up for disposal at major Buddhist temples such as that known popularly as Kawasaki Daishi, it is clear that the general population regard these institutions as being part of a continuum of religious culture in which they participate without sharp differentiation.

Not to be overlooked are the varied informal versions or editions of short formal texts which have a long history of their own. An obvious example of this may be seen in the various ways in which the ancient Mahāyāna Buddhist *Heart Sūtra* is presented in different Buddhist contexts. The local variations and special applications will be of interest here. Quite often the *Heart Sūtra* is found in the context of a hand-held, folding service book which appears in many variations, differing somewhat even within some of the larger denominations, but more so as between the main schools of Japanese Buddhism. A similar hand-held, folding format is in use in various new religions, even in cases where the main inspiration is Shintōist rather than Buddhist. In such cases the books may very likely be on sale for use by believers. Nevertheless, although the general characteristics are widely familiar, it is not really possible in most cases to trace the precise pedigree in a library. The character of such works, which under normal circumstances will be replaced sometime with an edition which is updated or improved in some respect, is essentially *ephemeral.*

Slightly more specialised, but very numerous, are the ephemera to be found on pilgrimage routes: pilgrims's slips for depositing at the temples, usually bearing a simple prayer formula, as a sign that one has been there, *nōkyōchō* (books for collecting temples' seals and calligraphy, as a proof of visit for the returning pilgrim), and *miei* (small pictures of the buddha or bodhisattva of each temple, used as devotional mementos).[3] The hanging scrolls which are also often used as a base for the seals and calligraphy of each temple are also in principle ephemeral, for they are often disposed of at the pilgrim's death. When analysing pilgrimage, especially in Japan, it is helpful to proceed in three stages, considering first the route and the journey, second the ritual actions or transaction carried out at each temple or shrine on the way, and third the question of the meanings which are important for the pilgrims. The relevant ephemera are of great value in the study of each of these. In particular, the *differentiation* of Buddhist and Shintō significations can conveniently be read off the ephemeral sources, because it is in these that alternative readings of the meaning of the act of pilgrimage are indirectly documented. Thus handwritten copies of the *Hannya Shingyō* (the Heart Sutra) will be seen in Buddhist contexts, while these are not desired at Shintō shrines. Indeed at one Shintō shrine a notice (no doubt an ephemeral one) was displayed reading "Please do not recite the Heart Sūtra here", betraying the point at which meanings are differentiated, or in the case of some enthusiastic visitors evidently *not* differentiated. Some visitors might recite the Heart Sutra in "the wrong place" through ignorance, but there is also a tendency for pilgrims in the Shingon, Tendai or Shugendō traditions to bring Buddhist meanings into non-Buddhist holy places, i. e. Shintō shrines or on sacred mountains mainly administered (nowadays) by Shintō authorities. And this is not always welcomed.

In spite of the rather massive ritual or accidental destruction of what *could* be of interest, there remains a limited availability of some older ephemera. Relevant travel guides, *nōkyōchō* (the seal and calligraphy books of pilgrims) or religious scrolls may turn up in flea-markets. Recitation booklets are not regarded as being the subject of ritual disposable and may be collected freely at second-hand bookshops. Other types of ephemera, e. g. the pilgrim slips mentioned above, cannot really be found in later years except when decaying on site. Nevertheless longi-

3 Fe examples of these, illustrated and translated, see Pye 1987a.

tudinal consistency can be assessed to some extent, even after the ritualised destruction of what for researchers would be potential source materials.

Ephemera in the presentation of research

Finally, given the fascinating complexity of ephemeral source materials for Japanese religious culture, consideration should be given to its later treatment. Ephemera are invaluable in research reporting or teaching because they can easily be transported and they make an immediate communicative impact. Seminar participants are thereby encouraged to handle and thus to consider "real things" from the field. Nowadays the real things can be valuably supplemented by innumerable digital images, which should however not displace the objects altogether. At the same time, in many hands such materials remains miscellaneous and eventually suffer from loss of context. It is therefore very desirable to document apparently unimportant materials as far as time and strength permit. As a simple example of this we may adduce a catalogue entitled *O-meguri, Pilgerfahrt in Japan* (Pye 1987a), listing the numerous small items of an exhibition on Japanese Buddhist pilgrimage in the university library at Marburg at that time.[4] A further temporary exhibition with a number of larger exhibits was mounted in the Museum of Religions (*Religionskundliche Sammlung*) of the same university from 2009 to 2011.[5] This time the main focus was on hanging scrolls (*kakejiku*) as religious artefacts in the context of pilgrimages and various forms of everyday religious practice.[6] This illustrates the fact that the concept of *ephemera* is quite broad, while it is always necessary to emphasise with respect to larger ephemera such as hanging scrolls, or posters, that these are not necessarily regarded in this perspective as works of art. Indeed many of

4 From the writer's own collections. In the meantime these have grown further; a web-based documentation is desirable and in the long run enquiries may be directed to the Museum of Religions (Religionskundliche Sammlung) of the University of Marburg.

5 This exhibition was jointly mounted with Katja Triplett and included many personally collected items as well as some others from the holdings of the museum itself. The illustrated catalogue (Pye and Triplett 2011) was entitled *Pilgerfahrt visuell. Hängerollen in der religiösen Alltagspraxis Japans*.

6 A particular stimulus for the concept of the exhibition was Brian Bocking's work on the variations in a particular set of hanging scrolls in his *The Oracles of the Three Shrines: Windows on Japanese Religion* (2000).

them would have no chance of being taken up into fine exhibitions. Financially well-endowed connoisseurs with an artistic bent might regard them as rubbish. However, I regard them as fascinating sources which tell us a great deal about religious ideas and practices. Seen in this way, they also become visually interesting into the bargain.

Conclusions

Such ephemera as all or any of these are often despised, on the one hand, by historians, who do not usually regard them as major sources, especially if they have not yet acquired any notable antiquity. Needless to say, they would be regarded differently if they were centuries old and were printed by order of a member of the royal family, like the tiny copies of the *Dhāraṇī Sūtra* printed in Japan in the year 770 (the oldest known multiple printing) and distributed to temples all over the land! They are also often disregarded by those social scientists who prefer only to ask people verbal questions, or to arrange for others to ask questions.

We may conclude however that there are several reasons why ephemera can take on great significance for the study of religions. First, they are evidence for the communication which is taking place between the religious organization and the individual participant in religious behaviour, or between the participant and the gods, or between the participant and his or her own family, colleagues and associates. Second, the information provided by such ephemera does not only have a qualitatively interesting character; it also takes on a quantitative value because of the sheer mass of material which is constantly being produced, but which is only visible in the field. For example, pilgrim slips can be considered as documents of individual journeys, but they can also be *counted.* Third, such information often escapes the directive policies of the publication and public relations departments of successful religious organisations. Even when it is printed centrally, it is intended for common religious use rather than for conscious publicity purposes. Finally, and above all, materials of this kind are not published, selected, edited or otherwise adjusted for the benefit of researchers who happen to be foreigners. Thus, at the confluence of historical and social-scientific method, such ephemera provide a particularly reliable and valuable answer to the problem of access in the study of Japanese religions.

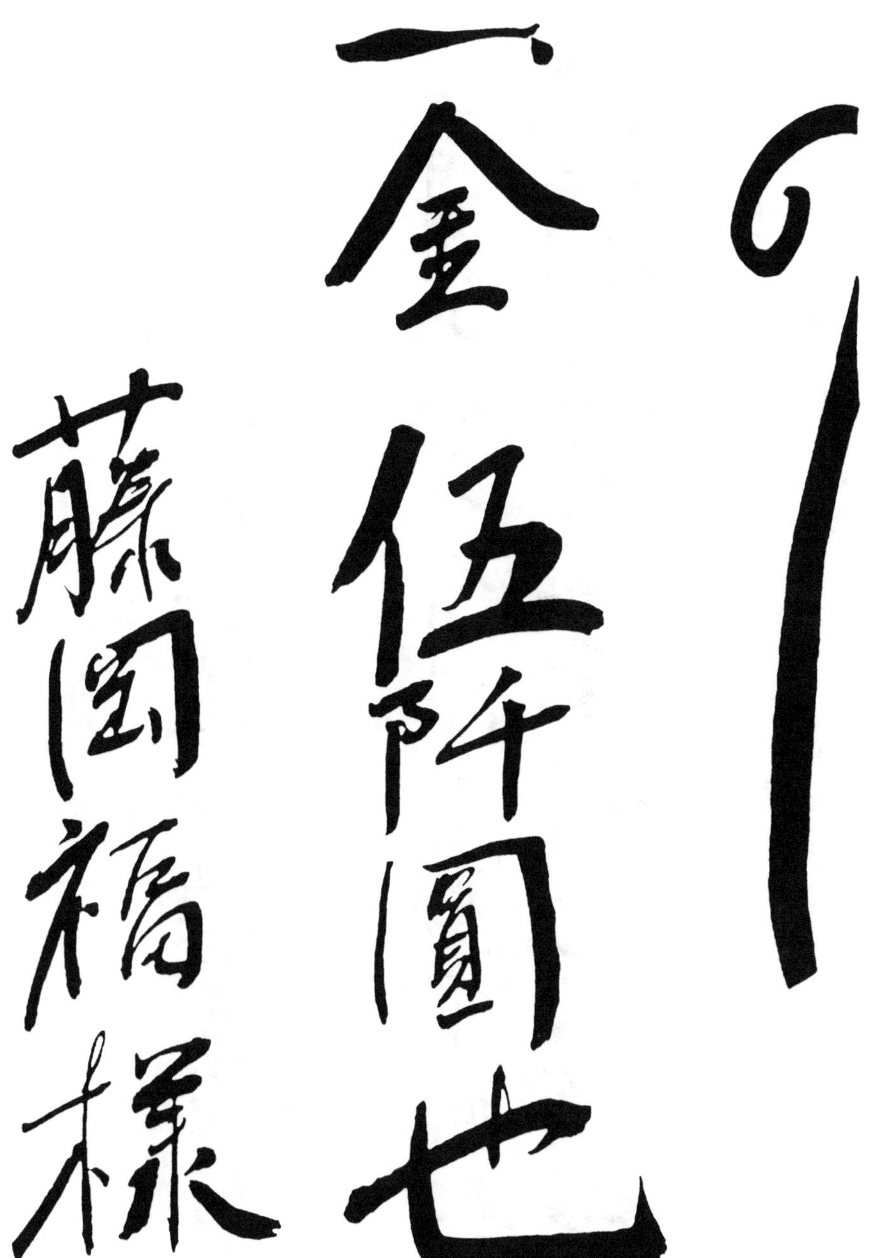

Illustration 1. Ephemerum at village (Shintō) shrine summer festival.

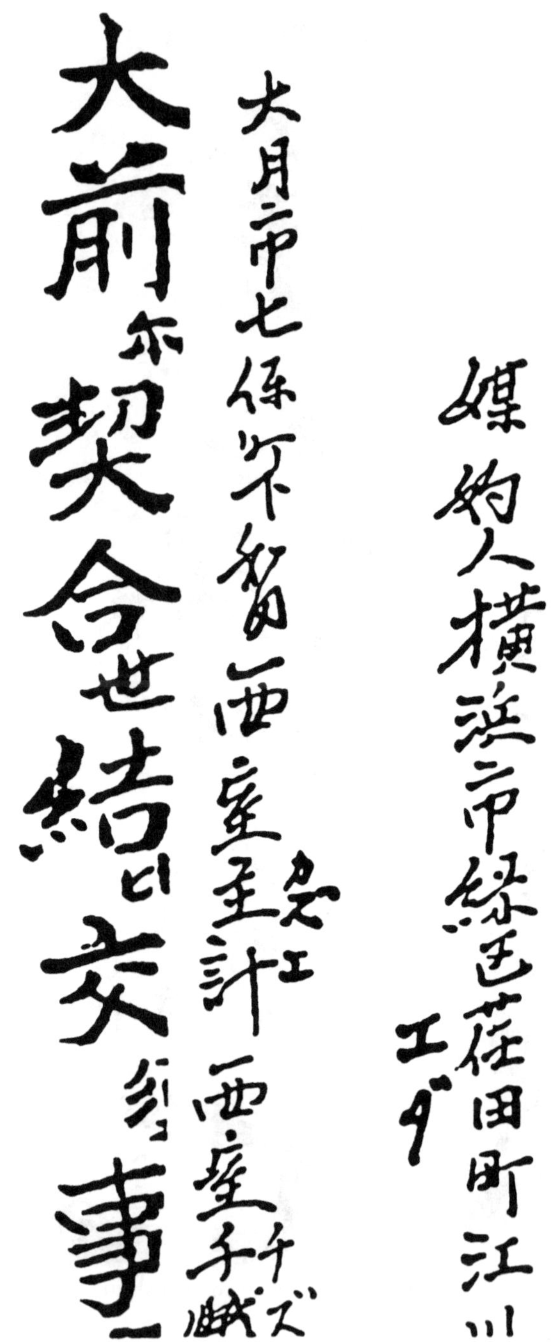
媒妁人横浜市緑区荏田町江川
大月市七保町下和田西室至計西室千歳
大前尓契合世結ヒ交須事

Illustration 2. Fragment of a *norito* text used many times over.

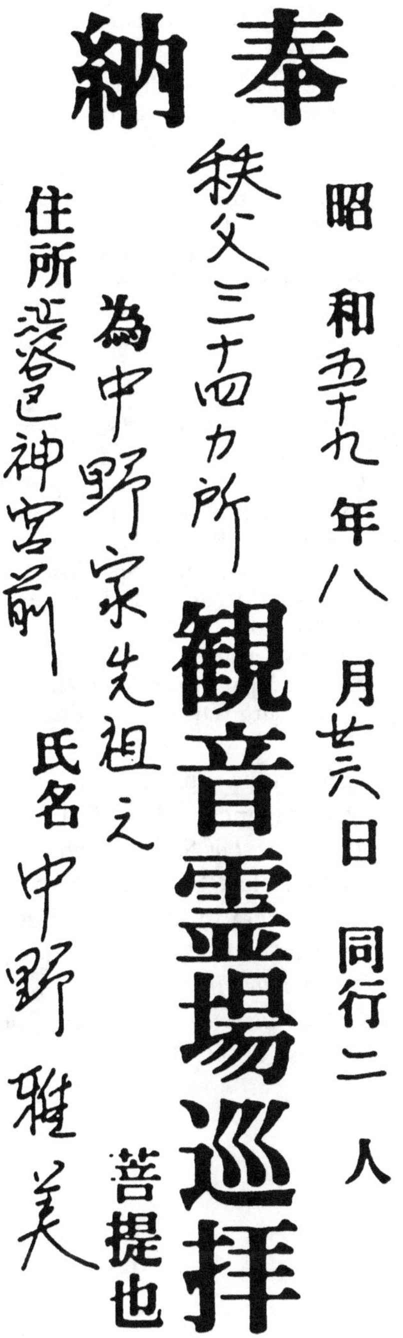

奉納

昭和五十九年八月廿六日　同行二人

秩父三十四カ所

観音霊場巡拝

為中野家先祖之菩提也

住所渋谷区神宮前

氏名中野雅美

Illustration 3. Pilgrim slip from Chichibu Buddhist pilgrimage circuit temple no. 34, reprinted from *O-meguri, Pilgerfahrt in Japan*, 55.

Bibliographical references

Earhart, Byron H. 1970. A Religious Study of the Mount Haguro Sect of Shugendō: An Example of Japanese Mountain Religion. Tokyo (Sophia University).

– 1989. Gedatsu-kai and Religion in Contemporary Japan, Returning to the Center. Bloomington and Indianapolis (Indiana University Press).

Hardacre, Helen 1984. Lay Buddhism in Contemporary Japan. Reiyūkai Kyōdan. Princeton (Princeton University Press).

– 1986 Kurozumikyō and the New Religions of Japan. Princeton (Princeton University Press).

Bocking, Brian 2000. The Oracles of the Three Shrines: Windows on Japanese Religion.

– Richmond (Curzon).

Philippi, Donald L. 1959. Norito, A New Translation of the Ancient Japanese Ritual Prayers, Tokyo (Kokugakuin Daigaku).

Pye, Michael 1987a. O-meguri, Pilgerfahrt in Japan. Katalog einer Ausstellung. Marburg (Universitätsbibliothek der Philipps-Universität Marburg).

– 1999a. "Methodological Integration in the Study of Religions" in: Tore Ahlbäck (ed.) Approaching Religion, Scripta Instituti Donneriani Aboensis XVII (1), Åbo/Turku, Finland (Donner Institute for Research in Religious and Cultural History): 188–205.

Pye, Michael and Triplett, Katja 2011. Pilgerfahrt visuell. Hängerollen in der religiösen Alltagspraxis Japans (Veröffentlichungen der Religionskundlichen Sammlung 5), Marburg (Diagonal Verlag) 2011.

Precursor versions of this article were published as: (a) "Philology and fieldwork in the study of Japanese religion" in: Tyloch, Witold (ed.), *Studies on Religions in the Context of Social Sciences. Methodological and Theoretical Relations*, Warsaw (Polish Society for the Study of Religions) 1990: 146–159; (b) "Ephemera in Japanese religion with special reference to Buddhist pilgrimage" in: Baskind, James (ed.) *Scholars of Buddhism in Japan: Buddhist Studies in the 21st Century. The Ninth Annual Symposium for Scholars Resident in Japan*, Kyōto (International Research Center for Japanese Studies) 2009: 67–78.

1.5 Participation, Observation and Reflection: An Endless Method

This paper offers some reflections on the methodology of field work which is carried out with a view to developing comparative perspectives in the study of religions. It was conceived in honour of Juha Pentikäinen, the well-known Finnish specialist in the study of religions who among other things has studied shamanism in various contexts.

Insiders, outsiders and specialists

When invited to contribute to this volume of essays I first conceived the goal of presenting an account of *civil religion* in the wider context of Mexican religiosity, based on some observations which I carried out recently in various cities. In other words, I intended to report some *results.* And in all brevity, I will indeed do so below. However, I am neither a specialist in Mexican studies, nor an *americanista.* While developing the presentation therefore, I realised that a methodological reflection is needed on the relation between field observations in an area where one is a specialist and field observations in an area where one is not a specialist. As far as I know this has not been thought about very much. It is important, however, because the way in which the relation between these two is understood relates to the general question of balance in the study of religions. Without achieving some balance, comparative perspectives cannot be reliably or interestingly developed. Without comparative perspectives general questions about religion cannot be sensibly formulated or answered. I decided therefore to concentrate here on the methodological aspect, with some illustrative examples, and to present a fuller account of the extremely complex Mexican materials at a later date.

"Fieldwork is a hard rite" (or orthodox-liturgically, "a heavy rite"), they are saying.[1] And so it is, not least, for the comparativist in the study of religions. We are commonly supposed to have command of a specialism in relation to a particular country or region such as Siberia, Japan, Greece, Brazil or Nigeria, with knowledge of a relevant language or languages, and years of experience in the field. We are supposed to have made various attempts at reporting back, wherever "back" is, once we have really lived somewhere different from where we started! On the other hand we are also supposed to develop our knowledge more widely in order to be able to put specialised knowledge into a comparative perspective. Of course there are also those specialists who do everything backwards, being experts about the field within which they themselves were born and formed, and seeking the comparative perspective elsewhere as far as time permits. But then, in these cases, quite often time does not seem to permit. Obstinately, the comparative perspective fails to materialise.

Provocatively, I have just used the word "backwards". In the course of studying subjects such as Mahāyāna Buddhism or astronomy, it is possible to learn that the apparent difference between forwards and backwards may be deceptive. This is instructive, metaphorically, for understanding the methodology of the study of religions. Field research in the study of religions consists of a pattern of three key elements, namely participation, observation and reflection. Participation may be more or less intensive, ranging from mere attendance to playing a full role in some religious practice like meditation. Observation may be quantitative or qualitative. Reflection may be discursive or take the form of compact models of analysis. However all these variations do not need to be pursued now. What I wish to emphasise here is that while the sequence "participation, observation and reflection" might seem at first sight to stand in a logical order, in real life and work the three elements may be learned and put into practice in various sequences.

For example, a person might be born into and grow up and participate in one society, more or less without reflection, and then through study and experience learn to participate, to observe and to reflect *elsewhere*. This may lead, in a later development, to greater observation and reflection on the initial society, and thus to a different kind of participation. But it is also possible to put all three elements into practice with-

1 I.e. in the title of the multi-authored work in which this essay first appeared: *Ethnography is a Heavy Rite* (Holm et al. 2000).

in the society into which one was born. In one's own society of origin participation will inevitably occur before reflection, which in turn may occur before observation in any sustained and intended sense. In a society beyond the society of origin, however, it is quite possible that observation will occur first, reflection second and participation only later, leading in turn to more observation and more reflection. In other words, it is maintained here that experience in "field research" relevant to the study of religions can be gained in varying sequences, both in the society into which one is born and in societies of which one becomes aware only later.

Moreover even this is over-simplified. Significantly increasing numbers of people, and this includes some of the small number who study religions, are not born and bred in one single society at all, but are aware from an early age of the plurality of societies and cultures. To illustrate, my own eldest son was born in Japan, both parents being European but of differing nationality, so that for almost the first three years of his life he was regarded, in Japan, as a foreigner, that is, in colloquial Japanese, a *gaijin*. The literal meaning of this word, for which there are equivalents in other East Asian languages, is "outside person". When, shortly after birth, he was first registered as an alien at the "alien immigration office", one of the questions to be answered on the form was where he had immigrated from! This was a metaphysical puzzle indeed. On the basis of an *ad hoc* decision he had already been granted a British passport, following the father's nationality. So the bureaucratic solution was to return the false answer "Britain", as country of origin. Nearly three years later he arrived in Britain for the first time, at the sea port of Southampton. After a few days of bemusement, he concluded, speaking Japanese, that the country was full of *gaijin*. The right wing politician of the day in Britain, Enoch Powell, was at that period running a vicious campaign against immigration into Britain which included his notorious "rivers of blood" speech. The statistics which he constantly quoted, raising the level of anxiety among the population, were based on the numbers of "persons born abroad of foreign mothers". This included our son, the *gaijin*. Such experiences contain all the above-mentioned elements of participation, observation and reflection, and illustrate the complexity of the relationship between them.

Naturally these complications play havoc with any simple view of the so-called "insider-outsider" problem. How do we know, when engaging in theoretical discussions, who is "inside" and who is "outside"? And what are they inside or outside *of*? There is of course a simple answer to these questions. Usually people are trying with such terminology to refer, distinctively, to the participant on the one hand and to the observer on the other hand. This is important. Moreover the century-old work of distinguishing the study of religions from "being religious", doing theology, or promoting a religious point of view requires this or similar distinctions to be made. The abiding virtue of the so-called phenomenological tradition in the study of religions, now unpopular with younger writers, has been to emphasise the self-understanding of believers (or participants, as I have always added) and to regard this as being of significance for the study of religious systems. This approach has to be distinguished from theories, or indeed very often theologies, which from the start would inflict an alien interpretative scheme on to systems of religious behaviour or thought. Unfortunately, as has often been pointed out, the work of the very representatives of the phenomenological school who pleaded for this was itself often structured, if unconsciously, by theological perspectives. Nevertheless they led the way. There is no need whatever to turn the clock back on this well-worn discussion, which has been an important factor in the emergence of a discipline of the study of religions which is independent of religions themselves.

Observant participation

Nevertheless, a simple view of the opposition between outsider and insider will not do, as the attraction of the equally well known phrase "participant observation" has also shown over many years. Valuable though this concept has been, not only in ethnology, but also specifically in the study of religions, it needs to be adjusted or complemented in an important respect. This correction is needed because the *sequence* may be more complex than is often realised. When people refer to "participant observation" they are usually talking about the idea of going out of one system into another system, participating in that "other" system and thereby putting themselves into a position to observe it. But this oppositional approach is not really adequate for an inclusive study of religions. Not only "participant observation" should be recognised as a normal feature in the study of religions but also, to use a phrase of my own coinage, *observant participation*. This phrase is intended to suggest that for some people, in particular those who seek sensitively to study religions, that in which they already participate provides a basis for the development of observation and then for further reflection. This is because, by simple reflection, they have already observed that they are participating. This is not really difficult. Indeed I would claim that I discovered it for myself during adolescence, although I only later knew that I had done so. No doubt others have done the same. But it is desirable, for the study of religions, to become conscious of it. The importance of this variation in the methodological models available lies in the fact that it enables the specialist in the study of religions to escape from the traditional and still rather strong idea that he or she is expected to study what are known as "other" religions or even "foreign" religions (suggested by the dreadful German expression *Fremdreligionen*). *Any* religions can be studied by means of participation, observation and reflection, and the order of these may be varied. The results will depend to a varying extent on all three. Participation may be relatively low. For some enquiries it may not be necessary, and for others it may be indispensable to some extent.

It is fundamental even to the classic idea of participant observation, though not always noted, that "reflection," the third element referred to above, is also essential for the research endeavour to remain scientific. In a formally conceived research process, reflection should involve both analysis and report. Without these, participant observation is scientifically useless, though it may be interesting as a way of life. I have personally lost sight of not a few promising students who did not quite understand this. They went off to participate and observe, but never came back. They are probably living to this day on various sunny islands, participating. But let us return to the question of the *sequence* of the three elements which, I have suggested above, does not necessarily always have to be understood to be the same. Reflection, too, may well occur at various moments in the whole complex process. By applying flexibility in our understanding of the sequence, we can arrive at very useful and appropriate variations in our understanding of the relations between "insiders" and "outsiders", "participants" and "observers", "starting point" and "field", without giving up the conceptual independence which has been gained over the decades for the discipline of the study of religions.

On the basis of these fundamental considerations my argument now progresses to a consideration of the relationship between research in fields for which specialised knowledge is already available to the researcher and research in fields where this is not the case. In view of the above arguments it should be noted that a sub-question arises about how to position research in a field which is quite familiar (in my case some of the counties of England, for example) but concerning which no specialised academic knowledge is claimed. In the interests of keeping the argument simple enough to follow, this sub-question will not be addressed in detail.

Fieldwork never ends

Let us presuppose, then, a certain depth of experience in either quantitative or qualitative research in the context of one particular society, so that the main problems of field research have been resolved in some way or other. These questions are not my subject just now. What I want to suggest is that the extension of methodological experience to other, less well known fields is not only possible but also desirable, and may be consciously pursued in the interests of achieving a more broadly based comparative perspective. Moreover the argument is that this extension is of particular importance in the discipline known as the study of religions (or *Religionswissenschaft*, etc.). It may not have the same importance in some other disciplines. I do not assert that archaeologists, for example, should go around digging all over the place. It may be that archaeologists should restrict their digging to sites in regions in which they have specialised knowledge. Here we would see, therefore, one of the distinctive features in the "methodological clustering" characteristic of the study of religions.

In the study of religions fieldwork never ends. Yet it can become easier. How relaxing it is, on such a basis, to pay visits to countries less well known to the researcher than the area of his or her main specialism, still mysterious, fascinating, where one has the great advantage of a certain *naiveté*. Relative *naiveté*, however, may be combined with a much higher degree of reflection, which is informed through comparisons, than is brought to the subject matter even by intellectuals residing within the country itself. To illustrate from personal activities, although the success level and the documention are uneven, I have tried it out to some degree in Korea, China, Siberia, Poland, Finland, England, Germany, South Africa and most recently Mexico.

In such situations one can discover things which are only half known to the intellectuals of the country itself. It may seem that such discoveries occur by chance. Partly it is by chance, but partly it is by intention. In South Africa, for example, I investigated the overwhelming

Voortrekker Monument outside Pretoria with an Afrikaaner colleague, who out of sheer liberalism had not been there himself for decades. He was reluctant to go there, and only his personal kindness and liberalness permitted him to agree to my request. Now it was most unfashionable, in 1994, even to mention this astounding example of civil religion (centred on the idea of "Ons vir jou, Suid-Afrika!" etc.). Participants at a conference in Pretoria were visibly shocked at the mere mention of the Voortrekker Monument at the beginning of a plenary address. It seemed best to compare it to the Stalinist Palace of Culture and Science in Warsaw (which I have also observed from without and from within during the communist period). The comparison lies in the Polish joke that it is *from there* that one has the best view of the city at large. However even this was barely understood in South Africa, for few South Africans at that time had visited Poland during the communist period. Nor would the comparison have made sense in Poland, for very few Polish people visited the Voortrekker Monument during the apartheid period, I believe. And since Poland has also changed, it is now too late for the two populations to share their jokes. It seemed prudent therefore to omit this reference in my own contribution to the South African publication entitled *Religion and the Reconstruction of Civil Society* (see "Religion and identity: clues and threads" 7.2 below). Notice in this very title the interest in "civil society", the central recognition that it needed to be reconstructed, and the idea that this problematic complex has something to do with religion. And the Voortrekker Monument was there all the time, in its dramatic studiability, raising the reflective questions, at least for this observer, as to what should be done with it, or how it should be presented, in the post-apartheid era. Warsaw's Palace of Culture and Science, another embarrassing attempt to insist on a civil religion, was also still there, raising the same questions for the future. What should the construction or the "reconstruction" of civil society be like, and what could or should religion have to do with it, if anything? In the meantime we have seen some of the developments in both countries. Observers of Polish culture during the communist period will know that an alternative civil religion was also being encouraged, namely a nationalist one. I observed the workings of this directly, by participating in activities organized by the lay association Pax, which provided a syncretistic context for the dynamic correlation in tension (which is how I understand syncretism to function) of Catholicism, Communism and Patriotism. A more straightforward symbol of the alternative civil religion, however, evident to any visitors, was the precise restoration of the old square in Warsaw including the "Royal Palace".

It was worthy of note that the People's Republic of Poland, without a royal family, should at that time require a "Royal Palace". Unfortunately the English designation "palace" obscures the difference between *pałac* (with a hint of the French *palais*) and *zamek* (more like the German *Schloss*). To use a more recently popular term, there was a lot of "negotiation" going on in Poland in those days. The methodological point here is that only field observation carried out in each of these two fields gives rise to comparative reflection on the role of the above mentioned monuments in the changing fortunes of civil religion. The "insiders" at the time did not notice or reflect on these things in the same way. Possibly, they just "knew" them. As to "outsiders" there are probably few researchers in the study of religions who happen to have *specialist* field knowledge of, specifically, just these two societies, Poland and South Africa. In any case there are certainly not enough researchers in the study of religions to cover all possible combinations of countries and regions as specialists.

Or consider the beautiful Finnish city of Turku, or Åbo, where inside the cathedral a most interesting juxtaposition of protestant hymns in Swedish and Finnish can be experienced. Of course the inhabitants *know* about this, as one congregation makes way for another. But do they *think* about it? I suspect that the large majority know about it, without even noticing it, not to mention "observing" it, or "reflecting" upon it. Indeed, no colleagues or acquaintances ever drew my attention to it on my various visits to Turku/ Åbo! Probably they thought I was just giving some lectures, taking part in an examination, or attending a conference, and did not realise that I was also doing field observations. Thanks to Grimm's law and various orthographic decisions, the Swedish hymns are easier to follow with regard to the meaning, but from the point of view of phonetics, the Finnish hymns are easier to "participate" in than the Swedish ones. This has to be done very quietly of course. One has to pretend to be an old man with a small voice and an uncertain sense of music, so that any small mistakes might pass as normal behaviour by such a helpless old fellow. Which congregation cares most about the singing? To what extent do people care, or do they care at all, about the meaning of what they are singing? In most of my informal enquiries about this, the majority of people do not care about the meaning of what they are singing. However the question has not been sufficiently explored in the study of religions. The relation between knowledge of the content, commitment to the performance and whether people are good or bad singers would be interesting factors to investigate.

These are just a few simple illustrations of the practice of participation, observation and reflection. The fundamental point, important for a good understanding of method, is that there are so many practical aspects to the discovery of all the subtly interconnected features of religion in societies, large or small, pre-modern or modern. Of course not all of these are to be found in buildings such as those referred to above. Suggestions to beginners in fieldwork may very profitably begin with instructions like "Ride around on the metro" or "Switch on the television." But perhaps there is no television and no metro, the reader may object, for example if you are afloat on the river Ob or Irtysh in the Siberian summer. This too provides a valuable opportunity for checking over the relative delapidation or state of repair of some local churches along the shoreline. So here the suggestion would be: "Get out there and see how tough the mosquitoes are, and don't forget your *repellentni*". Juha Pentikäinen is also aware of this problem, as I know from a common acquaintance in Novosibirsk. Yes, fieldwork is a heavy rite.

Civil religion in Mexico: Green Indians and the Empress of the Americas

In September 1999, mainly as a result of a very kind invitation by a colleague, I was able to travel around for some time in Mexico. After a short while, in search of civil religion and related matters, I left the Ciudad de Mexico (Mexico City) and took a first class bus to the harbour city of Veracruz. That was the easy, comfortable part. After that: the walking, the looking, the asking, the listening, the uneven paving, searing pains in my left foot, the endless fascination of the people. In Veracruz the whole new, old world is there to discover, the immense secularity of a vulgar harbour city, Catholicism, El Señor de la Viaje, the architecturally impressive customs office and post office, the lack of religion, the religion where there is no religion, the civil religion of the museum of the naval college. After Veracruz the journey took me back inland to the cities of Puebla and Tlaxcala, and then back to the impossible City of Mexico itself.

So where is the civil religion of Mexico? What are its main elements? And how does it relate to the wider spectrum of religion in the country? In fact it is quite possible for the non-specialist observer to discern it, even if naively, for the simple reason that civil religion itself is essentially naive. In Puebla for example, in September 1999, a festival with much loud music was in full swing at the Zócalo (central square). The official banners proclaimed: "Puebla: una ciudád para todos" (Puebla: a city for all), while others displayed the slogan of an ethnic identity organisation stating: "Nuestras raices viven" (our roots are alive). It appears that the distinctively ethnic element had sought, and had been given a place under the overall civic idea of "a city for all," though the relation between the major and the minor civil religions was not quite resolved.

Puebla has a number of famous churches, beginning with the Cathedral. Here there is a prominent alms box near the door surmounted by the torso of a male person of most desperate appearance. Who is this sad figure who requires our support? The text indicates that these alms are destined for masses for deceased bishops and priests (*los señores obispos y sacerdotes difuntos*). The priests and bishops are expected to join the heavenly population in the end, but may need assistance in between times. Out in the streets of Puebla on the other hand, volunteers are organising relief parcels for the *damnificados*, i. e. the victims of the recent extensive floods. In short, the chantry principle remains firmly present in the religiosity promoted by the cathedral, but outside there is competition from a charity principle which appeals to civil solidarity and civil virtue. Such elements of civil religion often go unnoticed, except to the inveterate observer, suffering from uneven pavements, unaccustomed noise and all those other things which make fieldwork a hard rite.

Further illustrations may be drawn from the underground metro system in Mexico City itself. Metropolitan transport systems provide excellent opportunities for getting to know the symbolic orientations which are taken for granted by the population of the city, as I learned years ago through thousands of rides in Tokyo. While mainly not "religious", my various friends in Mexico City were extremely well informed about the remarkably named metro stations in Mexico City such as "Insurgentes", "Revolución", "Niños Heroes" (meaning "Boy Heroes") and even "Indios Verdes" ("Green Indians")! On this basis, we considered how very significant the map of the Mexico City metro might be for reflecting on civil religion. This map however, is very hard to acquire. It cannot be bought. Rather, it is given away free of charge. From this we can at least deduce that *citizens* have a right to get it. Unfortunately however there were none left. A few days later there were also none left. In fact it became quite interesting to discover how many information stands there were at which it was impossible to acquire this map. In the end I managed to acquire a commercially offered metro plan in a little plastic wallet, for about five *dollares mexicanos*. It should be noted that *dollares mexicanos* are more correctly known as *pesos*, but by calling them *dollares* a statement is made on behalf of all Mexicans, rather like building Tokyo Tower to surpass the Eiffel Tower by a few metres.

Not a few of the metro station names are important symbols in Mexican civil religion, suspended in a state of institutionalised revolution, like "Insurgentes", memorialised in a major traffic route. The "Niños Heroes" are young men who romantically laid down their lives in a hopelessly lost war against "the north". An intellectual, atheist friend was, thankfully, able to explain the historical associations of almost all the metro stations which we passed through, though it was hard to hear him speak above the noise of the train. Moreover he fully appreciated the civil force of many of these names. Only at the reference to "Indios Verdes" did he resist firmly. This really had no particular meaning, he argued, plausibly. In one sense the informant is always right, of course. Yet after all the years of talk about Mexican independence and identity, overcoming the ethnic contradictions etc., which are not entirely overcome, the question remains how there can possibly be any such thing as "Green Indians"! I wanted to go there. However, when the metro held still for a moment or two I was informed that "Green Indians" is nothing more than a rather boring sculpture in the middle of a very noisy traffic concourse, so that going there would be a complete waste of time.

This reminded me of Bloemfontein in South Africa, which was so boring, I had been told in 1994, that I was more or less forbidden to go there too. In fact, however, Bloemfontein is rather interesting. It all depends on what one is interested in. My own informal report on the matter was entitled "The battle of Bloemfontein", on the basis that I had to battle to get there, and that if the *new* South Africa could emerge at all, the decisive battle would have to be won in places like Bloemfontein, a classic city in the apartheid tradition. For example the local museum would need revision to make sure that all the varieties of *homo sapiens* get into the same part of the exhibition. At the time of observation, models of black humans were shown together with other high mammals, while whites did not appear until the next room. Outside the museums, it is in cities like Bloemfontein that the poor will have to be brought in to the university from the outlying shanties (a process which had already begun in 1994), and the rich will eventually have to live without their fences and their hidden guns.

But to return to the "Green Indians" of Mexico, it has to be revealed to readers not familiar with Mexico that they are no more and no less than a group of sculptured *Indios* who have oxidised and turned *green!* And after they had turned green, a metro station was named after them! What we can see from this is that they are so integrated into the overall pattern of symbolic names in the City of Mexico that they can be referred to by anybody as "Green Indians", indifferently, and yet so easily and affectionately, even while underprivileged persons of mainly "Indian" extraction are running up and down the trains trying to sell matches, electric batteries, or leaflets calling for political *change!* Although the sculpture had no specific religious intention when it was created, I regard the "Indios Verdes" of Mexico City as an item which has been unconsciously and successfully incorporated into Mexico's civil religion. How would it be possible to observe and reflect upon this without the benefit of a comparative perspective?

Naturally there is a great deal more to civil religion in Mexico than the names of a few metro stations. Moreover some of it is very much more obvious and can easily be documented by means of posters printed for educational purposes. Some of them show the history of the Mexican flag, for example, incorporating all its religious and secular variations into one grand story. Others show portraits of nationally important figures such as Venustiano Carranza, Lazaro Cardenas and Benito Juarez, each emerging out of a glorificatory cloud.

While visiting a superb exhibition of artefacts from the now highly respected, but crushed Maya civilisation with three kindly students the conversation again turned to "civil religion". The subject arose because it was quite evident that an immense pride about Mayan culture has been building up in Mexico, and this pride could be regarded as an aspect of its current civil religion. Naturally, this is debatable. It is a matter for detailed cultural assessment by specialists. Now interestingly, although the concept of civil religion was not well known to the Mexican students, it was readily understood. While explaining it briefly, apart from drawing attention to the writings of Robert Bellah, I recalled the inscriptions around the immensely high ceiling of the Victorian Town Hall of the city of Leeds in northern England, birthplace of the Industrial Revolution. Fortunately I had hastily noted them down, one day long ago, and was able to send them to Mexico later by e-mail. Here they are:

> Weave truth with truth / Forward / Goodwill towards men / Magna Charta / Deo Regi Patriae / Industry overcomes all things / God in the highest / In union is strength / Honesty is the best policy / Auspicium Melioris Aevi / Trial by jury / Labor omnia vincit.

In addition we find at the two ends of the hall the Psalmic quotations: "Except the Lord build the house they labour in vain that build it." and "Except the Lord keep the city the watchman watcheth but in vain." Similarly, if with greater secularity, I found civil religion in a poster published by the Electoral Institute of Tlaxcala, advertising and describing in detail the following values:

> Pluralidad
> Tolerancia
> Diálogo
> Respeto
> Igualdad
> Libertad
> Patriotismo
> Solidaridad
> Legalidad
> Participación

Above all, civil religion in Mexico is intensely visible in the unofficial, but national cult of the Virgen de Guadalupe as the "Queen of Mexico" and the "Empress of the Americas", the astonishingly successful successor to the pre-conquest goddess Tonantzin. Guadalupanism is based on Juan Diego's visions of the Virgin of Guadalupe in Mexico itself. Without going into any details here on this much documented subject, suffice it to add a quotation from Francisco de la Maza's book *El Guadalupenismo Mexicano* (1953):

> Guadalupanism and barock art are unique, authentic creations of the Mexican past, different from those of Spain and the rest of the world. They are the mirror fabricated by the men of the colony in order to see and discover themselves.
>
> (El guadalupanismo y el arte barroco son las únicas creaciones auténticas del pasado mexicano, diferenciales de España y del mundo. Son el espejo que fabricaron los hombres de la colonia para mirarse y discubrirse a sí mismos.)[2]

2 De la Maza 1953: 10. This fascinating work explores the gradual development

This quotation was exhibited magnificently at the conclusion of a substantial exhibition mounted by the Museo Nacional del Arte in 1999, directly opposite a painting of the installation of the virgin's *imagen*, the normatively revealed painting, at the sanctuary, in the year 1709. In other words, by means of this quotation the exhibition concludes, in full accord with the cultural tradition, by claiming its subject for the Mexican identity. This exhibition was concerned with the origins of New Spain, and covered the period from 1680 to 1750. The Guadalupan iconography appeared in diverse forms, suggesting quite prominently the correlation of the sun and moon, being male and female principles in the pre-Spanish mythology, and also showing the supporting role of the friars in getting the Mexican Virgin of Guadalupe installed as a focal symbol. This itself was part of a wider pattern of Mary's, for example La Virgen de los Zacatecos, La Virgen del Pueblito, and La Virgen de Loreto or Santa Maria de Nueva España.

This in turn throws up the question of the relationships between civil religion and other forms of religiosity in Mexico, which are extremely complex and interesting. Catholicism is a part of the spectrum, but is itself not monolithic. From the point of view of the study of religions Catholicism is undoubtedly polytheistic, at any rate in Mexico. Leaving aside other evidences, the relationship between Catholicism and Guadalupanism illustrates the point, for it can easily be argued that this particular *virgen* is a goddess in her own right. The matter has been further complicated by the recent visit of the Pope [John-Paul II], who was evidently attempting to recoup the loyalty offered to this cult for the benefit of the Church based in Rome. A huge statue was erected on the plaza of the Guadalupe's Basilica, so there he stands himself, now, like a new member of the pantheon. Another significant element is the revival of interest in pre-conquest culture through dance, music and artefacts. This is in part ethnically based, but in part is a wider cultural movement on the part of the mixed urban population, who also have other interests. Guadalupenism plays a key role in mediating between the diverse elements across the whole spectrum, but these intricate relations cannot be explored further just now. Here a synoptic list of the main elements of Mexican religiosity, without regard to their mutual interactions, must suffice. Any rounded view of Mexican reli-

---

of the symbolism of the Mexican Virgin of Guadalupe from the sixteenth century onwards, emphasizing the interplay of Mexican Indian and Spanish Catholic contributions.

giosity, with special reference to civil religion, would have to include consideration of the following elements:

Pre-conquest elements
Assimilated pre-conquest elements
Resurgent pre-conquest elements
Reinvented pre-conquest elements
Evangelizing Catholicism
Architecturally dominant Catholicism
Catholic polytheism
Guadalupenismo as a vehicle of pre-conquest elements
Guadalupenismo as Catholic inculturation
Guadalupenismo as Mexican identity (Criollos)
Guadalupenismo in fusion with civil religion
Secularism (anti-Catholicism)
Civil religion (including some of the above)
Amuletism
New Age themes
Charismatic movement

No sooner are these elements mentioned than new questions arise, partly about the historical sequence, which could be charted without too much difficulty even by non-specialists in Mexican history. For analytical reasons however the above list does not attempt a historical sequence. Rather, the variations on pre-conquest elements and on Guadalupenism are grouped together for convenience of comparison. Resurgent and reinvented pre-conquest elements are of course modern, and the presence of New Age themes and the charismatic movement is relatively recent. The correlation of all these elements within the pattern is particularly difficult to follow, not least because the overall pattern has undergone various interesting changes from time to time. In some cases the various elements overlap and mediate with each other, while in others they conflict with each other as options. Thus what is going on at any one time, for particular population segments or even for individuals, has to be a matter for detailed study. The various elements may be activated as more or less obligatory features of the primal religious pattern, or they may be denied on intellectual or political grounds. It hardly needs to be stated that socio-economic status, and change in socio-economic status, play a part in determining the positioning of groups and individuals within the whole. *Resurgent* pre-conquest elements are of interest to the relatively deprived while *reinvented* pre-conquest elements are promoted by a mobile urban class. The charismatic movement is attractive to a wide range of people partly because of its direct appeal to the emotions and partly because it is in some cases rather well-funded from without. The thesis maintained here however is that in some sense, whether more or less clearly in consciousness, all the named elements are available within the overall range of Mexican religiosity. Moreover, whatever the degree of affection or disaffection, of involvement or alienation, the whole pattern taken together amounts to a certain cultural force which creates a Mexican identity. For example, the Catholic elements are part of the cultural identity even of those Mexicans who are ideologically anti-Catholic and therefore have a negative attitude towards them.

Methodological implications

This extremely brief account of some interesting features of Mexican religion, and in particular of civil religion, is intended here only to illustrate further the methodological considerations which were developed at the beginning of the paper. These considerations, concerning the role of field work in the study of religions, will now be summarised by way of conclusion. There is an intricate relationship between participation, observation and reflection, and these do not necessarily have to be carried out in that sequence. Participant observation should be complemented, as appropriate, by *observant participation*. Both participant observation and observant participation require reflection in order to reach their completion as a research act. However, reflection may also occur at an earlier point in the sequence. Naturally, field work in this sense may be carried out by a person with specialised knowledge in one particular field. On the other hand, in order to develop comparative perspectives, it is desirable for the same processes to be attempted in other "fields", i. e. in countries and regions other than those in which the researcher has specialised knowledge. Needless to say, such attempts can only complement the researches carried out by specialists in those fields. Yet, as experience shows, unless specialists perform their own comparative work they may not always be sensitized to the same theoretical questions. The increasing irrelevance of a firm ideological or religious starting base for the specialist in the study of religions means that the old paradigm of "home" and "field" or "insider" and "outsider" is seriously weakened. By contrast, the recognition of the intricate relationship between participation, observation and reflection, wherever one is, and the increasing possibilities for mobility between diverse yet comparable fields amount to a new methodological paradigm for the study of religions.[3]

Bibliographical reference

De la Maza, Francisco 1953. *El Guadalupenismo Mexicano.* Mexico D. F. (Fondo de Cultura Económica).

First published in: Nils. G. Holm et al. eds. *Ethnography is a Heavy Rite. Studies of Comparative Religion in Honor of Juha Pentikäinen* (Religionsvetenskapliga skrifter 47). Åbo (Åbo Akademis Tryckeri) 2000: 64–79.

3 Retrospective foonote. For an extended example of this kind of work see "Syncretism in Chinese temples of South-East Asia and Taiwan" at 6.6 below (Volume Two).

1.6 Getting into Trouble with the Believers: Intimacy and Distance in the Study of Religions

This article is based on a lecture given to a varied academic audience at the University of Lausanne, Switzerland in 2002, and some informal stylistic features are retained. The subject is the relationship between an academic view of religion, as represented (broadly speaking) among those present in the audience, and views of religion held by those who through belief or actions participate in it.

Getting close to the believers

If we want to get to know a living religion we have to get to know its believers and practitioners. The religion does not exist by itself, but rather in the consciousness and the lives of human beings. So the study of religions may in part be understood as being a kind of anthropology. However it is a special kind of anthropology, one which includes and respects complex, long-term history, and which therefore includes not only social scientific studies but also philological, textual studies, and various additional methods besides. Field-based anthropology is normally related to the present or the recent past, while religious systems often refer to a distant past, in which they may already have existed. Thus we have believers dead or alive. As argued in "Methodological integration in the study of religions" the study of religions has mainly oral, material and written sources, and to study these three kinds of source appropriately, a variety of methods is required (Pye 1999a and 1.2 above; see especially the section "Sources and methods" and its diagram). The study of religions has no single specific method of its own; rather it selects a cluster of methods which are appropriate to the particular sources. Furthermore, the study of religions is a dynamic process. It is important to understand that the first step involves getting to know the religion in question, while later steps include analysis and correlation. Without the initial steps of elucidation and characterization, the later steps of analysis and correlation will be worthless (cf. diagram 2 below).

While a living religion is to be found in the consciousness and the lives of human beings, these are not isolated individuals (or at any rate, not usually), and so "the religion" in question is more than just what one individual person thinks, feels or does. Because of the innumerable interactions between individual believers and practitioners it is in fact a system which can be perpetuated whether or not particular individuals continue to play a part in it. To recognise this is not to subscribe to what is sometimes referred to as "essentialism." What it does imply however is the recognition that various routines and symbolic complexes have a power which is greater than that ascribed to them by any one individual. Rather, the systems continue, in various processes of development and adjustment, on the basis of the support given to them by very many individuals, each of whom has particular interests and motivations. Because of this it is often necessary and appropriate to speak of "Buddhism", "Islam", etc. and of course of subsections of these major traditions such as Tiāntái Buddhism or Shi'ite Islam by name. The problem as to what may or should be referred to by such names is not easy to solve, as has often been remarked. Yet, while it certainly cannot be avoided, it is not insoluble.

To understand a religion we have to be somewhere near its heartbeat. To know "Buddhism", for example, I have to have some kind of an appreciation of meditation, detachment and emptiness. Assistance may be provided by calligraphic circles, as in Zen Buddhism, or Won Buddhism. But as far as meditation is concerned it is best to sit down and learn how to *do* it.[1] To know Shintō I have to walk from the profane world of the village or city through the symbolic gateway or gateways (*torii*) into the ever more sacred area, knowing that entry into the holiest place of all is forbidden. I should purify myself with water, or allow a ritual specialist to purify me with a white paper wand. To understand Christianity I have to have some idea of what it means to pray. I have to sing the hymns in various languages, English, Japanese, Swedish, German, Afrikaans or French. To understand Orthodox Christianity I have to stand there, taking in the beauty of the music, the glorifying iconography and the sanctifying incense, recognising the repeatability of liturgy as a symbol of eternity. To understand Islam I have to have some idea of what it means to pray, to rely on God alone, to understand the crucial importance of Mohammed as the messenger (*rasul*) (peace be

1 Personally, I have brief experiences of meditation in the context of Sōtō Zen Buddhism and Won Buddhism.

upon him) who received the Koran in unalterable language. To understand Scientology or the Hare Krishna movement I have to have some idea of what it means to be a lost person, young or not so young, and how to make progress in the inner life. To understand Judaism I have to have some idea about what it means to belong to a people, whether I "believe" in "God" or not. To understand the Virgin of Guadalupe in Mexico I have to travel on the underground railway to the Basilica, recognizing that Mexicans are not just Catholics but also Mexicans. The Virgin is their Queen, and also the Empress of the Americas – La Reina de Mexico y l'Imperatriz de las Americas. To understand shamanism I have to understand how to die, and how to fly, at least in the imagination, how to develop non-notatable rhythms on a drum, and how to find lost objects.

And who will teach me all these things? Why, the practitioners and believers themselves. Just as, when I visited a mosque in Turkey, an elderly gentleman took me by the sleeve and taught both myself and my wife how to pray, one each side of him, while tourists passed by elsewhere. In another mosque, in another country, I tried to stand unobtrusively at the rear, near a column, but the latecomers came along and stood next to me, forming a new row of worshippers, so that I had no alternative but to take part as before. Or when we ascended the Japanese volcanic mountain named Ontake (literally "honoured peak") the pilgrim leaders refused me permission to observe their ritual but expressly gave me permission to *participate* in it (*sanka shite mo yoi*), which I did, discreetly, from a modest position at the rear. At another time, while observing a summer festival (*natsu-matsuri*) in the world of village Shintō, the men and the women were separated. The men were seated in the small hall of the rough-hewn shrine, and each of them had the privilege of offering an evergreen *sakaki* branch to the gods (the *kami*). At the end of the row was the foreigner, the observer. What more natural than that he too should be invited, and should accept, to offer a *sakaki* branch to the *kami*. It is difficult to avoid intimate situations in the study of religions. In general, if we respect our fellow human beings, we welcome these situations. Indeed I have little patience with theorists in the study of religions who tell us how to carry out research among believers and practitioners, but who, apparently to avoid embarrassment, never do it themselves.

Notice, however, that the situations mentioned above are not all the same. Nor is there one single religious self-understanding. Religions are diverse. Not every religious experience is an experience of the numinous. Rudolf Otto's brave effort to assert this, though his book *Das Heilige* became famous, was profoundly wrong. The museum of religions which he founded in Marburg illustrates exactly the opposite.[2] It illustrates, in an incremental, cumulative way, without further analysis or structure, the more or less miscellaneous diversity of religions. Not every religious experience is an experience of grace. On this many agree, for they think that others have not experienced grace in the same profound way as themselves. Not every experience is a mystical experience. Here too many agree, especially when they see a hierarchy of validity in mystical experience. I mention grace and mysticism because these were themes which Otto pursued in his other writings. However rituals, in which Otto seems to have had less scientific interest, also have diverse meanings and diverse functions. In other words, religious believers and practitioners do not all think and do the same things, even though strong theoretical interests often seek to reduce the phenomena to singularities. The same warning must be addressed to those who are thrilled by the development of new theories such as those of cognitive science, for here too there is a danger of minimizing the phenomena which we are supposed to be studying and not taking account of their full cultural diversity.

Taking part in religious activities as an observer will probably immediately suggest the phrase "participant observation," and so it should. Participant observation is an essential element in the methodological resources of the specialist in the study of religions. Note however that, in many cases, the counterpart which I have frequently called "observant participation" may also easily occur and be very worthwhile. In this case the emphasis is subtly shifted to the aspect of participation, on the assumption that many researchers are able to develop reflective, scientific observation on situations in which they would have or might have participated anyway because of their own personal formation and situation. In the first case one participates, as far as possible, in order to observe. In the second case one learns to observe while participating. The two are complementary. As experience accumulates there

2 Die Religionskundliche Sammlung, founded in 1927. First maintained in rooms in the castle at Marburg it was moved (in 1982) to its present position in the "neue Kanzlei" (Landgraf-Philipp-Strasse 4). From 1982 until the time of this lecture in 2002 the exhibitions remained practically unchanged. Nowadays revisions have been undertaken and special temporary exhibitions have demanded reorganisation of the available spaces.

may not be very much difference between the two. In any case, the idea that there is some terrible problem about how to understand "the other" recedes dramatically for, after all, the situations in which one participates in order to observe are human situations into which one might have arrived anyway through the accidents of birth and socio-cultural formation. And the situations in which one finds oneself in the early years of life are never exactly repeated because there is social, cultural, even geographical movement which leads the individual into ever varying situations.

So participating is a natural activity in many respects, whether it is a matter of observant participation, which is rather normal, or participant observation, which over-nervous anthropologists sometimes regarded as stressful. Autobiographically I may be permitted to add here that I have rarely experienced participant observation as stressful, although I can imagine that there could be extreme situations, for example in deeply isolated jungles, or in military contexts, where this could be so. This does not mean that there are no limits to participant observation. It simply is not possible to take part in any and every religious activity as an observer. There are two main reasons for this. First, a particular situation or activity might imply a degree of cognitive dissonance on the part of the researcher such that it cannot reasonably and ethically be maintained. In this case a reserved or retiring position should be adopted. As a result it may not be possible to "see" everything. Second, some levels of participation may not be permitted by the relevant authorities. For example, it is only possible to perform the Hajj in Mecca if one is a Muslim, or if one is disguised as a Muslim. There are no goodwill visitors as such, just Muslim participants. But this raises the question of membership. Of course it is possible to become a Muslim. But in this case we would be talking about observant participation, not participant observation. Going to Mecca in disguise, though it has been done, is not a good idea. The stress of being in disguise might be exciting and adventurous, but it would not be conducive to worthwhile participant observation, which needs to be genuine, honest and natural.

To return to the main theme, what we learn from real life situations in the field is that the modest student of religion may come to be closer to the believers and participants in one particular case than religious persons in general are to each other. Yet this intimacy is provisional. Distance is also required. For without distance there can be no independent reflection, analysis or explanation.

The centrality of the believer's self-understanding

Not the grand theory, therefore, but the self-understanding of the believer or the practitioner is central, in the first instance. To understand this was the partial achievement of the "phenomenologists" of religion, whether they called themselves that or not. As William Brede Kristensen wrote: "For the historian only one evaluation is possible: 'the believers were completely right'."(Kristensen 1960: 14). Unfortunately, courageous though this assertion was, it is untenable. Believers have often been wrong about many things, including various aspects of their own religions. Similarly we must qualify carefully the statement of Wilfred Cantwell Smith, that great respector of persons, who wrote: "...no statement about religion is valid unless it can be acknowledged by that religion's believers." (Smith 1959: 42) We must note here above all that the religion does not exist by itself –it only exists via its believers and practitioners, as Cantwell Smith himself understood. To think otherwise is to fall into the trap of essentialism. So the question always arises as to which believers are to be asked, and about which religion or religions. Now this question can be answered. But it can only be answered with respect to particular sets of believers, chronologically and demographically defined, who may not be in a position to confirm or deny statements relating to other sets of believers. This means in turn that statements about particular religions may well be correct in themselves, even at the level of the consciousness of believers, which do not meet with the approval of other believers subscribing to the same "religion" who regard them as incorrect.

Of course we know what Kristensen and Cantwell Smith were after. In principle the same is affirmed by Jacques Waardenburg when he emphasizes the intentionality of the believers themselves as a central datum for the study of religions (see especially Waardenburg 1986). This requirement avoids reductionist approaches which drive forward immediately to "explanations" contradicting the believers' beliefs but thereby fail to take any account whatever of the religious consciousness as a datum. To claim that such "reductionism" is an essential presupposition of the study of religions is grossly misleading, indeed a catastrophic misunderstanding of what is needed. Remember that the noted anthropologist Clifford Geertz also insisted in his well-known essay "Religion as a cultural system" that there should be two main levels of theoretical activity. Before going into functional explanations, which might well be regarded as reductionist by the people concerned, the symbolic system of beliefs and rituals must be known and understood in its own right. To give an example not adduced by Geertz, the ecumenical movement should be understood in its own terms as a sincere attempt to restore the unity of the Christian Church *before* the theory is advanced that it is economic pressures which lead to the joint use of church buildings. If *only* the latter theory is advanced, then the ecumenical movement in general will not be understood. On the other hand, when the theory of economic pressure is adduced, tension with the self-understanding of the believers and practitioners will occur.

Now Clifford Geertz referred mainly to the writings of famous anthropologists (Durkheim and Malinowski), sociologists (Weber) and psychologists (Freud). If he had taken note of specialists in the study of religions he would have found that this fundamental matter had already been rather clearly seen by those characterized as belonging to the so-called phenomenological school. Some of the interests of that school in the study of religions, which, in spite of some shared intellectual roots, should not simply be identified or confused with philosophical phenomenology, may nowadays be regarded as inappropriate, notably the wish to identify a general "essence" of religion within all the particular religions. Such views have long been clearly criticized (e. g. Pye 1972a). On the other hand the idea of placing the consciousness of the believers at the centre of attention, rather than some intellectual framework, belief system or explanatory theory which might interest the observer, was of great value. It was mainly thanks to this emphasis that the older "phenomenologists of religion" in the Netherlands, such as Kristensen, van der Leeuw and Bleeker, helped to develop and stabilize the study of religions. Unfortunately they still failed to free themselves from the dominant influence of Christian theology at the level of morphology and typology. But they did see that the beliefs and theories of the observer have to be, as far as possible, set aside in favour of the beliefs of the believers and participants. First then, the meaning of the religious system for the believers and practitioners must be ascertained. This does not mean, of course, that their beliefs are true or that their values are to be applauded. But the system itself, in all its complexity, has to be ascertained and elucidated. In short, we have to know what it is we are talking about. That is, we have to know how it fits together, how it works, and what it signifies for the believers and practitioners themselves. Note that the word "practitioners" should always be added to "believers". This is because constant talk of "believers" can easily lead to a logocentric view of the phenomenon, while, as we know, religion is practice and behaviour just as much as it is belief and thought. In sum, it is the intention of human beings as believers and practitioners which has to be taken into account at this stage of the enquiry.

However, if only the statements of believers and practitioners were to be regarded as valid, the study of religions would be reduced to a completely insignificant minimum. In such a case, we might as well just let the representatives of religions tell their stories and leave it at that. If we literally accepted the dictum of Cantwell Smith quoted above we would be limited to a simplistic positivism. It may be agreed that the cross-checking of statements about religious systems by the believers themselves, in so far as linguistic diversity permits, is valuable. But it is only valuable up to a certain point. Looking further ahead, a serious science of religion will not be able to avoid making some statements which will *not* find favour with the believers and practitioners. This may not happen immediately, but it will happen sooner or later.

Tension created by parallels and comparisons

One of the most obvious reasons for the emergence of tension with the believers and practitioners is that the researcher is aware of parallels and comparisons which play no part in the self-understanding of the believers. Yet these parallels suggest that any one case is less important in the history of human consciousness than particular believers think with respect to their own case.

For example, we might observe, and wish to say, that there is a similarity between the assumption of Elijah, the assumption (or ascension) of Jesus, the assumption of the Virgin Mary and the assumption (or ascension) of Mohammed, who according to the legendary narratives were all taken up into the heavens in a similar way. Moreover there was possibly a tradition concerning the assumption of Moses, as mentioned in the title of a work entitled *The Assumption of Moses*, of which only fragments remain. Later, founders of little known religions are believed to have ascended into heaven, e. g. the foundress of the Japanese religion Tenrikyō, Nakayama Miki.[3] But not all of the believers of the three main religions mentioned above, Judaism, Christianity and

3 The term used for ascension is *shōten*, the same expression which is used by Japanese Christians for the ascension of Jesus.

Islam will be happy with these statements. So a certain tension arises.The great majority of Christian believers are not aware that "ascension" is a common theme in various religions. They believe that the most important person or persons in their *own* religion ascended into heaven, above all Jesus who, as a consequence, "sits at the right hand of the Father." Protestant Christians are not happy to be told that Mary also was taken up into heaven and therefore left no bodily remains on earth. This is not so much because they cannot imagine such a thing, as because there is no narrrative about it in the New Testament. In the liberal protestant reference work *A New Dictionary of Christian Theology* there is a distinctly theological article on "The Ascension of Christ" by John Tinsley, a professor of theology who later became Bishop of Bristol in England. This article contains no reference whatever to any ascensions into heaven other than that of Jesus Christ. In the reference work entitled *Wörterbuch des Christentums* there is not even any entry at all concerning ascension. In the *Macmillan Dictionary of Religion* (or *The Continuum Dictionary of Religion*), on the other hand, there are entries both on ascension and on assumption. According to the latter, belief in the assumption of the Virgin Mary into heaven was elevated into a formal doctrine of the Roman Catholic Church by Pope Pius XII in 1950. Now that is rather late, considering that the event is supposed to have taken place not many years after the death of Christ himself. Catholic readers will also not be happy to read that belief in the assumption of the Virgin Mary has been widespread since the 7th century. This is a correct statement in itself, but the implication which disturbs belief is that before that time it was not widespread. Moreover the article points out that the belief "is rejected by Protestants as being entirely non-Biblical." In the *Encyclopedia of Religion* edited by Mircea Eliade there is no entry on "assumption," but there is a substantial article by Ioan Petru Culianu, who links "ascension" with shamanic flight and with the ascent of the soul. Yet these really are rather different matters. After all, "ascension" is usually about the assumption of the body into the heavens, without any physical remainder on earth. On this subject therefore the views of specialists in the study of religions are variously closer, or less close, to the leading interest of the religious persons who entertain such notions. Moreover it is not really possible for any specialists in the study of religions simply to share the notions of religious believers on this subject, because no religious believers, for their part, are likely to take account of the spectrum of related beliefs. If we think about these various alternatives, we cannot rest with the simplistic statements of Brede Kristensen or Cantwell Smith about the believers being right. We have to ask, which believers and which religion? Who was it or is it, who is supposedly "always right"? Which statements about the ascension of Christ, in the history of religions or the scientific study of religions, could conceivably be valid, or invalid, on the basis of such a criterion?

There are numerous cases where the doctrinal positions maintained by some representatives of a religion diverge from religious practice in real life, as may become evident to observers. For example, observations of Catholic Christianity easily lead to the recognition that it may be regarded as polytheist. This is what Muslims tell us about Christian doctrine in general. It is the Muslim response to the doctrine of the Holy Trinity. Naturally, this interpretation of the Holy Trinity will be rejected by Christian believers and especially representatives of the historic Christian churches. Indeed it is really not countenanced in the historic creeds. But there is more. The concept of polytheism becomes increasingly relevant as soon as various metaphysical beings are addressed in prayer, as especially in Catholicism. Here it is thought to be quite natural that Mary should be addressed in prayer, as a being who is in a special realm. The same holds good for various other saints and angels. Thus the whole question of what should be regarded as polytheism is very complicated. In the study of religions we have to recognise that there are theological statements about polytheism made by believers, as for example when Christian priests declare that Christianity is of course not polytheist, but monotheist. Such statements may be misleading for the independent study of religions. In particular, there is often no black-and-white choice. In an observer's analysis of a particular religion we have to be prepared to see that there may be a complex symbiosis of "monotheism" and "polytheism", as in some forms of Christianity, in Zoroastrianism (cf. the article on Zoroastrianism by Gnoli in the *Encyclopedia of Religion*), or for special reasons among the religions of Indonesia.

To conclude this section in more general terms it may be said that the validity of various religious concepts is compromised for the believers when it is pointed out that comparable teachings may be observed elsewhere. The same may apply for practices. Not all believers will experience this to the same degree, but many will experience it to some degree, simply because they believe that their own experience is of normative value.

Examples from Japan: Zen Buddhism and Shin Buddhism in the wider pattern of Japanese religions

As a detailed example I will turn now to the problem of locating Zen Buddhism and Shin Buddhism in the general pattern of Japanese religions. These two major traditions in Japanese Buddhism have particular points of emphasis, which the student must of course make every effort to understand. On the other hand, in what we might call "Buddhist Studies" there are many Buddhist purists who have no interest in the general study of religions and tend to reinforce a religiously positive understanding of Buddhism within their particular perspective. Very often these specialists do not wish to recognize that there are aspects of Buddhism as a religion which do not fit with their official presentation of it.

First, and briefly, Zen Buddhism cannot be understood without some attention being paid to *zazen*. It is difficult to learn anything about *zazen* without going to a *zen* meditation hall and practising it, which in turn means submitting to the guidance of the meditation teacher. Now this exercise is very popular among people who are interested in Zen Buddhism, existentially, so to speak, but who have no intention of studying Zen Buddhism as one religion among others. Such enthusiasts of Zen Buddhism on the other hand, especially in the western world, are not very interested in the extensive funeral activities which Zen Buddhism supports, especially in Japan. These funeral activities, and the idea of the veneration or care of ancestors (*senzokuyō*) simply are not important for Zen Buddhism in the minds of westerners. Indeed some westerners are quite shocked when they visit Japan for the first time and come to understand the importance of the funeral business for the maintenance of the temples. Thinking that Zen Buddhism is supposed to lead into the path of enlightenment, they are disoriented when they discover that many millions of registered supporting families never have anything to do with meditation but pay over substantial sums in connection with the veneration of ancestors. Such a divergence of interests is not infrequently supported by representatives of Zen Buddhism themselves, who tour western countries and teach about Zen thought and practice, without ever suggesting that the main part of the temple organisation in their own country has other functions. This is an example of the happy promotion of "orientalism" by representatives of the orient.

In the case of Shin Buddhism (i. e. Jōdo Shinshū) the problem is, if anything, more acute. The main point of Shin Buddhism is reverence for and trust in Amida Buddha, based on the idea that human beings can do nothing of religious value for themselves. According to this tradition, the only way forward is to believe and trust in the "other power" and the saving compassion of Amida Buddha. For this reason, the practice of praying for "this-worldly benefits" (*genzeriyaku*), which is widely current in Japan, is frowned upon. Moreover the equally widespread Buddhist idea of making spiritual progress, or making merit by means of special practices loses its force. Nevertheless Shin Buddhism is in some particular ways located within the general pattern of Japanese religions, and this may seem more evident to the observer than to the believer.

To analyse this problem, let us first consider the practice of circulatory pilgrimage, and the way in which Shin Buddhism relates to it. A contrast may be seen between Shin Buddhism and Shingon Buddhism, the leading form of "esoteric" Buddhism in Japan. Very popular in Shingon Buddhism is the lengthy pilgrimage around eighty-eight temples on the major island of Shikoku. So well-known is this pilgrimage that there are also smaller imitations of it, which can be carried out in a short time, as for example at Omuro in northern Kyōto, just behind the attractively laid out temple, Ninnaji. It takes about two hours on foot to go round the eighty-eight miniature temples. Such pilgrimages are all thought to assist in the development of spiritual powers, or at least to be helpful in the search for this-worldly benefits such as healings or success in business or other enterprises. This is but one well-known example of a very widespread phenomenon. Other important pilgrimage routes are based on the thirty-three appearances of Kannon-sama (Chinese: Guānyīn). The leading example of this is the route known as the Saikoku Thirty Three Spiritual Places, which covers a wide area in western Japan, but this route too has its imitations of varying length in many parts of the country. The very idea of circulatory pilgrimage, which seems to be almost a Japanese speciality, is so firmly established that it is practically impossible for Shin Buddhism not to have some kind of relation to it. Doctrinally however, this is not acceptable, for no merit-making activities are admitted. Moreover, as observers we should recognize that this principle of no merit-making is really important for all who participate in Shin Buddhism. So what about pilgrimage?

Shin Buddhism was founded on the basis of the teaching of Shinran (1173–1262) and there are a number of specific places in Japan which are associated with the story of his life and work. These are grouped in three areas. One area covers Mount Hiei and the city of Kyōto, one is based on the coastal region to the north of Kyōto where Shinran spent his time of exile (i.e. in the ancient provinces of Echigo and Echizen), and one is in eastern Japan, the Kantō region, being associated with the activities of twenty-four of his leading followers. Guides and maps are issued which show these various sites, encouraging people to visit them. In the case of a map showing many of these sites in the coastal region, we can even see that three different "model courses" are suggested.[4] Thus the concept is very close to that of circulatory pilgrimage, known in Japanese as *o-meguri*, a word which is even used in the title of the popularly conceived maps. The pilgrimage places of Shin Buddhism may all be regarded as belonging to the circulatory pilgrimage type, even if the sites are visited individually or variously, rather than in a strict sequence.

In August 2001 I was fortunate enough to have the opportunity of visiting one of the most famous of these sites, namely the spot where Shinran "landed" after he was sent into exile from Kyōto during the suppression of *nenbutsu* Buddhism. In Shinran's time this was a serene coastal beach, whereas now it is much exploited by holiday makers, many of them parking their cars directly on the sand and screaming around the waters in motorised sea-craft. But the on-shore remembrance hall (*kinendō*) is of interest and evidently attracts quite a number of visitors. There is no provision for entering seals and calligraphy in pilgrims' books although, as I heard, this is not infrequently requested. Such a service is not provided because it would imply the recognition of a meritorious work on the part of the pilgrim, which is not considered to be appropriate in Shin Buddhism. However this does not mean that paying visits is discouraged as such. On the contrary. Moreover, the *nenbutsu*, the special formula for calling on the name of Amida Buddha, is recited in the memorial hall, thus following in Shinran's tracks.[5]

In addition to these tentative forms of pilgrimage we should note the practice of encouraging believers in large numbers to visit the head temples (Honganji) of the major denominations of Shin Buddhism

4 Hosokawa 1983: 167.

5 This subject was set out in detail in the present writer's "Traces of Shinran Shōnin" (Pye 2002b).

in Kyōto, including Shinran's mausoleum. Using an observer's phrase, this practice belongs to the single-goal type of pilgrimage. Looking further afield, a considerable interest has developed in modern times in visiting the historic sites of Buddhism in India. This is also a form of pilgrimage. It is favoured in many Japanese Buddhist denominations and can also be documented for Shin Buddhism. In fact it is particularly popular with specialists in the teaching of Buddhism and their university or college students. The pilgrimage goals in such journeys to India include one or more of those sites which were designated in ancient Buddhist tradition as places to be visited, namely those four places where the historical Buddha was born, where he achieved enlightenment, where the first preaching of the Dharma took place, and where he entered the state of nirvana.

We have to ask ourselves whether travels to these sites by Shin Buddhists, or travelling from one site to another, should properly be called "pilgrimage" at all. It was already suggested that the difference between religious activities in Shin Buddhism and in other denominations of Buddhism lies in the intention. It is frequently stated in Shin Buddhism, and also widely understood by the believers, that ordinary human beings cannot, in their own strength or of their "own power" (*jiriki*), achieve anything significant for themselves or others through religious practices. Only the "other power" (*tariki*) of Amida Buddha is effective. As one who studies religions, I respect this stated position, of course. In fact it was through a helpful friend in the community of Shin Buddhist believers that I learned about these places to begin with. Thus Shin Buddhism provides an excellent example of the importance of taking intentionality seriously as a characteristic of good methodology in the study of religions. On the other hand this does not mean that the existence of pilgrimage in Shin Buddhism can simply be denied altogether. So this leads into a further question of analysis.

Shin Buddhism has a very specific teaching about salvation through the grace and compassion of Amida Buddha. It is believed that human beings can only be saved through reliance on the "original vow" (*hongan*) of Amida Buddha. This is thought to be especially so in these latter days when the Dharma has declined and the tendency to evil-doing is so strong. Meritorious activities are therefore not only hard to put into effect, they are even misleading and obscure the need for reliance on the "original vow" alone. This is undoubtedly the self-understanding of the believers. At the same time, the observer notices, perhaps more than the believers themselves, that Shin Buddhism is located within the overall pattern of Japanese religion. The believers either deny this or take it for granted. While recognizing that Shin Buddhism on the one hand adopts a dialectically critical position vis-à-vis many standard features of Japanese religion, there are some important ways in which it participates in the general pattern.

Three may be mentioned above all. First, as we have already seen, the idea of making religious journeys to special places associated with the faith is really quite strong. Second, Shin Buddhist temples, like Zen temples, play the usual role in funeral rites and the veneration of ancestors. This includes participation in the standard seasons for ancestor veneration, namely *higan* at the spring and autumn equinoxes, and *o-bon* in high summer. It also includes the use of Buddhist altars (*butsudan*) in private houses, the main purpose of which is ancestor veneration. The furnishings of the house altars are carefully designated to avoid any idea of meritorious worship, but then this stipulation is part of the common pattern in that each Buddhist denomination in Japan has its own recommendations about what to put on the altar. Third, the social structure of the religious institutions is quite similar to that of other well established religions in Japan. Apart from the importance of the central temples in each of the main Shin Buddhism denominations, we may note that both the general leadership, following Shinran himself, and the local temple management are as far as possible hereditary. Of course there are also special features, such as the rather significant administrative role played by the wives of temple priests. However temple priests have to have at least one son in order for the provision of temple services to continue. If there is no son to take on this role, one must be adopted. The role of the educational institutions such as schools and universities, which have been developed in modern times, is also quite typical for the way in which Japanese religions are organized. From this we can see that while Shin Buddhism is distanced, in its intentionality, from common patterns of Japanese religion, it also participates in these patterns. This participation is not part of the self-presentation of the believers. It is a matter which becomes evident in the analysis of the observer. To the believers it is just common sense. But when it is thematized in the analsyis, some resistance is met with, because it is not supposed to be the main point. This is a simple, but real example of "tension with the believers".

Various questions which cause tension with the believers (TWB)

It is time to broaden the discussion again. In one short paper not every kind of problem can be discussed which may cause tension with the believers (TWB). So far we have seen two kinds of problem. First, there is tension which arises because of general comparative considerations which are not the main interest of the believers themselves. Second, there is the tension which arises when believers are not aware of, or fail to draw attention to important factors in their religion which are relevant to an analytical understanding of it. These factors, such as ancestor veneration in Zen or Shin Buddhism, will be particularly evident to students of religion because of their non-confessional, comparative standpoint (and less evident to religious enquirers and converts). Two other main types of problem can be stated briefly.

The challenge of historical factuality is probably the most evident source of tension with the believers, so evident indeed that it is hardly necessary to give it detailed attention here. Did religious founders or leaders really say particular things ascribed to them? Frequently not. Can the Lotus Sutra be attributed to the Buddha? No, at least only very indirectly. Does the New Testament contain the teaching of Jesus in his very words? Stated simply, no, even though it contains numerous fragments which could be attributed to him. Did Lǎozǐ go to India to teach the Way to the Indians? No. Have the Vedas been in existence for thousands of years? No. Is oral tradition always completely accurate? Of course not. But simply to raise such questions can be very irritating for believers. My own simple book about the life of the Buddha (Pye 1979a), unusual in not beginning with the unhistorical narratives about his presumed conception (through his mother's thigh) and nativity (from the armpit), led to an irate questioner demanding to know whether I had "any religion at all." On the other hand one kind reader sent me a packet of tea from Sri Lanka. More substantially, the specialist in Sikh studies, Hew Mcleod, has experienced considerable controversy with believers as a result of advancing historical perspectives on the development of Sikh traditions which do not coincide with the religious version.

The other main problem is that of identifying consistency, and its corollary, innovatory departures, in religious traditions. Various different "religions" have been referred to above, and it has been indicated that within the major traditions it is necessary to specify just which sub-traditions, sometimes formally defined as denominations but not always forming distinct organizational strands, are being considered at any one time. Thus arises the well-known puzzle as to who counts as being a believer in any particular tradition. Who is a Buddhist? Who is a Christian? Who is a Muslim? Thus posed, these questions are undoubtedly too simple. Yet they cannot be avoided. When reflection takes over, many academics become impatient and declare that they should not be formulated at all. If someone says they are "a Buddhist" then so they are, the argument goes. Yet this is too simple. We ought to be able to say whether Aum Shinrikyō, a religion whose leaders arranged to have poisonous gas released in the Tokyo subway, is "Buddhist" or not. The answer: it is not. This clear example, as I have argued in detail elsewhere (Pye 1996b), shows that the believers' own statements on such questions are not necessarily to be accepted. Are modern lay movements such as Sōka Gakkai and Won Buddhism Buddhist, or not? In these two cases arguments could be advanced in both directions. My own conclusion is that it is not unreasonable to regard these movements as Buddhist, just as Zen Buddhism and Shin Buddhism may be so regarded. At the same time it may be accepted that Won Buddhism is a "new religion", as its own representatives also argue. It is both a new religion and Buddhist (Pye 2002c). Of course there is the question of criteria. An easy criterion is whether a major new source of revelation is dominant. This is so, for example, in the case of the *Book of Mormon* in the Church of Jesus Christ of the Latter Day Saints. Because of this, the term Christianity is no longer applicable to this religion. In less obvious cases, the main question is whether there is a plausible degree of consistency with the wider tradition with which identification is claimed. The intentionality is important. However the explicit intentionality is not alone determinative. In other words, it is too simple to say that everybody who says he is a Buddhist, or a Muslim, is one. Academics who propound this "solution" are simply being historically or scientifically irresponsible. This issue, in its various detailed forms, may give cause to tension with the believers. In research, we have to accept that such tension may arise, and it is valuable to know when and how it is likely to arise.

There are therefore various kinds of reasons why the historian of religions and/or the systematic investigator into religions might feel obliged to make statements which diverge from those of the believers or practitioners. This can lead to serious *trouble with the believers*. Nevertheless, these questions must be asked in the interests of a reliable and informative history of religions. The history of religions cannot be built on purely positivistic phenomenological studies alone. Even if these are carried out sequentially through various historical periods tension will arise because of the sequential comparisons between present consciousnesses and our knowledge about earlier periods – comparisons which may not suit the current believers at all.

Finally, quite a lot of attention has been paid to the question of the relation between the world-view of the observer, which is supposedly scientific, and that of the persons observed, which has been thought of in many cases, variously, as pre-logical, magical, religious, unscientific, superstitious, etc. Needless to say, condemnatory terminology should not be selected. For example, "superstition", though it is an interesting term in itself, since it has a distinctly pejorative implication, is not a part of the vocabulary of the scientific study of religions. However the basic problem about the relation between a scientific world-view and any other kind of world-view, pre-logical, visionary, or whatever, is quite an easy one for the researcher because, quite simply, he or she does not need to solve it at all. If this is a problem, then it is one for the believers.

The TWB factor (The tension with believer factor)

Some of these points, though not always exactly the same ones, have been discussed elsewhere in terms of "insider" and "outsider" accounts or as "emic" and "etic" accounts of religions, world-views, etc.. So the problem-field is in general quite widely known. However, many people discuss it without ever having done any field work or indeed any specific historical studies. Moreover the specific points of interest relating to the study of religions are often overlooked.

One other differentiation is necessary. Field work in the study of religions is sometimes understood as a kind of dialogue, and this has been referred to as "the dialogue model". However the simple model of immersion in the field is to be preferred to such an understanding. The dialogue model can easily end up either in agreement with believers and practitioners (about something) or in disagreement (about something), and this is not the purpose of scientific research into religions. The so-called dialogue model can also create, or at least permit the emergence of its own tension with the believers (that is, in such cases, the other believers!) which is an extra burden on the research process. This is not the tension, should it arise, which is being referred to in this paper.

In conclusion therefore I return to the "tension with believer factor" or TWB factor, as explained here. The correct positioning of this factor in the research process is important, and therefore its changing location should be followed in accordance with the diagram below.[6]

At first the TWB factor is *low*. This is because the researcher is close to the believer or practitioner. He or she may even be drawn into the religious situation and be invited or requested to participate in some way. He or she may share journeys, rooms, food, family information, etc. with believers. A certain degree of intimacy is involved and creates trust. Such trust is of course valuable, not only because it implies respect, but also because it facilitates observation. The TWB factor is low when the main emphasis is on elucidation and characterization. Both of these steps correspond to the best practice of the older "phenomenological" approach. The intentionality of the believers or practitioners is important. The process of characterization may however lead to an initial tension, because terminology may be used which is other than that which is preferred by any believers who have a representative function.

Thereafter the TWB factor increases. This is, first of all, because the internal analysis of the system requires non-believer terminology with comparative reference points. The believers may not like it. Second, when it comes to functional correlations, clear contradictions with the self-understanding of the believers are likely to arise. Buddhist temple priests help people to care for the ancestors for religious reasons, but also for economic reasons. The people sometimes even complain about the economic reasons themselves, but this does not invalidate the religious reasons in their own minds. Thus there is an emergent tension which finds a clear place in the observer's account.

In general, the existence of the TWB factor has not gone unremarked in methodological discussion. However I believe it is helpful to name it. Above all, it is necessary, in the study of religions, to understand where, why and how the TWB factor arises, where it should be resisted as inimical to the research process, and where it should be expected and tolerated as a natural feature of it.

---

6 © Diagram by Michael Pye (used in lectures and internet teaching unit from 1997 onwards).

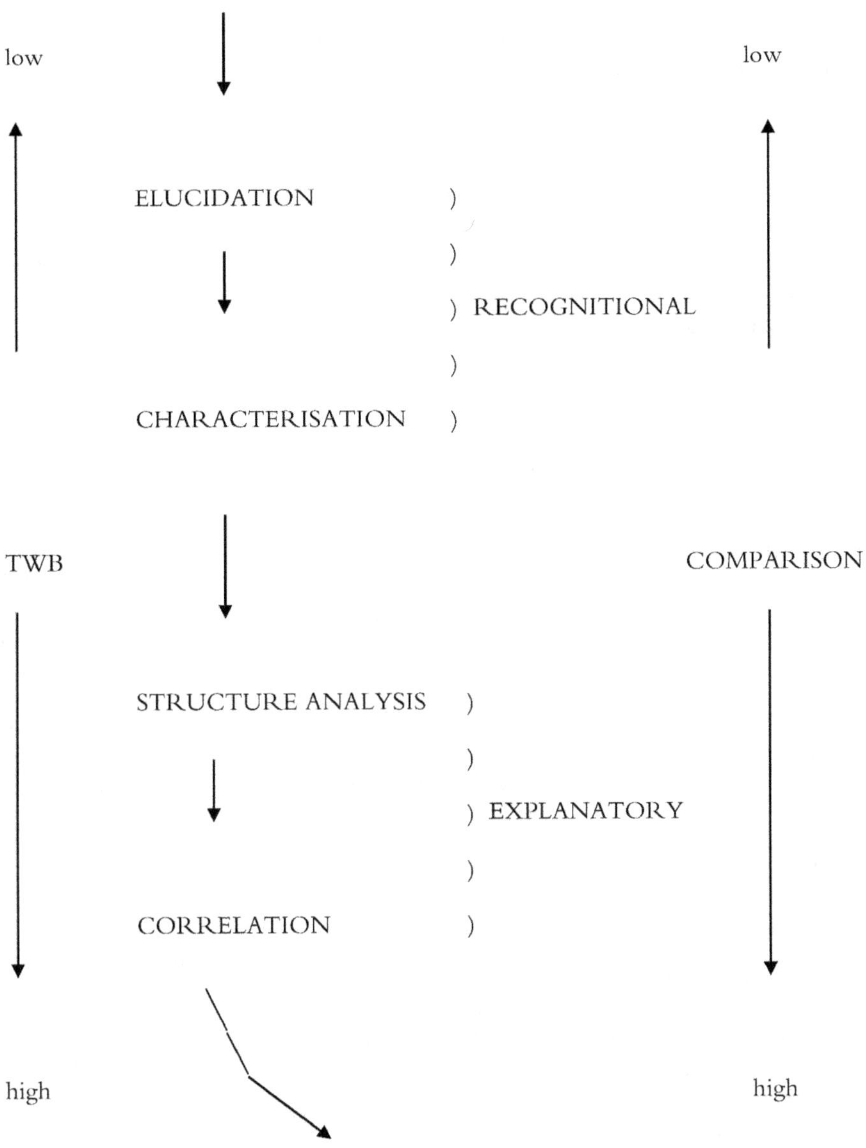

Diagram 1: Study of religions and TWB-factor (TWB = tension with believer)

Bibliographical references

Drehsen, Volker (et al. eds.) 1988. *Wörterbuch des Christentums*. Gütersloh (Gütersloher Verlagshaus) and Zürich (Benzinger).

Eliade, Mircea et al. (eds.) 1987. *Encyclopedia of Religion*. New York (Macmillan).

Hosokawa, Gyōshin (ed.) 1983, 1996. *Kojijunrei Gaido, Shinran*. Kyōto (Hōzōkan).

Geertz, Clifford 1966. "Religion as a cultural system" in: Banton, Michael (ed.) *Anthropological Approaches to the Study of Religion*. (ASA Monographs 3). London (Tavistock Publications): 1–46.

Hosokawa, Gyōshin (ed.) 1983, 1996. *Kojijunrei Gaido, Shinran*. Kyōto (Hōzōkan).

Kristensen, W. Brede 1960. *The Meaning of Religion: Lectures in the Phenomenology of Religion*. The Hague (M. Nijhoff).

Pye, Michael 1972a. *Comparative Religion: An Introduction through Source Materials*. Newton Abbot (David and Charles) and New York (Harper and Row).

1979a. *The Buddha*.London (Duckworth).

– (ed.) 1994e. *The Macmillan Dictionary of Religion*. London (Macmillan) and as *The Continuum Dictionary of Religion*, New York (Continuum).

– 1996b. "Aum Shinrikyō. Can Religious Studies cope?" in: *Religion* 26 (3): 261–73.

– 1999a. "Methodological integration in the study of religions" in: *Approaching Religion, Scripta Instituti Donneriani Aboensis XVII (1)* Ahlbäck, Tore (ed.) Åbo Finland (Donner Institute for Research in Religious and Cultural History): 188–205.

– 2002b. "Traces of Shinran Shōnin" in: Thierfelder, Constanze and Eibach, Dietrich Hannes (eds.), *Resonanzen. Schwingungsräume Praktischer Theologie (Gerhard Marcel Martin zum 60. Geburtstag)*, Stuttgart (Kohlhammer): 215–24.

– 2002c. "Won Buddhism as a Korean new religion" in: *Numen. International Review for the History of Religions* 49 (2): 113–41.

Richardson, Alan and Bowden, John 1983. *A New Dictionary of Christian Theology*. London (SCM Press).

Smith, Wilfred Cantwell 1959. "Comparative religion: whither and why?" in: Eliade, M. and Kitagawa J. M. (eds.) *The History of Religions:* Essays in Methodology. Chicago (University of Chicago Press): 31–58.

Waardenburg, Jacques 1986. *Religion und Religionen: Systematische Einführung in die Religionswissenschaft* (Sammlung Göschen, Nr. 2228). Berlin (de Gruyter).

This paper has not been published previously. Diagram: ©Michael Pye (used in lectures and internet teaching unit from 1997 onwards).

Part Two
East Asian Starting Points

2.1 Introduction to Part Two

In Part Two we turn specifically to ways in which the academic study of religions can be seen to have deep roots in the intellectual traditions not only of Europe but also of East Asia. This is sometimes disputed, either by those with little knowledge of East Asian thought or Asian scholars who have invested in reverse orientalism. But what is needed is a balanced view. My own interest in the matter arose during the late 1960 s and early 1970 s, when I was engaged in translating a major essay by Ernst Troeltsch about the meaning of the term "essence of Christianity."[1] This essay focused on one of the major categories which was at that time used in reflection on tradition (see further in Part Five below), and Troeltsch was using his philosophy of history to clarify the issues raised by the widespread use of the term "essence" (in German *Wesen*) as applied to the Christian tradition. Though terminology has shifted a long way since then, his essay remains most instructive. In the same period, I took note of the brief selections from writings by Tominaga Nakamoto (1715–46) in *Sources of Japanese Tradition* edited by Tsunoda, de Bary and Keene.[2] While Troeltsch referred frequently to the European Enlightenment as the major starting point for the reflective and relativizing historicism typical of modernity, this being one aspect of the emphasis on reason in general, what was evident even in those brief selections from the Japanese was that Tominaga (that being his family name) was at the same time mounting a historical critique on the traditions known to him, Confucianism, Buddhism and Shintō, which was remarkably parallel to the European movement of thought. When mentioning this parallel to others, the usual response was scepticism. The assumption was that there just could not be any such parallels based on independent Asian thought, because one had learned that the

1 "Was heißt 'Wesen des Christentums'?" (i. e. "What is the meaning of 'Essence of Christianity'?"), to be found in Vol II of Troeltsch's *Gesammelte Schriften* (Troeltsch 1913 and 1922) and in English translation in Morgan and Pye 1977. The essay was originally published in the journal *Die Christliche Welt* in 1903.

2 Tsunoda et al. 1958, 479–488.

latter was totally different from western thought. Thus either such an impression was a regrettable illusion, it was argued, or any similar ideas must have been derived from the western world itself. The position that there were indeed such parallels was first staked out in my article "Aufklärung and religion in Europe and Japan" (Pye 1973, but not included in the present volume), in which the attempt was made to identify major points of similarity in the work of Tominaga and his near contemporary Gotthold Ephraim Lessing (1729–81). Still, a common response was scepticism, based on a rather primitive assumption of the uniqueness of European thought, and for this reason the writer decided it would be necessary to make an independent study of Tominaga's works and to translate them into English. This took much longer than the translation of Troeltsch's essay and the results were published much later under the title *Emerging from Meditation* (Pye 1990a), this being an abbreviated version of one of Tominaga's own titles. In the introduction to that work will be found a circumstantial investigation into the regularly posited matter of western influence on Tominaga's thought. The result: there was none. Neither Jesuit scholars nor Dutch merchants peddled the ideas of the European Enlightenment. Also to be found there is an analysis of the intellectual preconditions thought to be necessary for the emergence of Enlightenment-style thinking with respect to religion. The result: there are several. This study therefore has affinities to the earlier comparison made with Lessing, in "Aufklärung and religion in Europe and Japan" (Pye 1973a) and nowadays should be consulted in connection with it.

Both while the work of translation was being advanced, as well as later on after the little remarked publication of *Emerging from Meditation*, a number of lectures and conferences provided opportunities to develop the argument for varied audiences. However, since there is naturally considerable overlap in content, only a simple selection of such papers is included here. We begin with "An Asian starting point for the study of religions" (1992), which presents the main argument that the reflective study of religions is not just a European invention but a matter which arose independently in more than one cultural context.

This is followed by two papers concerning the perception of the plurality of religions. One of the key presuppositions for modern, rationalizing reflection about "religions" or religious traditions is the simple perception that these are somehow present in their plurality. In Europe and East Asia the religions in question have traditionally been different ones, and yet the questions are fundamentally analogous. Hence, unknown to each other, both Lessing and Tominaga reflected carefully upon them in their respective, different worlds. All German schoolchildren know that Lessing's play "Nathan the Wise" is about the relations between the three religions Judaism, Christianity and Islam, handled adroitly by a wise rabbi. This had already been thematised in the above-mentioned "Aufklärung and religion in Europe and Japan" (1973a). Here the matter is set out from the Asian perspective with different religions, Confucianism, Buddhism, Daoism and Shintō, in "Tominaga Nakamoto and Religious Pluralism" (2.3 1984). In fact Tominaga was not the first person in East Asia to address the question of the plurality of religions, although he was probably the first "early modern" (or Japanese *kindai*) thinker to do so with the fully critical reflection which parallels the European Enlightenment. The intellectual heritage upon which he drew can be seen at least partly in that, in one chapter of *Emerging from Meditation*, he takes up a long-standing Chinese concept, namely that of the "three teachings" (*sānjiào*). This had first developed in the context of attempts to find some kind of harmony between Confucianism, Buddhism and Daoism, but for Tominaga it became a reflective, analytical tool.

The present argument is therefore taken a step further, and set in a wider context, in the next article given below, entitled "Three teachings (*sānjiào*) theory and modern reflection on religion" (2.4). Here we see that the concept of three "teachings" (*sānjiào*) had already been taken up in a reflective manner in China itself at the latest since Ming times, i.e. from the late 14th century. Indeed it was evidently espoused by no less a figure than the first Ming Emperor, Míng Tàizǔ himself. The "Treatise on the three teachings" (*Sānjiào lùn* 三教論), possibly fictively ascribed to the emperor, significantly predates Tominaga's writings. It is also shorter, more politically motivated, and less overtly intellectual. Nevertheless we can see that even then the concept was beginning to emerge as a significant starting point and facilitator for reflection on religions in their plurality. Thus the Chinese option is in principle not dependent on the Japanese intellectual tradition, and it will be interesting to see if recourse is taken to this line of thought again in future as reflection on religions becomes less tied to ideological patterns.

If we take these perspectives seriously, remembering that we are talking here about a development of ideas which has quite evidently not been dependent upon western thought, then our view of the way in which the modern study of religions has developed outside Europe must be adjusted accordingly. Consequently, this part is concluded by

"Modern Japan and the science of religions" (2.5) in which the claim is made, and documented, that the study of religions emerged quite viably not only in Europe and America, but also in East Asia, especially in Japan. Of course, by the time we come to the nineteenth century the interactions between Japan and the western world became an important part of the picture. There is no doubt about that. Thus Japanese Buddhologists went to Oxford to learn from Max Müller, the current "western" concept of religion became part of the complex international and domestic political discourse, and so on. The importance of all this is not disputed. Admittedly there was much influence from the west from the nineteenth century onwards, and there were corresponding responses, but in the case Japan at least these occurred with relative speed on the basis of available patterns of thought which were already highly developed, and relevant. Erroneous perceptions and presentations arise when it is thought that all modern thought about religions, and in particular the critically reflective or scientific study of religions, have only western roots. This is simply not the case.

The fundamental problem about recognizing the significance of these parallels in the history of ideas, which are important for our contemporary perception of the intellectual positioning of the "study of religions" in general, lies both in the minds of Eurocentric or westernist writers on the one hand, and in the minds of Asians who adopt a Eurocentric viewpoint by proxy, in a form of reverse orientalism. Since these matters evidently continue to haunt many, I have made various attempts to tackle the misunderstandings, and these cannot be all included here. Still prior to the publication of *Emerging from Meditation* was a short text entitled "Religion and reason in the Japanese experience" (1982c).[3] This refers to questions about the internal rationality of religious systems as well as to rational reflection about them, both being matters which arise in the wake of modernisation processes in general.[4] Returning specifically to the study of religions as a discipline, two contributions to congress proceedings of the International Association for the History of Religions (IAHR) are relevant, namely "The significance of the Japanese intellectual tradition for the history of religions" (1983, from the Winnipeg Congress of 1980) and "What is 'religion' in East Asia?"

---

3 This was based on a public lecture at King's College, London.

4 An updating of some of these related questions will also be found in the Occasional Paper *Rationality, ritual and life-shaping decisions in modern Japan* (Pye 2003c).

(1994a, from the Rome Congress of 1990). The latter includes a terminological point about the early use of the Sino-Japanese term for "religion" (*shūkyō* 宗教) which may be problematic and currently remains unresolved; this does not however affect the main argument concerning the arising of reflective studies of religions. A more recent account of the general argument will be found in "East Asian rationality in the exploration of religion" (1997b).[5]

Needless to say there continue to be those who are in denial over this general argument. In the case of western commentators this is neither "orientalism" nor "reverse orientalism" or even "occidentalism" (from an Asian viewpoint) but may simply be designated "westernism." Westernism is the naïve belief that all significant intellectual progress has either been "western" or is inconceivable without western influence. The prevalence of such a view, especially in connection with the study of religions, was discussed in "Westernism unmasked" (2000a) and "Overcoming westernism: the end of orientalism and occidentalism" (2003b), but to avoid undue repetition these are not included here. The main point is that Asian intellectual traditions pertaining to systematic reflection on religions should be given full weight in their own right.

Bibliographical references

Morgan, Robert and Pye Michael (eds. trans.) 1977. *Ernst Troeltsch: Writings on Theology and Religion* London (Duckworth) and Louisville Kentucky (Westminster/John Knox).

Pye, Michael 1973a. "Aufklärung and religion in Europe and Japan" in: *Religious Studies* 9: 201–217.

– 1982c. "Religion and reason in the Japanese experience" in: *King's Theological Review* 5 (1): 14–17.

– 1983. "The significance of the Japanese intellectual tradition for the history of religions" in: Slater, Peter and Wiebe Donald. (eds.)*Traditions in Contact and Change, Selected Proceedings of the Fourteenth Congress of the International Association for the History of Religions.* Waterloo Ontario (Wilfrid Laurier): 565–77.

– 1984 "Tominaga Nakamoto and Religious Pluralism" in: Daniels, Gordon (ed.) *Europe Interprets Japan* (select proceedings of the den Haag conference

5 This also responds to commentary by others on Tominaga's works, of which a slightly revised second English edition would be desirable, if time were to permit.

of the European Association for Japanese Studies 1982). Tenterden (Paul Norbury): 191–7.

- 1990a (trans.) *Emerging from Meditation (Tominaga Nakamoto).* London (Duckworth) and Honolulu (University of Hawaii Press).
- 1994a "What is 'religion' in East Asia?" in: Bianchi, Ugo, Mora Fabio and Bianchi Lorenzo (eds.) *The Notion of "Religion" in Comparative Research: Selected Proceedings of the XVIth Congress of the International Association for the History of Religions, Rome, 3rd-8th September, 1990.* Rome ("L'Erma" di Bretschneider): 115–22.
- 1997b "East Asian rationality in the exploration of religion" in: Martin, Luther J. and Jensen, Jeppe Sinding (eds.) *Rationality and the Study of Religion.* Aarhus (Aarhus University): 65–77.
- 2000a "Westernism unmasked" in: Jensen, Tim and Rothstein, Mikael (eds.) *Secular Theories on Religion. Current Perspectives.* Copenhagen (Museum Tusculanum Press), 211–230.
- 2003b. "Overcoming westernism: the end of orientalism and occidentalism" in: Schalk, Peter et al. (eds.) *Religion im Spiegelkabinett. Asiatische Religionsgeschichte im Spannungsfeld zwischen Orientalismus und Okzidentalismus (Acta Universitatis Upsaliensis. Historia Religionum 22).* Uppsala (Uppsala Universitet): 91–114.
- 2003c. *Rationality, ritual and life-shaping decisions in modern Japan (Occasional Papers 29).* Marburg (Centre for Japanese Studies).

Pye, Michael (trans.) 1990a. *Emerging from Meditation (Tominaga Nakamoto).* London (Duckworth) and Honolulu (University of Hawaii Press).

Troeltsch, Ernst 1913, 1922. *Gesammelte Schriften* II. Tübingen (Mohr and Siebeck).

Tsunoda, Ryusaku, de Bary, Wm.Theodore and Keene, Donald (eds.) 1958. *Sources of Japanese Tradition* (Introduction to Oriental Civilizations LIV, edited by Wm.Theodore de Bary). New York and London (Columbia University Press).

2.2 An Asian Starting Point for the Study of Religions

This paper was first delivered in 1989 at a conference in Hamilton, Ontario, Canada, entitled Religion in History / La religion dans l'histoire, which was stimulated by writings of Wilfred Cantwell Smith, Michel Despland and Ernst Feil and devoted to an exploration of the historical development of the notion of religion.

A science of religions, western and non-western

It is true to say that the study or science of religion in an investigative, descriptive and theoretical sense, as opposed to the intellectual promotion of a specific religious tradition or theology, has been mainly a feature of western culture in modern times. On the other hand it would be a mistake to radicalize this assumption and to assert that such a science of religion is inherently linked to western culture alone and hence in principle alien to other cultures. The following paragraphs are intended to provide an antidote to this error by adducing the ideas of an eighteenth century Japanese thinker, namely Tominaga Nakamoto (1715–1746). Tominaga made a profound contribution to the historical, descriptive and theoretical study of religion, without seeking to provide a normative statement on behalf of any one tradition to which he was beholden.

The sheer honesty and self-watchfulness of some western specialists in religious studies, in recent decades, has led to special emphasis being placed on the otherness of the main Asian traditions, on the otherness of the religious consciousness and of the accompanying intellectual patterns. As a result it has usually been supposed that there is little room in these cultures for an autonomously reflective science of religions, standing apart from the religions themselves. It is well known that not a few western scholars, whether orientalists or theologians, have shown a strong tendency to impose their own assumptions on other cultures with which they have attempted to interpret. In reaction to this it has mainly fallen to specialists in religious studies to question the very appropriateness of their own discipline in the face of the autonomous strength of diverse religious traditions. William Cantwell Smith, to take a clear, leading example, in order to take seriously the self-understanding of Islam in particular, has sought to develop new models of interpretation, even to the extent of avoiding the very term religion and emphasizing instead the concepts tradition and faith. Thus precisely within that circle of scholars whose professional activity is consciously focused on the study of "religion" the application of this very term has been kept under critical review. Yet the very modesty of this self-critical discipline, which has certainly led to a more finely tuned understanding of religions previously caricatured in some European writing, has led to the uncritical view that the study of religion is itself essentially alien to most cultures. In particular it is often supposed to be alien to those complex Asian cultures which have given birth to many of the religions under study. This view, however, itself requires to be overhauled. It is in principle inaccurate.

Admittedly the detached, analytical study of religion is of marginal significance in most cultures, even if it appears at all, and it is particularly fragile where religion itself is a dominant force. As a result Islamic Studies, Buddhist Studies, etc. tend to become established, rather than an autonomous historical, comparative or phenomenological discipline. Such a scientific study of religion may be regarded as potentially misleading or even hostile to religion. This reaction is not exactly unknown in the western world, not to speak of other cultures. On the other hand it is important, with all respect for the various religious systems themselves, not to lose sight of the fact that such investigation may seem attractive and valuable to thinkers whose formation was not dependent on modern western culture.

Tominaga Nakamoto

That this is so may be clearly seen from the example of Tominaga Nakamoto, a Japanese thinker of great, if not indeed of fundamental importance in the development of modern critical thought about religion. His two major extant works display modern ways of thinking about the subject which represent an entirely autonomous achievement within the context of Japanese thought. Specifically, Tominaga was concerned with the dominant religions of his place and time, namely Buddhism, Confucianism and Neo-Confucianism, Shintō, and more incidentally,

Daoism. His historically oriented critique included a critique of origins, a theory of religious development, and a detached assessment of the puzzle of religious pluralism (a traditional theme in Chinese and Japanese thought about religion, but hitherto usually handled from a decisively religious viewpoint).

The very fact that his historical and theoretical critique of three religious traditions, advanced from a standpoint of neutrality, was developed in the context of the urban culture of mid-Tokugawa Japan, means that the evident parallels with aspects of European Deism (though without Deus) and the European Enlightenment take on a significance of which he himself could not but be unaware. The parallelism inescapably suggests that there is a tendency, given certain intellectual and social presuppositions, for a historical and theoretical (and in this sense rational) critique of religion to emerge, regardless of the widely differing patterns and specific content of the religious systems in question.

The very existence of Tominaga's works, hitherto greatly underestimated, indicates that it is appropriate to speak of an Asian starting point for the study of religion. It is "Asian" and not isolatedly Japanese in that he works with Mahāyāna Buddhist materials (as far as sources are concerned, Chinese, but in historical projection Indian), with a wide range of Confucian and Neo-Confucian topics, and also with the Chinese derived "three teachings" question.

That his work has gone relatively unnoticed is probably due to the fact that his major extant work, *Emerging from Meditation*, had previously remained untranslated into any western language. Since it has now appeared in a full English translation,[1] the following paragraphs will draw attention to a few salient points of this work, thus complementing earlier articles.[2] The work consists of twenty-five chapters of *kanbun* (here meaning text in Chinese used as a literary language by Japanese scholars). In translation it amounts to 110 pages of printed English text. The title is Tominaga's own abbreviation of the fuller title "Emerging from meditation and afterwards speaking," which implies that the Buddha himself, after attaining enlightenment under the bodhi tree,

1 Pye 1990: *Tominaga Nakamoto, Emerging from Meditation.* This volume contains a full translation of *Emerging from Meditation* (original Japanese title: *Shutsujōkōgo*) and of *Writings of an Old Man* (*Okina no fumi*), with an appropriate introduction.

2 Relevant articles by the present writer up to the date of this article: Pye 1973, 1982, 1983 and 1984.

emerged from his meditation and reentered the world of articulated discourse. This led to diversity in the forms of his preaching and above all in the forms in which it was transmitted by others. The monks themselves diversified his teaching in the course of the generations, even while claiming authoritative consistency with the original. In fact however, thus Tominaga, the claims to consistency are spurious, at least in secondary matters. Diversity naturally arises because of the point of view and indeed the self-importance of particular groups or religious leaders. Since the same can be said for Confucianism and for Shintō, this assessment amounts to a theory of tradition. This comes out clearly enough in brief in the other work on religion which has been preserved, namely, *Writings of an Old Man.*[3] A detailed exposition relating to Confucianism, entitled *Setsuhei*, has unfortunately not been preserved for posterity.

Tominaga on Buddhism

As for Buddhism, Tominaga's main argument is advanced in the first two chapters of *Emerging from Meditation*, entitled "The sequence in which the teaching arose" and "Differences in what the sutras say." He saw clearly, on the basis of a thorough grasp of the contents of a very large number of Buddhist writings, and contrary to the widely current dogmatic orderings of the texts favoured by different schools, that it was these schools themselves who had produced rival versions of the sutras and commentaries in order to compete with each other. Thus,

> "The appearance of the divisions among the various teachings came about because they all first arose by superseding others."[4]

He disputed claims to a special transmission favouring the authority of particular sutras supposedly deriving personally from the Buddha. Thus,

> "…the scholars of later generations vainly say that all the teachings came directly from the golden mouth (of the Buddha) and were intimately transmitted by those who heard him frequently."[5]

On the contrary,

3 See note 1 above.
4 *Emerging from Meditation* (hereafter EFM), 81.
5 EFM,81.

> "Everybody renewed the teaching according to their opinions and passed it on orally."[6]

As a result Tominaga challenges the trustworthiness of the phrase with which the sūtras always begin, namely "Thus I have heard," a phrase with which he entitles the third chapter of *Emerging from Meditation.* He pounces on the improbable arguments advanced within the sūtras themselves to come to terms with their own variety. Thus according to one sūtra

> "Ānanda four times entreated: 'May the Buddha please expound again the sūtras which I have not yet heard.' "

Another says

> "The Buddha stretched forth his golden arm from within the golden coffin, and repeated his teaching (for Ānanda)."[7]

Tominaga simply rejects the view that the sūtras were all collected up by Ānanda (the Buddha's closest disciple).

> "The reality of it is that the sutras collected by Ānanda were just a few chapters of the *Āgamas*....As to the rest, not only do they not stem from Ānanda, but they represent the claims of later parties."[8]

Thus the problem known in Japanese as the *daijōbussetsu-hibussetsu no mondai* (the problem as to whether the Mahāyāna was the teaching of the Buddha or not) was launched by Tominaga in the early eighteenth century, and was not first raised by western scholarship in the nineteenth.

It should be noted that the view documented above is both a historical assessment, which (it should not be forgotten) is in general correct, and also a theory about the generation of diverse forms in a religious-textual tradition. The theory lies in the term "superseding" (*kajō*), which *explains* the diversified sequence of texts in a manner not drawn from Buddhist teaching itself. In *Writings of an Old Man* this theory is applied to Confucianism and Shintō as well.

This theme may be conveniently illustrated from Chapter 22 of *Emerging from Meditation*, entitled "Heteredoxies". Tominaga here takes up the view widely current in Buddhist writings that there were ninety-six heteredoxies or literally "external ways," that is, paths

6 EFM, 83.
7 EFM, 86.
8 EFM, 87.

other than the path of Buddhism. As is clear from the *Fǎxiǎn Record*, he argues, these heterodoxies have also been handed down over many centuries and at least in this respect are parallel to the teaching of the Buddha.[9] The style of Tominaga's reflection on the different points of view within the Buddhist writings can easily be illustrated by quoting the opening paragraph of this chapter:

> There were probably ninety-six heteredoxies. *The Great Treatise* says, 'The ninety-six kinds of heterodoxy once conspired together to debate against the Buddha.' In the Sarvāstivāda Vinaya it says, 'The six teachers of heterodox ways each gave way to fifteen kinds, which makes ninety-six altogether.' The *Daiju Sūtra* says, 'In the three jewels the mind is held in respect, and this surpasses all the ninety-five ways.' Then again the *Bunbetsukudoku Treatise* says, 'Among the ninety-six ways the Buddha way is regarded as the greatest.' This is the utterance of yet another group who made it ninety-six including the Buddha. The *Laṅkāvatāra Sūtra* refers to one hundred and eight heretical views. They are not all given in detail. The *Vimalakīrti Sūtra* lists six teachers of heterodoxies…The *Nirvāṇa Sūtra* lists six heterodoxies of of asceticism as follows: fasting, frequenting a precipice, fire-walking, sitting in solitude, maintaining a tranquil silence, living like a cow or a dog. The *Great Treatise* lists sixteen kinds of false subjectivity, the *Yuga Treatise* lists sixteen divergent theories of existence, the *Dainichi Sūtra* lists thirty kinds of heterodoxy, and the *Gedoshojonehan Treatise* lists twenty kinds of Hīnayāna heterodoxy. These are all convenient summaries and do not amount to the full number of ninety-six. They are not handed down in the *Vedas*, nor did their people enter China.[10]

As is well known, Buddhism was characterized as the Middle Way between self-mortification and self-gratification. As the *Great Treatise* says (quoted by Tominaga):

> "If Śākyamuni Buddha had not first practised asceticism for six years the people would not have trusted him when he reproved those not following the way. Hence he himself practised asceticism more than other people."[11]

But as the *Inga Sūtra* says:

> "The prince (i. e. the Buddha) said of himself, 'I have now been doing ascetic practice for a full six years. If I now attain the way with an emaciated body I will have to say that self-starvation is the cause of nirvana. I must take food and then complete the way."[12]

9 Cf. EFM, 157.
10 EFM, 156.
11 EFM, 159.
12 EFM, 159.

For Tominaga this statement betrays the real drive behind religious change or development. He writes:

> "Hence we say that Śākyamuni's double practice of pleasure and of asceticism was in order to bring the heterodoxies to submission. Thus the exposition of what is called the middle way is also something which emerges at one level above."[13]

He finds this view directly confirmed in the *Chū-agon* which says:

> "There are two kinds of practice, that of the five passions and that of asceticism; departing from these two is called the middle way."[14]

Thus the mode of origin of Buddhism is in principle no different from that of the heterodoxies on the one hand or of the later sectarian divisions of Buddhism on the other hand. Tominaga regards it as important to realize this. Otherwise innumerable problems of interpretation arise when the attempt is made to justify one trend over against another or to achieve an apparent harmony between those expressions of Dharma deemed to be orthodox. That the historical Buddha, Śākyamuni, himself played this game of relating dialectically to teachings which he considered inadequate is not in itself reprehensible; but since it has to be understood in terms of the context of other teachings and the intention to go one better than these it implies a relativization of the new teaching which is to be regarded as one teaching among others and part of a normal process of religious innovation.

This fundamental perception by Tominaga was of course quite at odds with the normal Buddhist view, according to which the "heterodoxies," even if not so perniciously misleading as wrong views (*jaken*) within Buddhism, nevertheless were of distinctly secondary value and in principle to be avoided or displaced by the Buddhist way. Not that Tominaga found it inappropriate, in itself, that Buddhists should mount a claim to the superiority of their teaching. This is normal. At the same time such a claim tends to lead to a misreading of the historical development and to presentations of the relations between the different teachings which are oversimplified, for dogmatic purposes, and thus simply not correct. Such errors in retrospective view can be avoided if one realises that Buddhism, i. e. the victorious and now dominant tradition, itself arose as one among several or many alternatives.

---

13 EFM, 159.
14 EFM, 159.

This is in fact the very starting point of *Emerging from Meditation.* At the beginning of Chapter 1 Tominaga writes:

> "If we first consider the sequence in which the teaching [of Buddhism] arose we see that in effect it began among the heterodoxies."[15]

The various teachings rivalled each other in the presentation of a realm lying beyond this world, and since all the possibilities had been exhausted, right up to the idea of a state of "nor-non-conception" which was arrived at by transcending the "realm of non-existence." there was nothing left over for Śākyamuni but to opt out of this competition and to teach "detachment from the characteristics of birth and death, adding to this the remarkable power of great supernatural transformations."[16] Tominaga concludes dryly:

> "Pointing out that this was very hard to achieve, he got the heretics to submit and converted the Indians. This was how Śākyamuni's teaching arose."[17]

The supernatural transformations referred to here are considered in more detail in Chapter 8 which, interestingly enough, contains close parallels to the idea in *Writings of an Old Man* that particular countries (we would now say, cultures) have their own special propensities when it comes to the elaboration of systems of teaching. Thus he opens by saying:

> "The common people of India are very fond of magic, and similarly the people of China are fond of literature. All those who establish a teaching and expound a Way find they must put it forward in terms of such things, for if they do not the people will not trust them."[18]

This was unavoidable even for a profound teaching such as Buddhism.

> "As the other teachings of the time all made use of magic in their promotion, even though Śākyamuni surpassed them in his teaching, he could not avoid using magic provisionally when making it known."[19]

Under "magic", though thinking first of miraculous feats performed by exponents of Buddhism to impress people, Tominaga includes a wide variety of secondary religious forms, notably "teachings like karmic ret-

---

15 EFM, 73.
16 EFM, 74.
17 EFM, 74.
18 EFM, 105.
19 EFM, 105.

ribution and heaven and purgatory, originally started in non-Buddhist schools." Making use of such teachings implies a dialectical relationship with forms of teaching which do not themselves represent the ultimate intention of the teacher.

> "Śākyamuni used them to lead people with, thereby winning over people of the lower kind. He then set up the teaching of attaining Buddhahood by detachment from particulars, and leaving the lower level he won over people of the higher kind. This was possible because those teachings were not originally bad, and moreover the Indian people like them. Nevertheless the reality is that it was a skilful means."[20]

This statement shows that Tominaga's perception of the dynamics of religion is drawn in part from Buddhist self-understanding, in the following sense. The term "skilful means" is a technical term in Buddhism which refers to the presentation of the teaching in a manner which is at once acceptable and understandable to its hearers and true, given a satisfactory devolution of the sense, to its own inner intention. Thus in Buddhism, to regard an element of teaching as "skilful means" is to imply that some dialectical progression is still required in order to lead into the full meaning. This reflective acceptance of the value of particular forms of teaching within Buddhism while at the same time proposing a spiritual departure from them clearly implies a high level of self-conscious detachment from the system of teaching even while this is being propounded. It seems evident from this and other places in Tominaga's work that the degree of abstraction achieved here was one of the seminal features in his own formulation of a theory of the way in which religions work.

The same point may be documented from Chapter 4, which is devoted to a discussion of the diversity of teachings about the cosmos. Tominaga begins:

> "The teachings about Mount Sumeru were all handed down by brahmans. Though Śākyamuni used them to expound his Way, they are to be regarded as cosmic theory. Later scholars (i. e. Buddhists) have made much of this teaching while criticising others, and lost sight of the Buddha's intention. This is because the Buddha's intention is not to be found in such matters. He was urgently seeking people's salvation and had no time for such petty matters. What he did is what is known as skilful means."[21]

20 EFM, 107.
21 EFM, 88.

The implication of this is that the Buddha (Śākyamuni) expressed his teaching in cosmological terms without intending to assert any particular theory about the cosmos for his own part. The divergences about cosmology between the different texts of Buddhism, adduced in detail in *Emerging from Meditation*, are therefore not of any importance in themselves if Buddhism is properly understood. What they do show however is that the Buddhist writings are secondary products of the tradition seeking to outdo each other. Thus Tominaga:

> "Those discrepancies between what the sutras and treatises say are just there for the sake of giving names to the various divisions [of Buddhist teaching] and providing sayings for each school."[22]

In the same chapter such divergences are linked with the idea of superseding (*kajō*). This is significant in that it represents a displacement of the Buddhist idea that teachings of secondary importance may be understood dialectically in terms of skilful means. This is replaced, for Tominaga, by a more general theory about the relations between a series of teachings, viewed now as rival systems following on each others' heels.[23] The idea of skilful means is internal to the Buddhist system and is in principle subordinate to the intentionality of that system. The idea of "superseding" sidesteps the normative interest of the Buddhist system in itself and helps Tominaga to formulate an independent theory of tradition formation which can be applied to the origins of Buddhism, as one system among many, and to the diversity within Buddhism. This theory conflicts with many specific statements found in Buddhist writings, whether polemical or eirenic, which Tominaga correctly perceived to be inconsistent with each other and thus in many cases historically inaccurate. Whether, as an intellectual theory about religion, it conflicts fundamentally with Buddhism in a more profound sense must remain a question for Buddhists. It is a question which Tominaga did not directly address, though the indications are that he did not consider that a more reliable historical assessment would prejudice the value of Buddhism properly understood.

22 EFM, 89.

23 C.f. Pye 1983.

Science of religion not exclusive to western culture

With these few examples enough has been said to show that a historically and theoretically reflective study of religion has clearly emerged in the context of an Asian culture. This simple fact in the history of ideas should be given due weight. Taking cognizance of it may help to readjust the equilibrium which is sometimes lost when undue weight is given to the supposedly impervious otherness of other cultures. The emergence of a science of religion is not exclusively linked to a set of postulates available only in western culture, as is often supposed. On the contrary, it can only really come to itself when it ceases to be bound to one culture alone. Although by the nature of the case he could not foresee this at the time, the writings of Tominaga Nakamoto provide mighty assistance in the development of a truly independent and hence intercultural science of religion.

Bibliographical references

Pye, Michael 1973a. "Aufklärung and religion in Europe and Japan" *Religious Studies* 9: 201–217.
– 1982c. "Religion and reason in the Japanese experience" in: *King's Theological Review* 5 (1): 14–17.
– 1983. "The significance of the Japanese intellectual tradition for the history of religions" in: Slater, Peter and Wiebe Donald. (eds.) *Traditions in Contact and Change, Selected Proceedings of the Fourteenth Congress of the International Association for the History of Religions.* Waterloo Ontario (Wilfrid Laurier): 565–77.
– 1984 "Tominaga Nakamoto and Religious Pluralism" in: Daniels, Gordon (ed.) *Europe Interprets Japan* (select proceedings of the den Haag conference of the European Association for Japanese Studies 1982). Tenterden (Paul Norbury): 191–7.

This paper was previously published as "An Asian Starting Point for the Study of Religion" in M. Nowaczyk and Z. Stachowski (eds.), *Language – Religion – Culture. In Memory of Professor Witold Tyloch*, Warsaw (Polish Society for the Study of Religions) 1992, 27–35; and in Michel Despland and Gérard Vallée (eds.), *Religion in History. The Word, the Idea, the Reality / La religion dans l'histoire. Le mot, l'idée, la réalité*, Waterloo, Ontario (Wilfrid Laurier University Press) 1992, 101–109.

2.3 Tominaga Nakamoto and Religious Pluralism

This article introduces and considers the critically reflective attitude developed by Tominaga Nakamoto (1715–1746) towards the question of the plurality of religions as he perceived it in his own day. It was first presented at the den Haag conference of the European Association for Japanese Studies in 1982 and later published in its select proceedings. The present version has been slightly edited.

Historicism and relativism in the writings of Tominaga Nakamoto

There is clearly a strong affinity between Tominaga's two extant works *Okina no fumi* (*Writings of an Old Man*) and *Shutsujōkōgo (Emerging from Meditation and then Speaking).*[1] However, these works are very different in character. The *Shutsujōkōgo* is moderately long, written in *kanbun*, contains numerous quotations from other mainly Buddhist works and is devoted to a critique of the historical character of the Buddhist tradition. Chapter XXIV, entitled 'The Three Teachings', which deals with the relations between Buddhism, Confucianism and Taoism, is simply a section of a work which takes up in turn many different aspects of Buddhism. The *Okina no fumi* by contrast is written in Japanese, is rather short, does not use the scholarly quotation style, and attends directly to the meaning and rôle of the three religions of Japan: Buddhism, Confucianism and Shintō. As the real meaning of each of these 'ways' it presents the notion of 'the way of ways', which can be practised in present-day life (i. e. eighteenth century) in Japan. Thus, unlike the *Shutsujōkōgo* the *Okina no fumi* has the question of the relations between religions in the forefront.

1 Quotations from both writings in this paper were from the writer's own draft translations. For full English translations reference may now be made to *Emerging from Meditation*, Pye 1990a. For the *Shutsujōkōgo* the *Nihon shisō taikei* (43) edition is followed (Mizuta 1976) and for the *Okina no fumi* the *Nihon koten bungaku taikei* (97) is followed (Iwanami Shoten 1966).

Some fundamental assumptions found in both works may be briefly recalled. Tominaga's historicist and relativist viewpoint finds expression in both. Section IX of *Okina no fumi* sums it up as follows.

> 'Since ancient times it has generally been the case that those who preach a moral way and establish a law of life have had somebody whom they have held up as an authoritative precursor, while at the same time they have tried to emerge above those who went before.'

Tominaga saw the perception of these dynamics of tradition as a releasing explanation for the otherwise confusing diversity of religions, schools and sects. He applied this principle in the *Shutsujōkōgo* (where the term *kajō,* or superseding, is used) to the claims and counterclaims within the whole Buddhist tradition, as it was known to him. In Section X of *Okina no fumi* he even refers the reader specifically to the *Shutsujōkōgo* for more details on the subject. In the same way Section XI refers us to the lost work *Setsuhei* for more details of his critique of the Confucian tradition. Tominaga's basic idea in this connection was that religious teachers or leaders usually try to add some new gloss or twist to what has gone before, which in turn leaves the next generation with the problem of how to claim coherence for the tradition, a problem which they in turn solve with a new attempt at a normative version.

Together with Tominaga's historicist view of religious tradition there is also to be found a strand of relativism of a cultural or even psychological kind. In Chapter XI of the *Shutsujōkōgo* for example he advances a fairly complex theory of language according to which 'all words are conditioned by type, by milieu and by the individual'. The influence of this theory (the details of which are not my subject here) may be seen in the *Okina no fumi,* not only in incidental comments on terminology, but especially in the fun which he pokes at those who vainly try to live in a language world which is not their own in order to bolster their religious authority. A related feature not yet commonly noted is his account of cosmological ideas which has distinctly relativist and even projectionist features. Chapter IV of *Shutsujōkōgo* reviews various forms of Buddhist cosmology and concludes:

> 'Teachings about the cosmos are in actuality quite vague and go no further than describing the logic of the mind. There is no way of knowing whether they are right or wrong. Hence I say that the worlds arise in conformity with people's minds.'

While the seeds of this idea may lie in Buddhist thought itself, especially in the Mahāyāna and indeed more specifically the Yogācāra schools, it nevertheless takes on a quite new meaning in the context of Tominaga's trenchant criticisms of the Buddhist schools. It must be admitted that this idea is not present in the *Okina no fumi*. On the other hand the *Okina no fumi* gives very clear expression to the geographical relativism of language, customs and religion, as is already well known. In a broad sense these ideas all belong together and complement the diachronic relativism in terms of which Tominaga criticised the development of each specific tradition.

Cultural difference and religious diversity

One further common point will lead us into a more specific discussion of Chapter XXIV of the *Shutsujōkōgo* upon which I wish to concentrate below. Tominaga argued in both of his extant writings that the specific religions each had a special propensity. Thus in Chapter XXIV the Confucianists are said to exaggerate in letters while Buddhists are said to exaggerate in magic. These are the same propensities or habits castigated in Sections XIV and XV respectively of the *Okina no fumi*. It is interesting that while Shintō is castigated for its secrecy, in *Okina no fumi* Section XVI, Daoism is said to have an exaggerated concern with heaven, thus being similar to the so-called 'other ways' of India among which Buddhism first arose (c.f. *Shutsujōkōgo* Chapter I). Tominaga also saw the Daoists as followers of the Buddhist trail in their emphasis on magic.

As a matter of fact, Tominaga showed relatively little interest in Daoism, treating it as little more than a feeble attempt to imitate Buddhism.' This pretended Way,' he wrote, 'is moreover quite wretched and is fundamentally not comparable to Confucianism or Buddhism' (*Shutsujōkōgo* XXIV). Typically, he notes that the sutras of Daoism appeared later. Again this is an example of a kind of argument already available in the intellectual tradition but which takes on a special nuance in the context of Tominaga's theory of the formation of religious tradition. However, his main reason for almost ignoring Daoism altogether may have been that it was not a matter of consequence in the Japanese debates. Referring to Daoist teachings he wrote, 'They have not been handed down over here and do not need to be debated now.' Thus, although he was aware of some of the leading features of Daoist tradition, the interest in healthful life, the goal of immortality, the celestial court, and so on, he did not think it worthwhile to comment on these in detail. He was more interested in the relations between Confucianism and Buddhism. Not only that, he was more concerned with the nature of the arguments among the Chinese about the relations and relative merits of the three teachings, than he was with the substance of the various teachings.

This lack of strong interest in Daoism, despite his use of the conventional phrase 'The three teachings' in the chapter heading of Chapter XXIV of the *Shutsujōkōgo,* is quite consistent with Tominaga's very definite idea of relativism by country. As is well known this is firmly stated in the opening sections of *Okina no fumi.* Thus we read, 'In any case, Buddhism is the way of India and Confucianism is the way of China, and because of the difference of country they are not the way of Japan' (*Okina no fumi* Section I). Lest Tominaga be thought of as a mere chauvinist one should not omit the following sentence which runs 'Shintō is the way of Japan, but because it is of a different age it is not the way of today's world.' Tominaga followed this up by ridiculing, in Sections II-V, those who painfully imitate Indian or Chinese manners or who artificially pursue Japanese archaisms.

The same line of thought is given an anecdotal basis in *Shutsujōkōgo* Chapter XXIV as follows:

> 'A man asked Prince Ryū Mon (竜門 Lóngmén)[2], "He (i.e. the Buddha) may be a sage, but what is his teaching?" He answered, "It is western teaching; in China it is mud."'

Tominaga goes on to argue that we read 'In China it is mud' because of the value placed on magic in Buddhism. Similarly, he wrote in *Okina no fumi* (Sections XIV and XV) that Indian magic and China's high-flown language were not necessary in Japan. Returning to *Shutsujōkōgo* Chapter XXIV, we see that there, too, the argument is advanced to deal with the reception of Confucianism in Japan, thus:

> 'Someone asked me, "He (i.e. Confucius) may be a sage, but what is his teaching?" I answered, "It is western teaching; over here it is mud." This is because of the value placed on letters. Here we have a case of language having conditions. Because of this the way is divided. It is because countries have their customs that the way is divided. Thus the teaching

2 The Chinese pronunciation of Chinese names is not usually used in Japanese, and Tominaga would have scorned such extra information as pedantry, but it is given here (at first occurrences only) for the convenience of western Sinologists who may feel uncomfortable with the Japanese pronunciation.

> of Confucianism is mud over here. The teaching of Buddhism lies to the west of the west.'

In this last phrase, 'The teaching of Buddhism lies to the west of the west', we can see how the sense of geographical distance may have contributed to the way in which Tominaga conceived of the problem of religious pluralism. One would not expect it to be so dramatically stated in China. Notice also that we meet here the general idea of a *way*, divided because of natural differences. (It is of course not to be confused with the *dào* of Daoism, though the same character is used.) It is here that Tominaga comes nearest in the *Shutsujōkōgo* to the positive teaching about 'the way of ways' which is found in the *Okina no fumi*. He concludes this passage, 'Since what the Buddhists exaggerate in is magic and what the Confucianists exaggerate in is letters, if we reject these we shall advance to the Way.'

Tominaga on models of religious pluralism

As mentioned earlier, Tominaga was not so much concerned with the relations between doctrinal systems as such, but rather with the kind of arguments which people advanced to deal with such questions. He was hardly interested in the relative merits of different systems, except that he happened to have little more than scorn for Daoism. Nor was he an apologist for one system against another. Hence his statement: 'I am not a follower of Confucianism, nor of the Dao nor of the Buddha. I watch their words and deeds from the side and then privately debate them.' (*Shutsujōkōgo* Chapter XXIV, closing sentence.)

With this in mind, we turn now to a closer examination of Tominaga's discussion of models of religious pluralism in Chapter XXIV of *Shutsujōkōgo*. In this chapter he considers the arguments of several Chinese writers, especially those of the monk Myōkyō (明教 Míngjiào 1007–1072) on the relationships between Buddhism and Confucianism, and finds them wanting. It is interesting to see why. Overall the argument represents an interesting counterpiece to the position advanced in *Okina no fumi*.

Two models of debate between Buddhism and Confucianism attract Tominaga's attention. Firstly, there are the polemical writings which attempt to prove the superiority of the one or the other. Secondly, there are eirenic writings which attempt to create compromise or unity. Tominaga mentions several polemical writings briefly and gives them short shrift. Claiming to have read them carefully he concludes that 'they are nothing more than quarrels between magic and letters'. This has to be understood in terms of Tominaga's more widely-stated approach referred to briefly above. What he means is that the protagonists are debating in defence of one or other of the chronologically and geographically determined propensities which the religions in question display. Such a debate, however, falls short of a realistic understanding of the way in which religious systems operate and does not lead to a satisfactory perception or explanation of pluralism.

As to eirenic statements Tominaga rejects these also. One opinion, that of Shinsō (真宗 Zhēnzōng) of the Sòng dynasty, ran:

> 'The purport of what the three teachings set up is the same. In general they all urge people to do good. However only scholars of advanced consciousness can see them as a single reality, and those who stagnate in one-sided attachments get further from the Way.'

Similarly, the Sòng Dynasty monk Ekō (慧洪 Hùihóng) said, when honouring the stupa of Myōkyō (of whom more anon):

> 'I have compared my way to that of Confucius, and there is a difference as of a palm and a fist, opening and closing. In short they are like the hand.'

Tominaga put this view down to Ekō's reliance on Myōkyō who had attempted such mediation, but also to ignorance of the real problem, commenting sharply, 'He did not know that magic and letters in particular are as different as Ko and Etsu (胡 Hú and 越 Yuè).' (All quotations in this paragraph are from *Shutsujōkōgo* Chapter XXIV.) In sum, the specific historically visible propensities of each tradition pertain to its nature and are not to be simply slurred over by an idealist appeal to a deeper truth or a fundamental complementarity.

Tominaga's main attention, however, is drawn by the writings of Myōkyō (Míngjiào 明教), and it may be that here we have one of the sources out of which Tominaga himself formulated his ideas, albeit by way of disagreement. In general, Myōkyō seems to have engaged in seeing similarities between Buddhism and Confucianism where Tominaga felt obliged to stress dissimilarity. Three examples of this can be given.

Firstly, Myōkyō asks why it was that the way of the Buddha spread out beyond India, – an interesting question for Tominaga. Myōkyō argued that Buddhism was not merely transmitted by officials but 'followed the inner law (*ri* 理 Chinese *lǐ*) of the teaching', and that 'The Buddha founded his teaching in accordance with the divine way and had feeling for its contents,' while admitting, however, that 'It was hidden and hard to see, which is why the people did not all come to believe it fully.' Tominaga comments that what Myōkyō is talking about is the popularisation of Buddhism through the doctrine of karmic cause and effect which operates at the same level as magic and, he says, 'is not the true meaning of the Buddha'. In any case, he adds, if Buddhism were a kind of Brahmanism giving moral instruction it would end up in China just like the officially sponsored teaching of Confucianism. Either way, it seems, Tominaga feels that Myōkyō has underestimated the distinctive character of Buddhism.

For the second example it will be well to reproduce a fairly long quotation which Tominaga gives from Myōkyō:

> 'The ten virtues and the five precepts are one and the same as the five constants, benevolence, righteousness, and so on. The sages are different in respect of their teachings, but the same in respect of doing the good. All the teachings of the world amount to nothing other than the good. If the Buddha's Dharma were not the good, everybody would have to reject it. It is my wish that everybody should be for the public and not for arrogance. The teaching of the sages lies simply in the good. The Way of these sages is nothing but righteousness. It is not essential to be a monk. It is not essential to be a Confucianist. Being monks or Confucianists is a mere form. The ancient sages who spoke of Buddhism, Taoism and Confucianism, were one in mind while in form they were diverse. Their being one lies in their desire for men to perform the good. Their being diverse lies in their division into schools, each following its own teaching. It would not do if there were no Confucianism in the world, if there were no Lǎo Zǐ, if there were no Buddha. If any one of these were lacking it would be a loss of one of the ways of goodness in the world. If one of the ways of goodness were lost, then the evil in the world would increase. I think that the three teachings help each other and make society good. This is also the natural way things are ordained. It is not something which people can grasp immediately.'

This quotation has been presented at length because it might seem at first sight to be very close to Tominaga's argument in *Okina no fumi*. However, Tominaga rejects Myōkyō's eirenic approach very firmly, and therefore his argument at this point is important for the interpretation of his thought. He offers two reasons for rejecting it. For one thing, he says, 'If goodness is the main feature, why limit it to the three teachings? Do not some tens of other ways, some tens of heretics, all seek the good?' This critique is in tune with Tominaga's general deflation of religious authorities. Either the heretics are as well justified as the respectable teachings, or all are to be criticised. The intellectual problem posed by pluralism cannot be solved merely by forging an alliance between two or three respectable and influential traditions. This point serves to remind us that in Myōkyō's exposition there is no parallel to Tominaga's assumptions about the historically conditioned nature of religion and about the competitive development of diverse viewpoints in the course of time.

Tominaga then goes on to argue that even while the mind of Buddhism and Confucianism are said to be one it is precisely their differences which confuse people. It is all very well saying that both Confucianism and Buddhism teach the people the good, but they still seem to end up by exaggerating in letters or in magic respectively, thus leaving the problem of diversity unsolved. If the real purport of different teachings is the same, why is this not more evident? Again we see that Tominaga is concerned to insist on the specific historical appearance of the two religions.

This argument shows that if anything Tominaga's critical position in *Shutsujōkōgo* XXIV is harder than in *Okina no fumi* where more room is given for positive statement about 'the way of ways'. However, it should not be forgotton that his rejection of eirenic compromise is not made on behalf of any one tradition or by reversion to a one-sided polemic. It is his underlying critical relativism which determines his response.

The third example of Tominaga's dealings with Myōkyō centres on the classic Chinese problem of the nature of man, a subject which had taken new turns with the introduction of Buddhist ideas. Myōkyō had tried to relate a Confucianist teaching about the desirability of returning to man's original nature with the Buddhist idea of latent or fundamental Buddha-nature within man. Tominaga's own words will explain the point and provide his comment:

> 'Having read this *Fukuseisho* (a Buddhist work) myself, I find it says "If passions are not aroused, man's nature is unified; given undeliberate non-conceptualising the passions do not arise, and this gives right thought." This makes passions pertain to what is bad while the non-arising of passions is regarded as a return to man's original nature. This is the final teaching of Dhyāna (i. e. Zen). However what the Chéng brothers[3] meant was different. The Chéng brothers' meaning was that neither do the passions pertain to what is bad nor does one seek the non-arising of passions, and that a real return to man's nature entails the passions being good. This is what *they*

3 Literally, "The elder brother and the younger brother," two Confucianists cited by Myōkyō.

> called a return to man's original nature. Myōkyō was mistaken when, dazzled by the similarities of this writing, he declared the teachings to be the same. In recent times Itō Jinsai has also done this.'

This argument illustrates well how Tominaga refused to accept any easy equations between the religions which would blur their specific character. This point of view fits precisely with one which sees the diverse traditions as having developing identities through time subject to cultural conditioning of various kinds.

Conclusions

It is time to draw some conclusions, however limited, about Tominaga's response to religious pluralism as found in *Okina no fumi* and *Shutsujōkōgo* Chapter XXIV. In general the ideas expressed in the two writings are consistent. *Okina no fumi* shows a greater interest in the positive truth or good conveyed by religion even though the historicist and relativist critique is clearly present. *Shutsujōkōgo* Chapter XXIV gives a sharper rejection of the idea that diverse religions are merely different expressions of one common mind or central concern. It should not be overlooked that even *Okina no fumi* with its 'way of ways' set out in Section VI (which turns out to be little more than neo-Confucian morality for the layman) rejects any identification of this 'way of ways' with a specific historic tradition.

In *Shutsujōkōgo* Chapter XXIV Tominaga actually debates against a specific example of eirenic identity-theory, and this indicates clearly that his main concern is with the precise nature of specific, historic, religious tradition. This is not particularly surprising as the main thrust of the work as a whole is to show how the Buddhist tradition was articulated and developed through a series of partisan improvements. Historical criticism does not lead to an easy solution to the question posed by religious pluralism, one may observe, rather away from such. It is also evident however that reflection on the debates, both polemical and eirenic, which arose in China on account of religious pluralism were part of the matrix in which Tominaga's historicist ideas took shape.

Bibliographical references

Ienaga, Saburō (et al.) 1966. *Kinseishisōka bunshū (Nihon koten bungaku taikei* 97). Tokyo (Iwanami Shoten).

Mizuta, Norihisa and Arisaka, Takamichi (eds.) *Tominaga Nakamoto, Yamagata Bantō* (*Nihon shisō taikei* 43). Tokyo (Iwanami Shoten).

Pye, Michael (trans.) 1990a. *Emerging from Meditation (Tominaga Nakamoto).* London (Duckworth) and Honolulu (University of Hawaii Press).

This paper was first published in Gordon Daniels (ed.) 1984. *Europe Interprets Japan* (select proceedings of the den Haag conference of the European Association for Japanese Studies 1982) Tenterden, England (Paul Norbury Publications): 191–197.

2.4 Three Teachings (Sānjiào) Theory and Modern Reflection on Religion

This paper was presented at a regional conference of the International Association for the History of Religions in Beijing, 1992, on the subject "Religion and Modernisation in China," the proceedings of which were published in 1995. Relevant to this paper is a section in 3.6 below which includes a diagram of the "three teachings" as understood by the influential Míng Tàizǔ introduced here.

A Chinese frame of reference for religious theory?

The purpose of this paper is essentially to pose a question to those who study religion or religions from a Chinese point of view in the modern world. The term "three teachings" (*sānjiào*) is used as a kind of symbol in this question, as will be explained below. At its simplest, the question is whether there is such a thing as a characteristic Chinese frame of reference for the exploration of the phenomena of religion, and if so, what the implications of this might be.

It is understood that the main line of the sociological explanation of religion in mainland China today follows the leading ideas of Marxism and of Mao Tse-tung's thought. This is applicable when it comes to discussing the relationship between religion and economics from the point of view of historical political development. However sociological theory often leaves unclear precisely what it is that is being explained in this way. What is the character of the phenomenon which is under consideration? In one sense our widely ranging explanatory theories of religion might be thought to be valid in any country or continent, bearing in mind the specific stage of its historical development. Thus some will adopt a Marxist line of interpretation while others are accustomed to a Weberian or a Durkheimian model. But if any such theory refers to a phenomenon whose shape has first to be discerned, it is surely significant for our theoretical reflections that the *manner* in which this shape has been discerned appears to vary in accordance with the specific religious history of different continents and cultures. Even though we might try to disregard the shape which has been dominant in any one cultural tradition, this is not easy to do. It is probably not even desirable to disregard culturally determined frames of reference in the name of completely generalised abstract theories. Is it not far better to consider with some seriousness those frames of reference which have been influential in various cultures in order to benefit our more general theoretical understanding?[1]

Let us consider first two or three non-Chinese frames of reference for the development of theory about religion. In Europe the dominant features are a Christian tradition splitting into two competing strands, the catholic and the protestant,[2] accompanied by religio-critical movements of which atheistic materialism has been the most prominent. This frame of reference has been the background for the development of secularisation theory in various forms and subsequently for attempts to interpret the alternative religious scene of imported Eastern religions (through immigration and adoption) and "New Age" movements. Many specialists in religious studies in the west take this general pattern for granted.[3]

In Latin America it is different. There the main feature is the juxtaposition of a dominant Catholic Christianity with the many forms of popular religion which are still influenced or even determined by pre-conquest patterns among the Indian populations. Of course there are other factors too: some highly active protestant sects, cults which draw on beliefs and practices of African origin, and organised religions spreading from Japan such as Tenrikyō.[4] However even with these admixtures the dominant patterns are recognisable and determine the framework of many scientific investigations, the keywords being not secularisation but syncretism, interaction and transformation.

For most of Africa the dominant model is that of the competition between Islam and Christianity on the background and occasional resur-

1 Essentially the same point is made in "Intercultural strategies and the International Association for the History of Religions" (3.3 below), but with an emphasis on an African context rather than a Chinese one. Both papers are originally from 1992.

2 That is, the religions known in China as Lord of Heaven Teaching and Christianity respectively.

3 For a critique from the present writer's viewpoint see "A common language of minimal religiosity" in *The Journal of Oriental Studies* (Pye 1987); the whole issue of this journal is devoted to concepts of secularisation and their relevance or lack of relevance to non-European contexts.

4 Cf. "Distant cousins: transmitting new Japanese religions to Brazil" (5.8 below).

gence of traditional religious belief and practice. Again it is complicated by the appearance of many new religious organisations, though interestingly enough their prophets and prophetesses (Simon Kimbangu of Zaire, Alinesitoué of the Diola) play a major role. The overriding pattern is neither that of Europe nor that of Latin America. As a result secularisation theory is not of such great significance as it has been thought to be in Europe. Nor is there such a sharp focus on the relation between dominant and popular religion as anthropologists and sociologists have developed in Latin America. Rather, theoretical interest has been drawn particularly towards the problems of elucidating "traditional" religion on the one hand and "religious innovation" on the other hand.

What then of China? We all know that the frame of reference in China in most centuries has been different from those mentioned so far. We also know that today it is not the same as in some past period or other, before the republican, independence and communist movements. Far be it from me to attempt to describe the current situation in China with regard to the activities of religious organizations and their place in society. This is not my subject. Nor do I wish to bring up some past epoch in a romantic or nostalgic manner, though this is often done by western writers. However it does seem that the concept of "three teachings," upon which I wish to focus, indicates a frame of reference which has characterised Chinese views of religion for centuries and which has greatly influenced neighbouring countries such as Korea and Japan. In the last century or two we have got used to religions being counted differently, and not necessarily as three in number. On the other hand it is difficult to go back to a time in Chinese history when there were not at least two religions. Moreover the relationship between the various teachings has been a matter of discussion ever since Buddhism was introduced into China, and it is in this context that the concept of "three teachings" arose.

Of course one might also pursue other concepts which have played a particularly strong role in China such as *dào* 道, meaning way or path. The strength of this concept lies in its reference to activity or behaviour rather than to teaching or doctrine, which in some cases at least are less important in Chinese culture than elsewhere.[5] However, while *jiào* 教

5 The concept of *dào* as a specifically Chinese category for reflection on religion was adduced by Joachim Christian during the conference discussion in Beijing, and is referred to here for that reason. He justifiably emphasised the behavioural dimension over against the doctrinal.

admittedly emphasises "teaching" it should be remembered that it is after all a Chinese term, and not a foreign one. Moreover a particular *jiào* or teaching can easily be understood to have a behavioural, a self-disciplinary or a mystical dimension.

"Three teachings" as a critical reflection on plurality

It is important to notice that giving prominence to the concept of "three teachings" (*sānjiào* 三教) does not necessarily imply a particular standpoint or decision about just how the teachings are, or were, related. "Three teachings" is an interesting frame of reference precisely because it has been interpreted in various ways. Often it has been used to support a synthesist view of religion. This leads to statements such as "the three teachings are one." However it may also imply a critical recognition of the plurality of religions. The direction in which it is taken depends on which author one reads, and how one reads. My question is, can the concept of "three teachings" be regarded as summing up a frame of reference which, at its best, gives rise to critical reflection on religions in their plurality? If so, may it not be seen as one of the starting points for the modern study of religion in a Chinese perspective?

Whatever we may think of Emperors, it would appear that the very short "Treatise on the three teachings" (*Sānjiào lùn*) by the first Ming Emperor (Míng Tàizǔ, reigned 1368–1398) was quite influential in setting the frame of reference to which I am referring.[6] Needless to say, he adopted a concept developed by others which had already had a considerable history. However his views on the nature and place of religion in the empire may be compared in their importance to those of Aśoka (c.268–239 BC) for India and of Constantine (280? -337) for Europe. In each case the pragmatic, political interest is evident, in spite of the "conversions" of Aśoka and of Constantine and in spite of Míng Tàizǔ's personal interest in "immortalism." At the same time the decisive patronage of a statesman who in each case ruled a huge and com-

6 The text of the *Sānjiào lùn* was consulted in an edition of the *Ming T'ai-tsu Yü-chih Wen-chi* (Wade-Giles as in catalogue) held in the Staatsbibliothek, Berlin. The English translation by Romeyn Taylor was an essential key, see: "An imperial endorsement of syncretism, Ming T'ai Tsu's essay on the three teachings, translation and commentary" (Taylor 1983). Also very helpful is his "Ming T'ai Tsu and the gods of walls and moats" (Taylor 1977).

plex empire had an impact for centuries on religious developments not only within those empires but also beyond. Aśoka's adoption of Buddhism led to a certain view of state-Buddhist relations, based on the *cakravartin* ideal, becoming well established in South and South-east Asia. Constantine's adoption of Christianity effected a link between imperium and gospel which had far-reaching implications for the understanding of orthodoxy, crusade and mission long after the fall of the Roman Empire. Míng Tàizǔ's sympathies for Daoism and apparently to a lesser degree, Buddhism, were set in the context of a then inevitable acceptance of the Confucian social and ethical perspective. But it was his politically motivated integration of the three teachings, allowing popular beliefs but excluding other organised religions, which reinforced this concept as a framework for reflection on religion in China and beyond.

The text of the *Sānjiào lùn* makes the nature of Míng Tàizǔ's interest quite clear. He realised that Buddhism and Daoism were both subject to misunderstanding and indeed to misuse for commercial ends. However he wanted them to be better understood because there might otherwise be those among them who would cause trouble for the state. Buddhism and Daoism were useful, he thought, in that they complemented the laws and institutions defined by Confucianism. As sinologist Romeyn Taylor has made clear in his article "Ming T'ai Tsu and the gods of the walls and moats,"[7] the emperor managed to build an integrated view in which state religion and popular religion, each necessary in their own way, were supported by the "three teachings" understood to represent "the way of heaven."

It is my contention that because of his interest in social organisation and the functions of religion in the state of his time, Míng Tàizǔ entered into a process of reflection about religions in their plurality. That religions exist in plurality is one of the characteristic features of Chinese religious history. This had been noticed at latest since the arrival of Buddhism in China, leading in particular to the questions about its relation to Daoism. However the earlier forms of reflection on this plurality had mainly been from a religious point of view. The position taken in the *Sānjiào lùn* does not seem to reflect strongly any particular religious allegiance. On the contrary, the religions are regarded dispassionately as systems to be evaluated. This means that by the time this short treatise came to be written (whether personally by the new emperor or by an assistant) "three teachings" does not so much mean "the three teachings

---

7 See note 5 above.

(which are one)" (although this is not denied) but rather "on religions (being several)." In other words the expression "three teachings" is a cypher for what in English today may be called "religions in their plurality."

The "three teachings" concept had a later development in the critical works of the Japanese writer Tominaga (Nakamoto) who wrote during the early eighteenth century. He argued against a synthesist view of the three teachings, and questioned the restriction of positive interpretation to three only. The interesting point to note however is that when he used the term "three teachings" as a chapter heading to indicate his subject matter, what he meant was something like "religions in their plurality and in their interrelationships." Thus we see the beginnings of a science of religion in his writings, framed by this long-established concept, but not determined by a religious point of view.[8]

More tentatively, the work of the Vietnamese monk An Thiền may also be referred to here. In the third volume of his substantial work *Dao giao nguyen luu*, first printed in 1845, he is reported to have used the concept of the three teachings both to point out their similarities, and also to differentiate between them.[9] Moreover this diversity arises because "the saints create doctrine depending on circumstances, forces, the times, and the state..."[10] This may be reminiscent of the adaptive processes summed up in the Buddhist concept of skilful means, but at the same time it is the ability to differentiate specific religions from each other, reflectively and analytically, which provides an important starting point for modern studies of religion. (See diagram on p. 258 below.)

In some non-Chinese descriptions of Chinese religion there is a tendency to emphasise the practical harmony which has existed between the various religions in their plurality in China. Of course there is good reason for this, for Chinese religious masters have often stressed this view of the matter of themselves.[11] Sometimes the point is over-

---

8 Tominaga's works are available in English translation by the present writer under the title *Emerging from Meditation* (London and Honolulu 1990a), and this specific point is discussed in my article "Tominaga Nakamoto (1715–1746) and religious pluralism" (Pye 1984, and 2.3 above).

9 Minh Chi/Ha Van Tan/Nguyen Tai Thu 1999 (*Buddhism in Vietnam*), 213–4. The rare Vietnamese accent marks are omitted here.

10 *Buddhism in Vietnam*, 214.

11 For an excellent study of such a religious standpoint see Judith Berling's *The Syncretic Religion of Lin Chao-en* (Berling 1980). Note however that her key figure is

emphasised, perhaps understandably when the situation is different from the countries from which these observers themselves have come. In other words, people from outside China rather like the harmonious idea that "the three teachings are one," and may emphasise it rather more than the actual position, certainly in modern China, really warrants. Note that "religions in their plurality" today do not include Confucianism or traditional state religious rites; at the same time they do include both Christianity and Islam, neither of which are easy to push into a general synthesis.

However the main point being made here is a little different. I do not seek to emphasis the practical harmony of "three teachings." Rather I am suggesting that recognition of religions in their plurality is a fundamental frame of reference in terms of which the study of religions can be carried out. This is different from, for example, a frame of reference which conceives of the study of "other" religions (i.e. "other" than the dominant one) or of the study of "popular" religion (rather than the official one). These latter frames of reference are common in Europe and in Latin America respectively. In spite of the necessity for further, modern theory, especially of a sociologically explanatory kind, it would seem that such a frame of reference for identifying the phenomena to be explained has much to commend it in the wider world. Admittedly the number three has no inherent significance in this connection. It is the thought, that religions are at least three in number, which counts. Could it be that such reflections have something to do with the mode in which studies of religion (or of "world religions" as these are named in the title of the relevant institute of the Academy of Social Sciences) are carried on in China? If not, how does the current frame of reference in fact differ? Is there now some other perspective in which it is considered possible and appropriate to study religions in their plurality?

Bibliographical References

Pye, Michael 1984. "Tominaga Nakamoto and Religious Pluralism" in: Daniels, Gordon (ed.) *Europe Interprets Japan* (select proceedings of the den Haag

---

probably better described as a synthesist. There is a separate discussion about the use of the term "syncretism," to which Berling contributes, but where different conclusions and hence different applications are possible. On this also see Part Six of the present work.

conference of the European Association for Japanese Studies 1982). Tenterden (Paul Norbury): 191–7.
– 1987b. "A common language of minimal religiosity" in: *The Journal of Oriental Studies* 26 (1): 21–7.
Pye, Michael (trans.) 1990a. *Emerging from Meditation (Tominaga Nakamoto).* London (Duckworth) and Honolulu (University of Hawaii Press).
Taylor, Romeyn 1977. "Ming T'ai Tsu and the gods of walls and moats" in: *Ming Studies* 3: 31–49.
– 1983. "An imperial endorsement of syncretism, Ming T'ai Tsu's essay on the three teachings, translation and commentary" in: *Ming Studies* 16: 31–49.
Minh Chi, Ha Van Tan and Nguyen Tai Thu 1999. *Buddhism in Vietnam*, Hanoi (Gioi Publishers). 1999, 213–4.
Berling, Judith A.1980. *The Syncretic Religion of Lin Chao-en*, New York (Columbia University Press).

This paper, here with slight revisions, was first published in Chinese translation as "Sanjiaolilun yu duizongjiaode xiandai fansi" in *Shijie Zongjiao Ziliao* (ISSN 1000–4505) (1992/4), 1–3; and in English as "Three teachings (*sanjiao*) theory and modern reflection on religion" in: Dai Kangsheng, Zhang Xinying and Pye, Michael (eds) *Religion and Modernisation in China, Proceedings of the Regional Conference of the International Association for the History of Religions held in Beijing, China, April 1992*, Cambridge (Roots and Branches) 1995, 111–116.

2.5 Modern Japan and the Science of Religions

This paper was first prepared for a conference on Modern Societies and the Science of Religion" which was held at Leiden University in 1997. It was first published some five years later in a volume including additional materials which were solicited afterwards.

Introduction

There is a widespread assumption that the academic study of religion(s) is a western cultural project which has in some cases been adopted elsewhere in a derivative fashion. While there is some truth in this, it is not the whole story. Japan is a significant counter-example. The academic study of religion(s) in Japan has an extremely significant history with a complex relationship to its own intellectual traditions and to modernity. It is therefore of interest to discuss the Japanese situation as an important example in the wider pattern of the relations between "modernity" and the "science of religion". What is needed, for this wider discussion, is a broad perspective in which some of the various strands in the Japanese tradition of *shūkyōgaku*, "study of religion(s)", can be located. The Japanese term *shūkyōgaku* does not distinguish between the singular and the plural. In English, the name for the discipline under consideration here occurs in several variations: science of religion, academic study of religion(s), study of religion(s). No particular importance is attached to these variations here.

The presentation given here will lead to a very specific conclusion, which is as follows. The modern study of religion(s) in Japan is influenced not only by reaction to western models but also by underlying ideas available in the Japanese intellectual tradition itself. However in the Japanese literature reflecting on the development of the study of religion, its relation to developments in the western world is usually emphasised to the neglect of its roots in the Japanese intellectual tradition. The distinctive East Asian setting is not always clearly noticed or set out by Japanese scholars who, in general, are more concerned to locate their work by reference to western scholarship. Indeed, it is sometimes said by Japanese scholars that there simply is no indigenous tradition of scholarship relating to religion, and that as far as they are concerned it is an entirely western import. However, the views of individual Japanese scholars who adopt such extreme positions cannot be taken as normative simply because they are Japanese. Account has to be taken of the roles and stances which they are adopting in a complex cultural situation. Such positions are usually struck in order to set up an opposition between "Japanese" and "western" which is not necessarily justified. The aim of this paper is to correct this perspective at least in the main outline.

At the same time there are of course very important, informative and reliable sources emanating from Japanese scholars, especially in relation to the more recent history of the subject. To give but one leading example, there is the "Fifty Years' History of the Japanese Association for the Study of Religions" (*Nihon Shūkyōgakkai Gojūnenshi*, 1980), which contains contributions by various participants in the field and an important introductory survey by Gotō Kōichirō and Tamaru Nori-yoshi. (All names will be given here in the Japanese order, family name first.)[1] The fifty years referred to here run from Shōwa 5 (1930) to Shōwa 55 (1980). The association was founded in 1930, its first president being Anesaki Masaharu, to whom further reference will be made below. At the same time however, as will be seen, the academic study of religions had been in a process of formation in Japan for quite some time before that.

To some extent the definition of the very term "religion", with particular reference to the Japanese context, is relevant to the analysis. Considerable care is needed over this however. It has already been argued under the title "What is 'religion' in East Asia?" that this is all more complex than is sometimes supposed,[2] and that the Japanese term *shūkyō* has a relevant, if limited pedigree prior to the strong intrusion of western influence from the middle of the nineteenth century. It is desirable, therefore, to avoid the widespread oversimplification that this term merely reflects a certain western notion of "religion", though such a

---

1 This order is now once again widely used in international situations, and it is of course absolutely normal in Japan itself. Some years ago there was a stronger tendency to put transcribed Japanese names into the western order. Readers not familiar with Japanese names should therefore be alert to the confusions which have been engendered.

2 In a paper for the 16th Congress of the International Association for the History of Religions (Pye 1994a) published in the proceedings (Bianchi 1994).

meaning has admittedly been widely current since the early part of the Meiji Period (from 1868). The term "religion" should by no means be written off as a misleading western import, and *shūkyō* is a reasonable equivalent.

Another fundamental problem is that there are competing views about what the study of religions should be understood to be. Who are the Japanese specialists in the study of religion? Who they are, specifically, depends as in other countries on the very definition of "science of religions" or "academic study of religions". The problem may be illustrated simply by referring to the influential department for the study of religion at Tokyo University, which has a tradition of textual studies and of empirical social research into religions, and comparing with it the very "philosophically" oriented "Kyōto School" which looks back to Nishida Kitarō and continues to display a strong affinity with Zen Buddhist thought.[3] It is debatable whether this latter tradition of religious philosophy can really be counted as "science of religions", for its intentions are different, though some of its representatives such as Ueda Shizuteru have carried out studies comparing western mysticism with Zen.[4] This diversity of approach is reflected quite strongly in the relatively large membership of the Japanese Association for the Study of Religions, many of whose more than one thousand members undoubtedly have a religious motivation and a religious focus in their studies of religion. The specialisms and affiliations of these members were assessed on a statistical basis by the present writer many years ago.[5] It would be possible to test some of the leading points of that analysis statistically against more recent documentation, but overall impressions of the current situation do not lead one to anticipate any major shifts in the balance. In the present paper attention is restricted specifically to the development of the religiously neutral study of religions with its historical, textual, comparative, and social-scientific ramifications. This differentiation is not at all unique to Japan, and it is not particularly difficult to identify

3 A convenient overview is to be found in Heinrich Dumoulin's *Zen im 20. Jahrhundert* (1993), pp.31–82.

4 See especially his very well received work *Die Gottesgeburt in der Seele und der Durchbruch zur Gottheit. Die mystische Anthropologie Meister Eckharts und ihre Konfrontation mit der Mystik des Zen-Buddhismus* (Gütersloh 1965).

5 This was an analytical survey for a special issue of the journal *Religion* published on the occasion of the 13th Congress of the International Association for the History of Religions (Pye 1975).

the orientation of individual scholars or research programmes in the Japanese case.

The institutional frameworks are also important. Among the relatively large number of persons engaged in academic contexts today with the study of religion, it is clear that a high proportion of them have some kind of personal orientation within one of the available religions and that this colours their studies to a recognisable extent. At the same time, in the case of Japan we do not have a situation in which this religious background is itself largely dominated by one specific religion, as in North America, where there is a constant danger that "science of religions" will be swamped by "theology" under the flag of "religious studies". From a methodological point of view the same problems arise in various quarters in Japan, but the multiplicity of different religious traditions which run their own universities, often housing pertinent departments for research and teaching, means that overall a slightly more relaxed attitude can be taken over this recalcitrant problem. As the years go by, it is becoming increasingly clear that "the study of religion" is an enterprise in its own right in Japan.

The number of Japanese researchers occupied in some sense with the field of "religion" today is very large, and many are internationally active and known. It is quite impossible to attempt here a comprehensive survey of the relevant academic institutions and personalities, though some illustrative details will be found below. Rather, attention will be drawn in outline to the main steps with which this academic study of religions, or "science of religions", has come to develop in modern Japan. By this means, the idea that it is no more than a recent western import can be corrected. This is probably the most important point which needs to be emphasised in the present cultural situation.[6]

Wider considerations

An understanding of the development of the science of religion in Japan cannot be locked entirely into the Japanese context itself. There are

6 This paper was first drafted for a conference in Leiden on modernity and the study of religions which was held in 1997. In the meantime it has become even more urgent to correct widespread misconceptions, but no attempt is made here to restate the issue yet again in opposition to intervening publications.

wider considerations about the way in which the history of the discipline is written, and these affect the way in which the development in any one country is understood. It is indeed becoming increasingly widely recognised that the history of the "science of religions", referred to in much English discourse as "the academic study of religion(s)", is more complex than has sometimes been realised. Attention will be drawn here to three aspects of this complexity, and implications drawn out for the Japanese case.

First, at the most general level, the various intellectual threads which have been woven into the coherent strand which we now designate as "science of religions", or similar, are perceived to be more diverse and more subtly related to each other than some presentations have suggested. In the European context, for example, it is no longer adequate to see the science of religion as predominantly the product of nineteenth-century comparativism or evolutionism, as in Eric Sharpe's influential account in *Comparative Religion, A History* (Sharpe 1975). The Enlightenment, though its importance is nowadays often underestimated and indeed misconceived, should also be given full weight. So too, however, must the impact of Romanticism, falling approximately between these two. The emergence of the modern academic study of religions is inconceivable without reference to these significant intellectual movements, even though at the time the thinkers concerned with religion did not themselves specify that they were developing a "science of religions". By analogy, there arises the question as to where relevant ideas in Japan can be identified, prior to the formal establishment of the discipline. This means that the intellectual traditions of the Tokugawa Period, *prior* to the frenetic interaction with western thought which has taken place since the mid-nineteenth century, must be considered from this point of view.

The matter can be taken even further back, for these particularly relevant intellectual movements are themselves partly to be explained by significant shifts in standpoint made possible by, in Europe, the Renaissance, the Reformation and the subsequent recognition of confessional pluralism. Somewhat similarly, in East Asia, we find on the one hand an increasingly clear focus on the natural and social world and human ability to analyse it in Neo-Confucianism, and on the other hand the unfolding and consolidation of various Buddhist denominations whose diversity only served to illustrate, to impartial outsiders, the relativity rather than the absolute significance of their claims.[7]

Second, the social and political context must be taken more fully into account. The explorer, colonialist, imperialist and missionary periods were, in general, of immense importance for the development, in the western world, of the study of religions. The researches, translations, and writings of diplomats and missionaries often amounted to informal contributions to the study of religions in various parts of the world, and thereby to the development of that study as a science.

A classic, if relatively late example is the story of what for Europeans was the discovery of Tibetan religion, which is framed in the story of the prising open of Tibet as a land. Journalist Edmund Candler tellingly entitled his account of the Younghusband expedition of 1904 *The Unveiling of Lhasa* (Candler 1905) (though this was not the first European contact). In other words, for the British public "discovery" was still in the air, even while Candler asserted that "we" (i. e. the British) "were drawn into the vortex of war by the folly and obstinacy of the Tibetans."[8] Perceval Landon's more substantial account of the same events, also published in 1905, contains much interesting detail about aspects of religion. Admittedly, Younghusband's own later discussions about reincarnation and related matters with Tibetan lamas, in *India and Tibet* (Younghusband1910), though somewhat detailed, do not really amount to "science of religions." Nevertheless he had with him in the "expedition" Colonel L. A. Waddell, whose extremely detailed work *The Buddhism of Tibet or Lamaism* had already appeared in 1894).[9] This too had been written, outside the closed country of Tibet itself, but in Darjeeling under the protection of the British Empire, which he served in the Indian Medical Service. Waddell not only observed the practices of the Tibetan Buddhist temple on the spot in Darjeeling (or Dorje Ling, "the place of the thunderbolt") but also spoke with numerous Tibetan merchants and lamas, employed his own Tibetan assistants and even acquired and installed in his own residence the complete fittings of a Tibetan temple. It is easy today to scorn "colonialist" views of the reli-

7 An attempt to identify the prerequisites for the emergence of the reflective study of religions more systematically, for comparative purposes, will be found in the introduction to my translations of the writings of Tominaga Nakamoto (Pye 1990a).

8 Candler 1905, p.2.

9 In the second edition (1939), Waddell himself refers to his work having been first published in 1895.

gions of the colonised, and yet the detailed studies undertaken by Waddell with exemplary persistence remain even now a most important secondary source for the period. In fact Darjeeling was also a training post for British spies, of whom the Tibetans were, not surprisingly extremely suspicious. This is well documented in the most readable account of Tibetan life including many aspects of Tibetan religion by the Japanese monk Kawaguchi Ekai in his work *Three Years in Tibet*, published in English in 1909, but based on his diaries from the years 1900 to 1903, during which he managed to enter the country, from India, under the guise of being a Chinese monk. Interestingly, it was the Theosophist Annie Besant who persuaded Kawaguchi to publish his work in English (it had previously appeared in instalments in the Japanese press), even though he himself thought that it might be outdated by the British accounts from the time of the "expedition" and the expected publication of a work by Sven Hedin. While Japan was not politically involved in the Anglo-Russian tug-of-war in Tibet, the contrast between Kawaguchi's mentality and that of the Tibetans which he presents displays some features of the sense of superiority characteristic of colonialist powers. At the same time he also demonstrates not only fervent Buddhist devotion and single-mindedness in the wish to collect more versions of Buddhist scriptures, but also the humility of the persistent observer who undergoes personal hardships and dangers to be right there, in the field. In effect, the Buddhist monk Kawaguchi discovered "Tibetan religion" for a readership in Japan and beyond.

A similar relationship between explorer, colonialist, imperialist and missionary can be documented for most of the world, certainly all over Africa and Asia. The perception is therefore becoming increasing widespread that it is now possible, and indeed necessary, to give "post-colonialist" accounts of the study of religions.[10] Related to this need for retelling the history of the subject from new vantage points are the well-known contextual discussion of "orientalism," the now popular recognition of "exoticism" as a long-running literary theme ,[11] and the corresponding self-reflection on the part of social anthropologists treated by Karl-Heinz Kohl in *Exotik als Beruf* (1979) and *Entzauberter Blick* (1981). A balanced view is required concerning all this. As far as the observation and discussion of religion is concerned, or in

10 An interesting recent example is David Chidester's study relating to South Africa (Chidester 1997).

11 For an interesting introductory overview see Mathé 1972.

other words the incipient development of the science of religions, the following state of affairs should be noted. There simply has not been a time when foreigners were writing about Japanese religions, while Japanese writers themselves were not! In this, Japan appears to differ significantly from Tibet.

Less obvious, and yet particularly important in the case of Japan, is the obverse of the coin. While Japan was being "discovered," Japanese for their own part were discovering the western world, having already been aware of most of Asia for a long time.[12] Thus it is possible to see in Japanese culture a tradition of "Occidentalism." This may be considered to have got fully into swing in the eighteenth century with the rather secretive studies of the *rangakusha* (specialists in Dutch studies). Significantly however, although the *rangakusha* have been much studied, Japanese occidentalism as a cultural phenomenon has rarely become a subject of reflection. Rather, European orientalism itself has been seized on as interesting by the heirs of those who in their day were the objects of the European fascination. Thus it became the subject of a substantial study published in 1987 by Iyanaga Nobumi of which the Japanese title might be translated as "The East as Reverie" and the subtitle as "The Lineage of Orientalism." Here orientalism becomes an aspect of Japanese occidentalism.

Third, the attention given to colonialism should not be allowed to distract us from the problems of neo-colonialism. The above mentioned styles of reflection were themselves dependent on colonialist and imperialist privilege, which is now largely regarded as having dissipated itself. But what has taken their place? The effects of neo-colonialism on the study of religions has as yet been largely ignored. It could be argued that this is relevant to Japan in the form of its own economic dominance, which creates a context for the promotion of research. Also practically unrecognised, and even less well understood except by a very small minority, is the impact on intellectual life and hence on the academic study of religions of the "Cold War," which covered several recent decades. This led to a maladjusted view both of religion and of the supposed absence of religion, on both sides of the Cold War. Correspondingly there has been a maladjustment in the study of religion, which was itself widely assumed to be either ideologically positive or

12 It was probably Donald Keene who first used the phrase "the Japanese discovery of Europe" (Keene 1952, 1969).

ideologically negative.[13] It would be possible to reflect on this maladjustment in the Japanese context as elsewhere, but the research has not yet been done. Overlapping with the Cold War period, and continuing today, is what might be called the "oil age." This too has had a certain impact on the way in which at least one of the major religions of the world, namely Islam, is viewed. These features of international life have provided the context for most of the half century since the end of the Pacific War, so that it would be theoretically desirable to study the recent history of the subject in Japan against this background. The main point to be noted here is that during this period, as enshrined in the post-war constitution, there has been a strong emphasis both on religious freedom and also on the separation of religion and the state. While the latter is intended to avoid a totalitarian concentration of ideological forces at the centre of society, the encouragement of religious freedom, not only for the individual but also for religious associations by means of freedom from tax liability, has without doubt been intended to provide a pluralist bulwark against the possible influence of communism. Studies of religion in Japan have acquired some aspects of their character in this context.

Fourth, the social basis for the study of religion is increasingly perceived to be, nowadays, not merely global but, within this global perspective, intercultural. It is arguable that the intercultural *diversity* of reflection concerning religion is more significant than the integral global perspective which currently seems to be so influential. Even within the western world, which is often regarded from outside, e. g. from Japan, as being more or less an intellectual unity, there have been major variations in the way in which the study of religion has been developed in different countries. These variations have been related to the changing cultural and political fortunes of religion in the various countries, though insufficient attention has been paid to them in discussions of the history of the subject. When the development of the study of religion is regarded globally, such variations become even more apparent. Hence a global

13 Four years after this paper was first written (1997) an IAHR conference was held on the subject in Brno, Czech Republic (August 1999) (see Doležalová, Martin and Papoušek 2001). The present writer's contribution there, under the title "Political correctness in the study of religions: Is the Cold War really over?" (Pye 2001a) attempts to cross the frontiers of the Cold War, rather than discussing it from within one side or the other. For earlier intimations of this important subject see also Pye 1991b.

view of the development of the study of religion must take this diversity into account.

This is of interest, and indeed of great importance, in that the underlying perceptions of "religion", which inform the development of theoretical models in diverse situations, are not the same in various regions of the world. The overall religious "situation" in Africa, in India, in Latin America, and elsewhere, is diverse. On the situation in Africa and its implications for the study of religions, to take but one of these continents as an example, see especially works by Westerlund (1985) and Platvoet, Olupona and Cox (1996)[14]. It can be seen from such accounts that major themes carry a special weight in various parts of the world and influence the academic study of religions accordingly. In East Asia, for example, the twin ideas of the reality of religious pluralism and the responsibility of the state for maintaining order in religious affairs are quite widely current. No specialist in the study of religion in China, Korea or Japan can avoid them. This complexity in the range of available models for the study of religion is itself interesting, and valuable for the future development of the discipline.

We can see from these examples and observations that it is most important to maintain a flexible attitude over the question as to *which* intellectual and socio-political strands deserve to be considered in reflecting on the development of the discipline. This applies in the Japanese case no less than elsewhere. In particular it is misleading to take a one-sided view about the significance of the western impact in the nineteenth century, as will be shown in more detail below.

Modernity in Japan

Since the term "modernity," as implied in the phrase "modern society," has itself become increasingly difficult to use, some attention has to be paid to the problem of the periodization of Japanese history in this regard. The periodisation of Japanese history after the so-called Middle

14 The latter includes my own introduction to the conference held in Zimbabwe in 1992 (the first IAHR conference ever held in Africa) entitled "Intercultural strategies and the International Association for the History of Religions" (Pye 1996a) This work was not published until 1996, and it should be noted that the introduction by Jan Platvoet and Jacob Olupona was written from a perspective some time later than the conference itself.

Ages (*chûsei*) is usually presented as: (1) *kinsei* (early modern) (2) *kindai* (modern) and (3) *gendai* (present). "Early modern" refers to the the Tokugawa Period (1600–1867). "Modern" refers to the Meiji Period (1868–1912), the Taishō Period (1912–1926), the Shōwa Period (1926–1988) and the Heisei Period (1989-). What the "present" refers to depends on the history book and when it was written. One outline, for example, starts the present with the Potsdam Declaration of 1945 (which fell in the Shōwa Period). In general it may be observed that the beginning of the "present" shifts forwards as time passes. Thus nowadays it is often regarded as starting with the beginning of the present Emperor's reign, i.e. the Heisei Period.

What is the relation here between *kinsei*, *kindai* and *gendai?* All of these terms suggest modernity in some sense. But what is "modernity"? From when does "modernity" occur, and does it occur at different speeds in different fields? Is contemporary Japanese culture "modern", or "post-modern," or perhaps still in some respects "pre-modern"? The analysis of religious culture is important in this connection, but it is only part of a wider historical question. A perception of the location of Japanese scholarship on religion can only occur within an informed view of these matters.

The view taken here is that "modernity" in Japan did not begin only with the "opening" of Japan to the direct and sustained influence of the western world in the later part of the nineteenth century. On the contrary, modernity began in important respects during the "closed" Tokugawa Period. This period is therefore quite appropriately referred to as "early modern", the phrase usually adopted to correspond to the Japanese *kinsei.* During this time there were important intellectual movements which, in a very broad sense, correspond to those which were so important in the development of "modernity" in Europe. There was a new interest in the systematic exploration of the empirical world (cf. the European natural sciences), there was a critical analysis of economics, politics and history (cf. the European Enlightenment), and there was a re-examination of cultural origins from a sophisticated standpoint which implied distance from those same origins (cf. the European Romantic movement). In the "real" world of commerce and industry, rampant mercantilism led to features of capitalism such as the ability to trade in futures, while technological advances hinting at the industrial revolution to come were also made. Without any reference to western thought on the subject, Japanese reflection on the subject of religion also took new turns during this period which could comfortably be described as modern or at least as early modern.

As far as Japanese history is concerned, the external pressure of imperialist western powers during the nineteenth century certainly led to a quickening of the pace of development. The political revolution of 1868, usually known as the Meiji Restoration, set the scene for an overt interaction with western society and culture in all fields, with a view to adopting that which might be profitable in Japan's own interests. This was indeed not a mere "restoration" (of imperial power over against that of the shōguns) but rather a dramatic revolution which catapulted Japan visibly into the league of modern states. Within a very short time, as is well known, Japan was competing with the imperialist powers which had threatened it and forced it "open". The speed with which new ideas were adopted, but also adapted, was only possible however because of the preceding history. There was a class of successful merchants on the one hand and well-informed ex-samurai on the other hand who together provided the intellectual and managerial base for rapid change. New, intellectually, was the sense of a need to measure ideas against the ideas of the western world. There are many examples of Japanese thinkers who were able to do this, and thought it necessary, in their various fields. As a result of their very success, the value of the heritage which enabled them to do it has often been obscured. Hence the story is sometimes distorted.

Three phases in the development of Japanese "science of religions"

Returning specifically to the "science of religions," it was mentioned near the beginning that the Japanese Association for the Study of Religions was founded in 1930. In comparative terms this is quite a long time ago. The first International Congress for the History of Religions had been held in Paris in 1900, while the International Association for the History of Religions (IAHR), related to the series of congresses inaugurated in Paris, was not itself founded as an organisation until 1950. It was not long until, in 1958, an international congress in this series was hosted in Japan.[15] Anesaki Masaharu, the founding president of the Jap-

---

15 For details of the series of congresses and the relevant proceedings, including

anese association, had himself been appointed to the first professorship in this field, at Tokyo Imperial University, now Tokyo University, twenty-five years earlier, in Meiji 38 (1905). But this was itself by no means an absolute beginning. Such institutional decisions of course have a prehistory. From a historical point of view therefore we also have to ask what took place before then which made these particular developments possible. That takes us back earlier in the Meiji Period. The second half of the nineteenth century saw the rapid modernisation of Japan under the "hands-on" leadership of the Emperor Meiji and his governments. This involved energetic intellectual interaction with the western world, which included thinking about various aspects of religion, partly for cultural and partly for political reasons. But, as we have already seen, the dramatic events which had led to the "Restoration" of Imperial power in 1868 were themselves more than an opportunistic reaction to the pressure of the western imperial powers. They too had their domestic background in the Tokugawa Period. The major changes relating to what is commonly called "modernisation", already referred to above, were also accompanied, admittedly in the minds of only a few, by changes in the way in which religions was reflected on and indeed studied. We can therefore speak, altogether, of three broadly definable phases in the development of the "science of religions" in Japan, and these will now be briefly reviewed.

The three phases are therefore (i) antecedents in the Tokugawa Period, (ii) the period of intensive interaction with the western world during the second half of the nineteenth century and continuing into the twentieth century, and (iii) the period of the formal establishment and consolidation of the discipline during the twentieth century. These phases of thought about religion in Japan are in a very broad sense parallel to but, it should be noted, not dependent on contemporary western developments.

As to the *first phase*, I have sought to show in several previous publications that there are antecedents in the intellectual history of Japan during the Tokugawa Period (or Edo Period) which are very relevant to an understanding of the development of the "science of religions."[16] It was during the early eighteenth century that, for the first time in Japanese intellectual life, reflection about religion became significantly in-

---

the one held in Tokyo and in Kyōto in 1958, see my compilation in the archive section of the IAHR website [since updated by others].

16 See for example Pye 1973a, 1983, 1992a and 1994a.

dependent of religious thought itself, at least among a few. In particular the writings on religion by Tominaga Nakamoto (1715–1746), and their later reception, may be regarded as a kind of Japanese "Enlightenment" (in the sense of *Aufklärung*).[17] The basic materials for becoming acquainted with Tominaga's approach may be found in the book of translations by the present writer entitled *Emerging from Meditation* (1990). The main characteristics of his writings on religions are as follows. First, he perceived them to be plural in number and regarded this plurality as interesting, referring to Confucianism, Buddhism, Daoism and Shintō. Second, his approach was based on principles of textual and historical criticism, polemically pursued. Third, he mounted a historical critique of Buddhist origins, in which he argued among other things that the sutras of Mahāyāna Buddhism did not stem from the Buddha himself. Note that this critical thrust did *not* occur in dependence on nineteenth century western scholarship, as has often been supposed. The point was already made within the Japanese intellectual tradition. Fourth, he provided an analysis of diversity and innovation within the overall stream of Buddhism and explained this with a psychological motivation.

Tominaga was not alone, however, in pre-Meiji times. Also relevant are the beginnings of folklore studies in the context of "national learning" (*kokugaku*) and Shintō studies. This phase can be regarded as being akin, though not closely similar, to the Romantic period in Europe. A dominant figure here was Motoori Norinaga who, unlike Tominaga, worked in favour of the "national learning" and thus as an apologist for the Shintō religion. At the same time his approach was philological and displayed a consciousness of his own distance from the archaic past of Japan. He also quoted Tominaga approvingly, though only in connection with his historical critique of Buddhism.

It is of great importance to recognise the existence of this first phase, which is often completely ignored. During the subsequent Meiji Period it was commonplace to regard everything which had gone before as backward and negative, and above all not modern and progressive. In all fields, models were sought in the western world. The reverberations of this misleading view of Japan's own history have continued down to recent times

17 For a comparison with the European Enlightenment based in particular on the writings of Lessing and Tominaga Nakamoto see Pye 1973a, but note that it was written before I was able to prepare detailed translations of the latter's writings.

(see further below), and as a result, the Tokugawa Period has been underestimated, and is often completely ignored in Japanese presentations of the development of reflection about and the study of religion.

The *second main phase* is the period of direct interaction with western studies of religion. This phase began during the nineteenth century, especially in the latter part of it, i. e. from the beginning of the Meiji Period. However interaction with western thought on religion was complicated by the pressure of western powers to allow Christian missionary work to take place (after Christianity had been banned for over two hundred years), thereby leading to complicated questions about freedom of "religion" and the political status of religion.

This phase, being so important for the development of Japan in many respects, is sometimes erroneously regarded as the absolute beginning of Japanese scholarship on religion. This is suggested in the statesmanlike but misleading account provided by J. M. Kitagawa in his forword to Hori Ichiro's book *Folk Religion in Japan. Continuity and Change* (1968).[18] Kitagawa writes that

> …scholarly enquiry into Japanese religion and culture was pioneered in the latter part of the nineteenth century by a number of talented Western scholars. Some of them – for example Basil Hall Chamberlain, Karl Florenz, and Ernest Fenollosa – were academicians by profession, while others were what George B. Sansom called 'scholarly amateurs' – for example William G. Aston, Ernest M. Satow, Charles Eliot, John Batchelor, and Sansom himself.[19]

These writers contributed immensely, in their various ways, to western knowledge about Japanese culture including religion. However, by the nature of the case, they did not add very much knowledge to that already available to Japanese people themselves.[20]

In a rather general sense the writings of various influential people may be regarded as belonging to this second phase. A typical example

---

18 Hori's book consists of "Haskell Lectures" given at Chicago, where Kitagawa was professor of history of religions as a colleague of Mircea Eliade and Joachim Wach.

19 Hori 1968, vi–vii.

20 Nor were they specialists in the study of religions, and while a writer like Charles Eliot was very sympathetic to the various forms of Japanese Buddhism (Eliot 1935), it must be said that Aston's judgements on Shintō (Aston 1905) were really quite wide of the mark and did not assist in getting this religion correctly understood in the wider context of the study of religions. For a survey of the chequered story of western studies of Shintō, see Pye 1982b.

of the approach taken at the time is that of Inoue Enryō (1858–1919), who was born into the family of a temple priest belonging to the Jōdo Shinshū tradition of Buddhism (Higashi Honganji). He learned English, studied philosophy at the (then) Tokyo Imperial University, and was widely active as a publisher and a writer. Reacting against the pressure to pay attention to western thought, he emphasised a return to the philosophical roots of Buddhism and in 1887 he founded an institute for the study of philosophy, the Tetsugakkan, to promote his programme. This institute was later transformed into the modern Tōyō University located in Tokyo. Inspired by Inoue Enryō, Tōyō University symbolises its position in the intellectual universe by displaying plaques of four thinkers: the Buddha, Confucius, Socrates, and Kant. This choice displays the attempt to achieve a balance between east and west typical of the time. Inoue was particularly concerned to debate the nature of Buddhism in the modern world, but he did this with reference to wider issues in philosophy, education and religion, with titles such as (translated) "The Practical Study of Religion" (1890) and "The Ethical Study of Religion" (1891).

In a more specialised direction a number of Japanese Buddhist scholars took up, in a sustained way, the challenge of historico-critical research which, particularly with respect to Indian and Buddhist studies, was being developed strongly in the western world. A well known example is Nanjō Bunyû (1849–1927) (usually writing his name in western contexts as Nanjio Bunyiu), who benefited greatly from studying in association with Max Müller, with whom he published Sanskrit editions of two of the three most important sutras in Pure Land Buddhism. He became best known for his catalogue of the Chinese Buddhist Canon which appeared (in English) as early as 1883.[21] Also associated with Max Müller was Takakusu Junjirō, who translated the "Meditation on Buddha Amitayus" for Vol. XIV of the series *Sacred Books of the East*,

21 It should be noted that this has now been completely superseded by the catalogue published by the French-funded Hōbōgirin Institute in Kyōto (Demiéville, Durt and Seidel 1978). One of the difficulties with Nanjō's catalogue is that, no doubt following the stimulus of European scholars, he provided numerous Sanskrit "restitutions" of titles for which there is no evidence in known Sanskrit literature. Looking at this positively, in terms of his own times, it demonstrated a renewed interest in the Indian origins of Buddhism, which has been maintained unabated down to the present day, combined with an awareness of the importance of philological studies for elucidating this background.

published in 1894, and went on to be one of the chief editors of the *Taishō Shinshū Daizōkyō (The Tripitaka in Chinese)*, published in one hundred volumes from 1924 to 1935 in Tokyo. Murakami Senshō (1851–1929) came from a Jōdo Shinshū family, like Nanjō Bunyū, and took up modern Buddhist studies in a clearly critical intellectual manner. At one stage his priestly qualification was withdrawn by the head temple of the denomination, the Higashi Honganji, because of his published assertion that the Mahāyāna sutras did not stem from the Buddha but were later compositions.[22] Maeda Eun (1857–1930) took the same line over this issue and his priestly qualification was withdrawn in 1904 by the head temple of the other main Shinshū denomination, the Nishi Honganji. It was restored in 1905. These were prominent cases. Maeda had been appointed head of the (then) Takanawa Buddhist University (now Ryūkoku University), and in 1906 was appointed to be president of the Tōyō University founded in the spirit of Inoue Enryō mentioned above. Another well-known scholar in this field was Inoue Tetsujirō of the (then) Tokyo Imperial University who applied the methods of historical criticism to the study of the life of the Buddha. These studies all led to a certain amount of stress in the Buddhist world, especially as it became clear to all who studied the question that the sutras lying at the basis of most Japanese Buddhism did not emanate from the Buddha himself, even though prefaced with the words "Thus I have heard" which traditionally implied that they did. It is striking that this recognition only became widespread among Buddhist scholars after the exposure of a number of them to western scholarship. It is very significant however that the same point had already been argued long before with great irony, and indeed effectively proven, by Tominaga Nakamoto. This was long before any contact with western scholars over such questions.

The steady importation of critical criteria into research into Buddhism meant that a certain closeness could be achieved between Buddhist-oriented scholarship and the more general study of religion. This closeness has been developed in academic quarters down to the present. It is symbolic that in the present-day Tokyo University the Department of Indian and Buddhist Studies is next door to the Department

22 His main academic activities were in Tokyo, including being professor of Indian philosophy there from 1917. In 1924 he was reconciled with the Higashi Honganji and in 1926 became president of the associated Ōtani University (Kashiwara and Sonoda 1994).

of Religion. At the same time this closeness was not unequivocal in the sense of leading to a restriction of research publications to historical and philological studies or to the "science of religion" approach. Inoue Tetsujirō, for example, sought to combine the spirit of historical criticism with a modernising revitalization of Buddhism, attacking Christianity in the process. This position was adopted in a widely read article entitled "The conflict between religion and education" (1893), which Inoue wrote as a response to the Christian Uchimura Kanzō's refusal to bow before the Imperial Rescript on Education during a ceremony.[23] Although for Uchimura himself this was not the issue, the main Buddhist criticism of Christianity was, then, that it was internationalist rather than sufficiently patriotic. The wide spectrum of interests covering textual studies, the history of Indian religious thought, and studies in Japanese Buddhism continues to be reflected in the pages of the standard journal *Indogaku Bukkyōgaku* (Indian and Buddhist Studies) published from the base in Tokyo University.

A similar, partial rapprochement with "science of religion" on the part of Shintō-oriented scholars began much more hesitantly. Of considerable interest is the work by Katō Genchi entitled *A Study of Shintō. The Religion of the Japanese Nation* (1926). Katō sought to interpret Shintō in the context of a number of themes current in western comparative religion, such as animism, polytheism versus monotheism, and mythology, while at the same time concluding that it had a unique quality and a special role to play in the protection of the Japanese nation. The dominance of nationalist ideology, which mobilised Shintō heavily for political purposes, inhibited this discussion. Only later, after the end of the Pacific War, was the process of intellectual rapprochement gradually brought to maturity, as for example in the writings of specialists such as Sonoda Minoru.[24] This was made possible partly by the disestablishment of Shintō from a position of state privilege and partly as a result of

23 On this conflict, see Kishimoto 1956, 254–257.

24 A representative, if rather recent work is his *Matsuri no Genshōgaku* (i. e. "Phenomenology of Festivals") published in 1990. Sonoda is well known as a sociologist of religion who at the same time takes the "phenomenology of religion" seriously. Religiously, he succeeded to the position of chief priest at Chichibu Shrine, known in particular for its lantern-hung "night festival" (*yomatsuri*), while academically he has taught at the Shintō-oriented Kokugakuin University in Tokyo and in the graduate school of the state and hence secular Kyōto University.

the development of an independent study of religions, which had in the meantime begun to establish itself.

The *third* phase in the development of the science of religion was set in motion when, towards the end of the Meiji Period, the study of religion was formally set up as a university discipline and consequently became established on a non-confessional basis. At earliest, this development can be said to begin with lectures on "comparative religion" (*hikaku shūkyō*) given in 1890 (Meiji 23) by the aforementioned Inoue Tetsujirō at Tokyo Imperial University. In 1896 (Meiji 29) Kishimoto Nobuto and Anesaki Masaharu founded a "study association for comparative religion" (*hikaku shūkyō gakkai*). However the subject was only really firmly established in 1905 with the installation of Anesaki Masaharu with a professorship in the discipline of "study of religion" (*shūkyōgaku*) at Tokyo Imperial University (now Tokyo University).[25] This phase has a prewar and a postwar aspect in a more or less continuous development running up to the present day and including such well known names as Kishimoto Hideo, Tamaru Noriyoshi, Wakimoto Tsuneya, Yanagawa Keiichi and their successors in post.

Anesaki himself became well known among western readers for his work *History of Japanese Religion, With Special Reference to the Social and Moral Life of the Nation.* While this work was first published only in 1930, it was originally drafted for lectures given at Harvard University during 1913–1915. The preface makes interesting reading. We find here a typical sense of the presumed tension between western science and eastern spirituality.

> In putting this book before the Occidental public, the author, an Oriental, wishes to acknowledge his indebtedness to the modern science of the Occident. For it is modern science that has trained his mind in its methods and scope, and opened his eyes to many aspects of the present subject which otherwise would have remained unnoticed. At the same time gratitude is due to the sages and saints of the Orient whose souls and spirits have inspired and moulded the author's spiritual life, however meagre and unworthy it be.

Anesaki's work is also interesting because of his emphasis on the values of Prince Shōtoku (574–622), of whom a very positive appraisal was quite clear in the work just mentioned. It is interesting to see however

25 These details are drawn from Tamaru's *Shūkyōgaku no rekishi to kadai* (1987), a work which itself is mainly concerned with introducing and discussing the western history of the discipline for Japanese readers.

that at a time when internationalism was unpopular and an extremely nationalist form of Shintō was in the ascendancy, he emphasised strongly the universalism of Shōtoku's civilisational and religious values, which were derived from Confucianism and Buddhism.[26] Another Buddhist figure about whom Anesaki wrote with some sympathy was the controversial Nichiren (1222–1282). As a title for this work in the English language he chose *Nichiren, The Buddhist Prophet*, thus drawing on a concept from the western history of religions to characterise a Japanese Buddhist.

Currently the academic study of religion by Japanese scholars, which has some interesting specific characteristics, makes a lively contribution to public discourse, especially with reference to the new religions which are so numerous and influential in the country. There is an interesting spectrum to be considered here, as the question of the relative "religiousness" or "non-religiousness" of the population continues to be a fascinating theme in Japan itself. Leading contemporary specialists in the study of religion naturally highlight their particular interests. With apologies to them all, it is unfortunately not possible to develop a contemporary bibliography within the scope of this article. The following well-known names with their main specialities will illustrate the spectrum as it relates to the study of religions within Japan: Abe Yashiya (religion and political and legal questions; Araki Michio (new religions in Japan); Miyake Hitoshi (religious folklore and mountain religions); Shimazono Susumu (sociology of urban religion, and new religions); and the previously mentioned Sonoda Minoru (Shintō studies and phenomenology of festivals). Further impressions may be gathered from the Japanese language journal *Shūkyō Kenkyū*, published by the Japanese Association for the Study of Religions, or in English language journals such as *Japanese Journal of Religious Studies* or *Japanese Religions*, which are edited by foreigners but often carry articles by Japanese colleagues. Yet these sources can only go a small way in reflecting the huge quantity of writing by large numbers of specialists, engaged as they are in various aspects of Buddhist studies and in the study of various religions of the world, including Christianity and Islam. The main religious bearings in the background consciousness of specialists in religion are provided by Buddhism and Shintō. A number of Buddhist and Shintō-oriented univer-

26 See for example his article "The foundation of Buddhist culture in Japan. The Buddhist ideals as conceived and carried out by the Prince-Regent Shôtoku" (1943).

sities provide a base for scholars whose work is partly carried out in the service of the religion in question and partly pertains to the more general academic study of religions. But minority religions also play a role. For example, there is a tradition of the scholarly study of religion (and a superb, well-balanced and historically interesting library on the subject) at Tenri University, sponsored by the religion known as Tenrikyō ("Teaching of Heavenly Truth"). The well-established *Tenri Journal of Religion* contains articles directly presenting Tenri traditions and theology and also articles which deal with various problems in the general study of religions.

It has not been possible to present here a full historical picture of any of these three phases. The necessary documentation would go far beyond the scope of this paper, and indeed the research time is not available to produce it in a manner which would be both detailed and balanced. Much more would need to be said about Japanese studies of religions outside the East Asian context which has been foregrounded above. Such studies, e.g. of Middle Eastern religions from ancient times up to and including Islam, or of Latin American religions, were not taken up until after the interaction with the western world began to have its effect. The main thrust of this paper, however, is to point out the deep roots of Japanese studies of religions, which naturally, were directed in the first instance towards China, India and Japan itself. Among the reference points indicated above, some are well known and others less well known. The purpose of this brief account has been to locate such reference points in the context of more general questions about the periodization of intellectual history and "modernity" which can so easily be distorted and misconstrued.

The Japanese component in the science of religions

In this concluding section, the question of how to view the development of the "science of religion" in Japan will be linked up with the key questions in the wider view of its history and problematics mentioned above under "wider considerations."

It will be recalled that, first, the question was raised as to which intellectual threads should be considered to form a part of the modern history of the study of religions in the first place. In the case of Japan the story of the study of religions should certainly be widened to include those antecedents which were present in Japanese intellectual life itself.

This applies in particular to the stunning contribution of Tominaga Nakamoto in the first half of the seventeenth century. Such contributions are important in understanding the history of ideas, even if later persons have to learn the same lessons from elsewhere, as turned out to be the case in the nineteenth century. It was possible to suppress or forget Tominaga's ideas at the time in Japan, whereas later the power-laden confrontation with the western world led Japanese Buddhist scholars, painfully, to recognise the same points all over again. Though Tominaga was regarded as a threat to pious religion, it is far from clear that his arguments and his understanding of history were or are necessarily contrary to Buddhist teaching in the long run. Rather, his researches put the study of Buddhism on to a modern critical-historical basis, within the not inconsiderable range of information then available to him. Although the data at his disposal did not extend to Indian languages and texts in Sanskrit or other Indian languages, it is remarkable that he was able to demonstrate effectively that the Mahāyāna Buddhist sūtras did not stem from the Buddha himself but were the product of later schools. Not only this, he asked why it might be that a variety of schools and texts with varying teachings should appear, and gave his analysis of the matter without any recourse to normative religious judgements on his own part. The fact that such a breakthrough could be achieved should be honoured as one of the main starting points in the modern development of the study of religion in Japan. Since this case is in principle clear, it then becomes of interest to ask what elements in the Japanese intellectual world made his work possible, and in what ways these elements were also present among other thinkers. Renewed study of the work of Motoori Norinaga could well be undertaken from this point of view. Though he was a Shintō apologist, he was also modern (and "romantic") in the sense that he had to look back across a long bridge of several centuries to the mythological roots which he valued. The "distancing" involved here is what made it possible for him to come to be regarded as one of the early figures in the development of Japanese folklore studies. Since folk-lore studies are close to the study of religion, the question of what antecedents are to count in the formation of the science of religion is raised again in another way.

Second, the political context must be considered. The impact of western imperialist expansion on Japan was very dramatic, though it did not lead to colonisation. On the one hand Japan itself became a colonial power in Korea, northern Asia, and during the Pacific War years further afield. During the war the Ministry of Education published a book whose title may be translated as "The Religious Culture of Greater East Asia" which gave a survey, illustrated with a number of photographs, of the religions in the various occupied countries.[27] It is interesting to see here how the subject matter is objectified from within an imperialist perspective.[28] On the other hand the dominant theme from the nineteenth century onwards was for a long time how to deal with, partly by learning from, the evidently very effective western powers. Thus while many intellectuals sought to assert the independence and integrity of "eastern" culture and thought, there was at the same time a psychologically complex reaction which tended to shut out a perception of those very intellectual bases which made sophisticated interaction with western thought entirely possible. Even during the postwar period of the twentieth century the same reaction is often found, no doubt because of the shock and reorientation caused by total military defeat. Another motivation for playing down the Japanese intellectual roots of the study of religion lies in the wish to preserve cultural "difference." That is, there is a tendency to blame western scholarship for the emergence of dry subjects such as history and sociology, while imitating them assiduously, so that Japanese culture and thought itself can be presented in a more mysterious and attractive light. Suzuki Daisetsu was a great adept in this approach, which he learned in the aftermath of the World's Parliament of Religions held in Chicago in 1893.[29] In sum, just as there is a need for a "post-colonial" history of the study of religions, there is also a need for a "post-reactions-to-the-west" or post-occidentalist history of the same subject.

The third question of interest is about the inter-culturality of the study of religion. On the one hand it might be argued that the science of religion can be carried out in principle anywhere and by anybody, just like any other "science." On the other hand, the formation within specific cultural areas of specialists engaging in it, and in many cases the focusing of research on those same areas, means that strong, culturally

---

27 Edited for the Ministry of Education (Monbushō) by Furuno Kiyohito (1943)

28 Subjects dealt with range from Siberian shamanism to the Muslim tradition of Malaysia, as well as leading features of Chinese and Indian religions. Inside the cover the publication also advertises ideological works such as the influential *Kokutai no Hongi*, a normative statement of ideologised state Shintō (see Gauntlett and Hall 1974).

29 This gathering, though culturally influential, should be regarded as being of no more than marginal significance in the development of the academic study of religions, in spite of the importance sometimes attached to it.

influential models come into play. It is important for us to notice that this is happening, partly so that they can be adjusted or even counteracted if necessary, but partly because they may be heuristically enriching when compared with each other or transposed from one culture to another. Japanese scholars such as Tamaru and Yanagawa have gone to some trouble, for example, to consider the possible relevance of the secularisation model to Japan.[30] Looking at it in the other direction two major themes have long been of importance, as mentioned in the introduction to this paper. These are the recognition of (i) the reality of religious pluralism and of (ii) the responsibility of the state in regulating religious affairs. In the case of Japan the recognition of the pluralism of religions occurred at an early date, and indeed had Chinese models. It was a major theme in the writings of Tominaga Nakamoto in the eighteenth century, and it is of no less importance today. It may be reliably stated that while many academics concerned with religion in some way or other are mainly concerned with the fortunes of one particular religious tradition, the "science of religion" in Japan certainly is fundamentally aware of this plurality of religions. The other deeply set assumption, which is often though not always related to it, is that in some way or other the various religions will stand in a relationship to society and the state, and that the question as to how this is so is a valid and recurring question. As political fortunes have changed, the prominence of the various religions has also changed, and in recent years quite particular problems have emerged such as the legal border between "customs" and religion, or the range of activities permitted to small religious organisations. The continuing assumption is however, in Japan, that these are matters of public concern, and that specialists in religion are expected to be providers of relevant information in the formation of judgements about them. To notice this is not to say that similar models are not available elsewhere. However in the case of Japan no "science of religion" is disposed to overlook them. Perhaps specialists elsewhere can learn from observing this.

30 These contributions are found in a special feature issue of *The Journal of Oriental Studies*, published in 1987 by The Institute of Oriental Philosophy, an institution sponsored by the Sōka Gakkai.

Bibliographical references

Anesaki, Masaharu 1916. *Nichiren, the Buddhist Prophet.* Cambridge, Mass.(Harvard University Press).

– 1930. *History of Japanese Religion. With Special Reference to the Social and Moral Life of the Nation.* London (Kegan Paul, Trench, Trubner and Co.)

– 1943. "The foundation of Buddhist culture in Japan. The Buddhist ideals as conceived and carried out by the Prince-Regent Shōtoku" in: *Monumenta Nipponica* 6: 1–12.

Aston, W. G. 1905. *Shintō, The Way of the Gods.* London (Longmans, Green and Co.)

Bianchi, Ugo (ed) 1994. *The Notion of 'Religion' in Comparative Research (Selected Proceedings of the XVI IAHR Congress).* Rome (l'Erma' di Bretschneider).

Bianchi, Ugo, Mora Fabio and Bianchi Lorenzo (eds.) 1994. *The Notion of "Religion" in Comparative Research: Selected Proceedings of the XVIth Congress of the International Association for the History of Religions, Rome, 3rd-8th September, 1990.* Rome ("L'Erma" di Bretschneider).

Candler, Edmund 1905. *The Unveiling of Lhasa.* London (Edwin Arnold).

Chidester, David 1996. *Savage Systems. Colonialism and Comparative Religion in Southern Africa.* Charlottesville (University Press of Virginia)

Dai, K., Zhang, X. and Pye, M. (eds.) 1995. *Religion and Modernisation in China, Proceedings of the Regional Conference of the International Association for the History of Religions held in Beijing, China, April 1992.* Cambridge (Roots and Branches).

Demiéville, P., Durt, H. et al. (eds.), 1978. *Répertoire du Canon Bouddhique Sino-Japonais. Édition de Taishō (Taishō Shinshû Daizōkyō).* Paris and Tokyo (Librairie d'Amérique et d'Orient/Maison Franco-Japonaise).

Despland, M. and Vallée, G. (eds.) 1992. *Religion in History. The Word, the Idea, the Reality.* Waterloo Ontario (Wilfred Laurier University Press).

Doležalová, I., Martin, L.H. and Papoušek, D. (eds.) 2001. *The Academic Study of Religion during the Cold War: East and West.* Frankfurt and New York (Peter Lang).

Dumoulin, Heinrich 1993. *Zen im 20. Jahrhundert.* Frankfurt (Fischer Taschenbuch Verlag).

Eliot, Sir Charles 1935. *Japanese Buddhism.* London (Routledge and Kegan Paul).

Furuno, Kiyohito 1943. *Daitōa no shūkyōbunka.* Tokyo (Monbushō).

Gauntlett, J. O. and Hall, R. K. 1974. *Kokutai no Hongi. Cardinal Principles of the National Entity of Japan.* Newton, Mass.: Crofton Publishing Corporation.

Hori, Ichiro 1968. *Folk Religion in Japan. Continuity and Change.* Chicago and London (University of Chicago Press).

Inoue, Enryō 1890. *Jissaiteki Shūkyōgaku.* Tokyo (Tetsugakkan).

– 1891. *Ririnteki Shūkyōgaku.* Tokyo (Tetsugakkan).

Iyanaga, Nobumi 1987. *Gensō no tōyō. Orientalizumu no keifu.* Tokyo (Seidosha).

Kashiwara, Yūsen and Sonoda, Kōyū 1994. *Shapers of Japanese Buddhism.* Tokyo (Kōsei Publishing Co.).

Katō, Genchi 1971. *A Study of Shintō. The Religion of the Japanese Nation.* London and Dublin (Curzon Press). (First published Tokyo 1926).

Kawaguchi, Ekai 1909. *Three Years in Tibet.* Adyar Madras (The Theosophist Office) and Benares and London (The Theosophical Society).

Keene, Donald 1969. *The Japanese Discovery of Europe.* Stanford California (Stanford University Press). (first published in 1952 as *The Japanese Discovery of Europe. Honda Toshiaki and other Discoverers 1720–1798*).

Kishimoto, Hideo (ed.) 1956. *Japanese Culture in the Meiji Era. Vol II. Religion.* Tokyo (Ōbunsha).

Kitagawa, Joseph M. 1966. *Religion in Japanese History.* New York and London (Columbia University Press).

Kohl, Karl-Heinz 1981. *Entzauberter Blick. Das Bild vom Guten Wilden und die Erfahrung der Zivilisation.* Berlin (Medusa Verlag).

– 1986. *Exotik als Beruf. Erfahrung und Trauma der Ethnographie.* Frankfurt (Campus Verlag).

Klostermaier, K.K. and Hurtado, L.W. (eds.) 1991. *Religious Studies. Issues, Prospects and Proposals.* Atlanta (Scholars Press).

Landon, Perceval 1905. *Lhasa. An account of the country and people of central Tibet and of the progress of the mission sent there by the English government in the year 1903–4.* London (Hurst and Blackett)

Mathé, Roger 1972. *L'Exotisme.* Paris (Bordas).

Miyake, Hitoshi 1992. *Shūkyōminzokugaku e no shōtai.* Tokyo (Maruzen).

Nanjō, Bunyū 1883. *Catalogue of the Chinese Translation of the Buddhist Tripitaka.* Oxford (Clarendon Press).

Nihon Shūkyōgakkai Gojūshūnenkinen Jigyōiinkai 1980. *Nihon shūkyōgakkai gojūnenshi.* Tokyo (Nihon Shūkyōgakkai).

Nowaczyk, Miroslaw and Stachowski, Zbigniew (eds.) 1992. *Language – Religion – Culture. In Memory of Professor Witold Tyloch.* Warsaw (Polish Society for the Study of Religions).

Platvoet, J. Cox, J. and Olupona, J. (eds.) 1996. *The Study of Religions in Africa. Past, Present and Prospects.* Cambridge (Roots and Branches).

Pye, Michael (ed.) 1989a. *Marburg Revisited. Institutions and Strategies in the Study of Religion.* Marburg (Diagonal-Verlag).

Pye, Michael 1973a. "Aufklärung and religion in Europe and Japan" in: *Religious Studies* 9: 201–17.

– 1975. "Japanese studies of religion" in: *Religion* (Special Congress Issue): 55–72.

– 1982b. "Diversions in the interpretation of Shintō" in: *Religion* 11: 61–74.

– 1983. "The significance of the Japanese intellectual tradition for the history of religions" in: Slater, P. and Wiebe, D. (eds.), *Traditions in Contact and Change, Selected Proceedings of the Fourteenth Congress of the International Association for the History of Religions.* Waterloo Canada (Wilfred Laurier): 565–77.

– 1989b. "Cultural and organizational perspectives in the study of religion" in: Pye 1989a: 11–17.

– 1990a. (trans.) *Emerging from Meditation (Tominaga Nakamoto)*. London (Duckworth) and Honolulu (University of Hawaii Press).
– 1991b. "Religious studies in Europe: structures and desiderata" in: Klostermaier and Hurtado 1991: 39–55.
– 1992a. "An Asian starting point for the study of religion' in Despland and Vallée 1992: 101–9.
– 1994a. "What is 'religion' in East Asia" in: Bianchi et al. 1994: 115–22.
– 1995b. "Three teachings (*sanjiao*) theory and modern reflection on religion" in: Dai, Zhang and Pye 1995: 111–16.
– 1996a. "Intercultural strategies and the International Association for the History of Religions" in: Platvoet, Cox and Olupona 1996: 37–45.
– 1997a. "Reflecting on the plurality of religions (full text)" in: *Marburg Journal of Religion* 2: (virtual pages). (Also published in abbreviated form in *World Faiths Encounter* 14 (1996): 3–11.
– 2001a. "Political correctness in the study of religions: Is the Cold War really over?" in: Doležalová, Martin and Papoušek 2001: 313–33.
Sharpe, Eric 1975. *Comparative Religion. A History*. London (Duckworth).
Sonoda, Minoru 1990. *Matsuri no Genshōgaku*. Tokyo (Kōbunsha).
Tamaru, Noriyoshi 1987a. *Shūkyōgaku no rekishi to kadai*. Tokyo (Yamamoto Shoten).
– 1987b. "The concept of secularization and its relevance in Japanese society" in: *The Journal of Oriental Studies* 26: 51–61.
Ueda, Shizuteru 1965. *Die Gottesgeburt in der Seele und der Durchbruch zur Gottheit. Die mystische Anthropologie Meister Eckharts und ihre Konfrontation mit der Mystik des Zen-Buddhismus*. Gütersloh (Gütersloher Verlagshaus).
Waddell, L. Austine 1894. 1939 (2), 1971 (reprint). *The Buddhism of Tibet or Lamaism*. Cambridge (Heffer).
Westerlund, David 1985. *African Religion in African Scholarship. A Preliminary Study of the Religious and Political Background*. Stockholm (Almqvist and Wiksell International).
Yanagawa, Keiichi 1987. "Introductory thesis: beyond the 'secularization' theories" in: *The Journal of Oriental Studies* 26: 1–4.
Younghusband, Sir Francis 1910. *India and Tibet. A history of the relations which have subsisted between the two countries from the time of Warren Hastings to 1910; with a particular account of the mission to Lhasa of 1904*. London (John Murray).

This paper was previously published in: Wiegers, Gerard A. and Platvoet, Jan G. (eds.) 2002. *Modern Societies and the Study of Religions. Studies in Honour of Lammert Leertouwer*. Leiden (Brill): 350–376; and in *Method and Theory in the Study of Religions* 15/1 (2003): 1–27.

Part Three
Structures and Strategies

3.1 Introduction to Part Three

While there is nowadays widespread recognition that religions are a most important phenomenon which requires sustained study, it is often thought that such study can just be undertaken by anybody with skills in any more or less relevant disciplines. Consequently, the study of religions, or *Religionswissenschaft*, has usually been rather weak in institutional terms and has suffered from the inadequacies of structures which are unfavourable to its best development. Very often it has been seen as an add-on subject and has been dominated by others such as oriental studies, theology, sociology and so on. The way in which this has occurred varies from country to country, depending on the academic traditions and the dominant ideological trends of any one region or time. To counteract this instability both in national contexts and in an international and intercultural perspective, organisations such as the International Association for the History of Religions (IAHR) and its many affiliated associations have been developed. The writer has spent considerable time and effort in support of the activities of these associations, and this is partly reflected in the papers which are coordinated here.

The topic was first set up at a special conference of the IAHR held in Marburg in 1988, the proceedings of which were entitled *Marburg Revisited. Institutions and Strategies in the Study of Religion* (Pye 1989a). In the writer's introduction, "Cultural and organizational perspectives in the study of religion," it was argued that the organizational parameters for the study of religions should be directly considered, confronted, and constructed. The conference itself provided the first opportunity for the full International Committee of the IAHR to be called together in between its major international congresses, which themselves are held just once every five years. It seemed good that at a point three years after one such congress it is high time for accumulated business and policy matters to be attended to. At the same time, with two years to elapse before the next major congress, there is good time to prepare for forthcoming decisions by the General Assembly.[1] Since 1988 this pattern has in fact been

---

1 This has proven to be particularly relevant in connection with new affiliations and minor points of constitutional revision.

sustained, with mid-term meetings of the International Committee being held regularly since then in the context of an appropriate conference.[2] This has been a crucial part of the streamlining of the IAHR, helping it to function as a viable organisation in the modern academic world. But there is more to it than organisational streamlining. It has also been necessary to correlate and develop channels of communication between institutions which reflect the varied traditions of societies across the whole world. To do this, awareness of and reflection on cultural difference is crucial. Somehow, working procedures and customs have had to be worked out which are both culturally sensitive and organizationally effective. The relationships between political contexts, institutional arrangements and deep-seated assumptions about the study of religions are pursued in the papers below which have followed this process.

The paper "Religious studies in Europe: structures and desiderata" (3.2) was addressed to a largely North American audience at the University of Manitoba in 1989. It may be highlighted that in this title "Europe" referred to the *whole* of Europe east and west at a time when many still thought that the "cold war" divisions could not in any way be overcome. This theme was taken up retrospectively ten years later in the paper "Political Correctness in the Study of Religions: Is the Cold War Really Over?" (3.5). This paper, from a conference held in 1999 at Masaryk University in Brno, in the Czech Republic, not only provides relevant documentation but decisively questions the tendency after the end of the cold war to negate or brush out all relevant academic work which had taken place earlier. The cold war is now over, supposedly, though many continue with cold war assumptions. However a narrow western hegemony in the study of religions which does not include the perspective of east European countries and Russia is not appropriate and should be resisted. This is but one example of the importance of getting to know the variety of cultural and political contexts in which interesting studies of religion are possible, and to work for perceptions which are as correct as possible.

Interleaved with this discussion are other perspectives. The paper "Intercultural strategies and the International Association for the History of Religions" (3.3) was presented at the first conference of the IAHR ever to be held in the whole of Africa. This took place in 1992 at Harare, Zimbabwe, and was classified as a "regional conference" of the IAHR. Though the participants were few in number, it was a historic occasion

2 I.e. to date of writing, in 1993, 1998, 2003 and 2008.

in that participant scholars from various countries of Africa were present. It was also correctly anticipated by all that great changes were soon to occur in South Africa, just across the border. So it was that in 1992, at Harare, the African Association for the Study of Religions was called into being at an open meeting over which the writer presided as General Secretary of the IAHR. This is not the place for a historical documentation of the IAHR as such, but there was certainly a sense of fulfilment when some years later in 2000 its major congress could be held in Durban, South Africa. The third paper in this section was a presidential address given on that occasion: "Memories of the future. Looking back and looking forward in the history of religions" (3.4).

This pluriformity, without abandonment of the quest for methodological coherence and integration, is further explored in the remaining paper in this section, "Difference and coherence in the worldwide study of religions" (3.6), first presented at Boston in the United States. The deep-seated, divergent assumptions about "religion" which mark various cultural regions of the world were explored in a related paper for a European audience at Messina entitled "Memes and models in the study of religions" (Pye 2002a) which is however not included here. Though such matters may seem to be quite simple when spelled out, it is remarkable how rarely they are clearly perceived. Deep assumptions about the shape or profile of "religion" are simply taken for granted by most people, including academics who have experienced a specific cultural formation, and they need to be not so much questioned and rejected as recognized and relativized.

The still insufficiently recognized perspectives are extremely wide. While the quinquennial world IAHR congress prior to Durban (2000) had been in Mexico (1995), there has never yet been one of these major events in the whole of South America, either in a Spanish speaking country or in Brazil. Yet there too, as is perceived by many academics on the spot, there is a need to articulate the study of religions in a relevant manner. While sharing in the debate in São Paulo in 2008, it became very clear to the writer again just how necessary it is, in that context as well as some European ones, to distinguish the study of religions from theology and other normative disciplines.[3] At the same time Latin American approaches are in their own ways specific, and different

3 Cf. my paper "The Study of Religions: New times, new tasks, new options" published in Portuguese as: O Estudo das Religiões: novos tempos, tarefas e opções, (Pye 2011).

for example from those of Japan, where major IAHR congresses have in fact been held (1958 and 2005), or those of China, where a first regional conference of the IAHR was held in 1992. While many said that it would be just "not possible" to hold a conference of this kind in China at that time, it in fact worked out rather well (for the proceedings see Dai, Zhang and Pye 1995). It is of interest for the present discussion that an attempt by a well-funded external body to take over the conference and to transform it into a *religious* conference, rather than a conference for the academic study of religions, was successfully thwarted.

For many equally unexpected was a further regional conference of the IAHR held at a dual site in Yogyakarta and Semarang in Java in 2004. This was the first time that a conference of the IAHR had ever been held in Indonesia and, with war raging in the Middle East, the relations between western and Muslim academics were in great need of exploration and development. Readers interested in these matters will find much of value in the various contributions to the conference volume which emerged, being published first in Indonesian as *Harmoni Kehidupan Beragama: Problem, Praktik dan Pendidikan.* (Wasim, Mas'ud, Franke and Pye 2005) and then in English as *Religious Harmony: Problems, Practice and Education* (Franke, Mas'ud, Pye and Wasim 2006).[4]

Our task in the IAHR and its affiliated associations throughout the world is to communicate and to moderate the various understandings of the study of religion which are, quite properly, influenced by the surrounding cultures and their intellectual traditions, while at the same time holding together and developing an international corporate identity for the discipline. The mutual support of the participating associations is necessary for worthwhile future development. What the writer himself has learned, from the various situations out of which the papers in this section have emerged, is that very much hard organizational work is required to achieve this kind of coherence and balance, and to maintain a globally shared identity for the study of religions as an academic discipline.

Bibliographical references

Dai Kangsheng, Zhang Xinying and Pye, Michael (eds.) 1995. *Religion and Modernization in China. Proceedings of the International Association for the*

4 The excellent collaboration and hard work of Edith Franke, Abdurrahman Mas'ud and Alef Theria Wasim is gratefully acknowledged here.

History of Religions held in Beijing, China, April 1992. Cambridge (Roots and Branches).

Franke, Edith, Mas'ud, Abdurrahman, Pye, Michael and Wasim, Alef Theria (eds.) 2006. *Religious Harmony: Problems, Practice and Education. Proceedings of the Regional Conference of the International Association for the History of Religions, Yogyakarta and Semarang, Indonesia, September 27th – October 3rd, 2004*. Berlin (de Gruyter).

Pye, Michael (ed.) 1989a. *Marburg Revisited. Institutions and Strategies in the Study of Religion*. Marburg (Diagonal-Verlag).

– 1989b. "Cultural and organizational perspectives in the study of religion" in: Pye 1989a.

– 2002a. "Memes and models in the study of religions" in: Giulia Sfameni Gasparro (ed.) *Themes and Problems in the History of Religions in Contemporary Europe. Proceedings of the International Seminar, Messina, March 30–3, 2001*. Cosenza (Edizioni Lionello Giordano), 245–59.

– 2006a. "Models of religious diversity: simplicities and complexities" in Franke, Mas'ud, Pye and Wasim 2006: 23–33.

– 2011. "O Estudo das Religiões: novos tempos, tarefas e opções" in: da Cruz, Eduardo and De Mori, Geraldo (eds.) 2011. Teologia e Ciências da Religião. A Caminho da Maioridade Acadêmica. São Paulo (Ed. Paulinas): 15–24.

Wasim, Alef Theria, Mas'ud, Abdurrahman , Franke Edith and Pye, Michael (eds.) 2005. *Harmoni Kehidupan Beragama: Problem, Praktik dan Pendidikan. Proceeding Konferensi Regional International Association for the History of Religions, Yogyakarta dan Semarang, Indonesia, September 27th – Oktober 3rd, 2004*. Yogyakarta (Oasis Publishers) 2005.

3.2 Studies of Religion in Europe: Structures and Desiderata

This paper was first presented at a twenty-year celebratory conference of the Department of Religion of the University of Manitoba, Canada, in September 1989. The title of the conference was "Religious Studies: Directions for the Next Two Decades" and so the expression "religious studies" is used at various points and originally figured in the title of the paper. In some cases the usage has been re-edited to "study of religion/s" in tune with other parts of the present volume. Bibliographical details have also been streamlined. However, in order not to distort the picture provided at the time of writing, no up-dating of content has been undertaken.

Geographical and terminological considerations

It is impossible to give a detailed picture of the many activities and institutions which are in some way related to studies of religion in the whole of Europe within the short space of this paper. The very diversity which can be documented pitches us directly into problems of structure and intention, thus also throwing up problems about future directions. In turn, incipient judgments about desiderata for the future, which will certainly be advanced below, themselves have an influence on the way in which the present and the past are construed.[1] Since "the past" in this context includes the sometimes contradictory influences of the intellectual and social history of the whole of Europe, not forgetting the Euro-

---

1 A clear example of this is the essay by Christoph Elsas entitled "Religionskritik und Religionsbegründung; Religionswissenschaftliche Diskussion am Beispiel christlicher Offenbarungstradition und Mystik" (Elsas 1988) in Hartmut Zinser's *Religionswissenschaft: eine Einführung* (Zinser 1988). Here the author weaves short comments on various thinkers from the past and the present, philosophers, anthropologists, sociologists, psychologists and theologians, in such a way as to conclude that the key function of *Religionswissenschaft* is the critique of religion. While the present writer is not without sympathy for this orientation in a general sense, it is evident that a different selection of past writers on religion and the choice of specifica other than revelation and mysticism could support a quite different train of thought.

pean reception of all the other parts of the world with which it has been heavily engaged over centuries, and since "the" present of Europe continues to be culturally and linguistically pluralist in a very strong sense, any treatment is sure to be impressionistic and open to correction. At the same time this very diversity and range helps to accentuate certain structures which in a more limited context, i. e. within the range of a single national educational system with its own local problems of the day, might be taken for granted and hence be only half visible.

Even the geographical extension of Europe is greater than is sometimes realised. Edinburgh is about 1600 miles from Athens or Istanbul as the crow flies, and Lisbon about 2000 miles from Helsinki or Leningrad. Moreover the geographical extension of Europe, which by some standards, may still be regarded as modest, is compounded by what might be regarded as "political distance." This implies that some weight must be attached, in spite of the relative ease of modern travel, to where people *feel* that they are. The strains of political and military history may still be sensed in many ways, even decades after the second world war, and in some ways even *because* the passage of time has allowed further layers of reflection to occur, some humane and some, alas, of more doubtful value. *Wo Deutschland liegt, Eine Ortsbestimmung* (that is, "Locating Germany") is the title of a sensitive work by Günter Gaus, a former representative of the Federal Republic of Germany in East Berlin, a title which admirably sums up the subtle difficulty of achieving a sense of geographical and political position in "central" Europe, wherever that might be.

The dynamic political processes taking place in Europe at the present time [1989] seem to be demanding coherence within a complexity which is voluntarily accepted, and these processes will certainly influence the cultural and academic life of the next generation. Specifically, the radical promotion of academic interaction in the European Community by means, for example, of the Erasmus program in the humanities, is balanced, quite unintentionally, by a quite new perspective of open intellectual association between the countries of eastern and western Europe which will evidently take us far beyond anything which could be achieved under Cold War conditions.[2]

2 This was very strongly felt at a small conference organised in Warsaw in early September 1989 by the Polish Society for the Science of Religions in conjunction with the International Association for the History of Religions (IAHR) and delegates from academic institutions in various east European countries. As it happens

If Europe is a complex cultural base for reflection on the nature and future of any academic discipline it must be added that the other term in the [original] title of this paper, "religious studies", is hardly simpler. In Britain, where the designation has come into widespread use in colleges and universities over the past twenty-five years, it usually refers to open-ended studies of religion which are not theologically oriented or theologically controlled.[3] With this demarcation in mind it has sometimes seemed appropriate to give university departments the joint designation "Theology and Religious Studies," or at least to run two degrees adjacently.[4] This device was adopted when syllabus and staffing were extended to take account of so-called "non-Christian" religions. Clearly, such a solution leads to an imbalance which cannot easily be sustained intellectually, in that one religion is treated in terms of its own normative tradition (Christian theology, including Old Testament studies, New Testament studies and Church History, all of which are designations implying a religious position) while other religions such as Islam or Sikhism are treated, perhaps not unsympathetically, but dispassionately, without accompanying religious commitment. Actively committed reflection about contemporary questions of religious life and meaning, ethics, and so on, naturally falls in this case to the side of "Theology," thus compounding the imbalance. In other cases "Religious Studies" has been given priority as a designation for courses which embrace among other things those subjects which used to constitute theology. In such cases, "religious studies" cannot be easily or precisely defined;

---

this meeting took place just days after the appointment of non-communist prime-minister Mazowiecki, but on the much broader background of *perestroika* policy in the Soviet Union. Needless to say it was only possible because of the long-term association between the Polish Society for the Science of Religions and the International Association for the History of Religions (IAHR) and the efforts of various individuals over many years when conditions were less favourable. In particular, attention should be drawn to the conference held in Warsaw in 1979, of which the proceedings were edited by Witold Tyloch under the title *Current Progress in the Methodology of the Science of Religions* (Tyloch 1984). This conference was held under the auspices of the IAHR and brought together religious studies specialists from the non-communist and communist world in a significant way.

3 This was clearest, in the pioneering days, in the program of the Department of Religious Studies at the University of Lancaster, set up in the mid-sixties under the leadership of Ninian Smart, now of Santa Barbara, California. The point was quite unclear, on the other hand, in the usage of the term "religious studies" at the University of Sussex, where it was established a little earlier.

4 E.g. Leeds, London.

the adjective "religious" can easily suggest, and sometimes may be intended to suggest, that these "studies" are supposed to be religious in orientation and not simply studies of religion, thus running clean contrary to the earlier use of the term.

A comparable problem has arisen in Germany where the term *Religionswissenschaft* in the singular (science of religion) is rivalled in some universities by the plural form *Religionswissenschaften* (sciences of religion) which tends to mean religious sciences with a religious motivation, including Catholic and Protestant theology. In North and East European languages there is really no reason not to use the available singular terms: *Religionswissenschaft, godsdienstwetenschap, religionsvidenskap, religioznawstwo, religiovedenia*, etc. However this is more difficult in English since "science" is not used so freely in the humanities. In France the choice falls between *sciences religieuses*, which shares in the ambiguities mentioned above, and *histoire des religions*, matched in Italy by *storia delle religione*. These more tightly definable expressions can in turn be matched by "history of religions" in English, and Germanic equivalents such as German *Religionsgeschichte* or Dutch *godsdiensthistorie*. Unfortunately, these terms, which are in partial use, especially in Germany, are not always understood to include the systematic and theoretical studies which *Religionswissenschaft* clearly demands. It is partly for this reason that the designation "history of religions" has not established itself institutionally in Britain, as it has in France and Italy, and that in early 1989 the British Association for the History of Religions (BAHR) changed its name to British Association for the Study of Religions (BASR).

In this context it may be noted that the International Association for the History of Religions (IAHR), the umbrella organisation to which the BASR belongs, uses the word history to indicate a non-theological program, but that its constitution emphasises an openness to "all scholars whose research has a bearing on the subject" (Article 1). This means that "history of religions" is taken to include all necessary comparative and theoretical investigations of the object under study. Just recently (8th September 1989) this aspect was strongly emphasised in a concluding statement agreed at the previously mentioned meeting held in Warsaw with the co-sponsorship of the IAHR.[5] Needless to say, the IAHR is not simply a European organisation, though it has a strong basis in Europe. The interests demonstrated at IAHR congresses and in the IAHR journal *Numen* are in fact more closely matched by the North American

5 See note 2 above. The statement is given as an appendix at the end of this paper.

journal *History of Religions* than by the British journal *Religious Studies*, whose strong penchant towards philosophy of religion sometimes seems to give way altogether to what has been called philosophical theology. Curiously enough, the phrase "science of religion," though unpopular in Britain, has also found partial acceptance in English-speaking North America, as in the name of the *Journal for the Scientific Study of Religion*.

These terminological reflections could be pursued in greater detail. Suffice it to say, however, that the terminological situation seems to be more complex in Europe than in either North America or in East Asia, as a result of diverse linguistic and cultural traditions. Thus "religious studies" covers a multitude of possibilities. The standpoint of this paper is that within these possibilities it is necessary to have a clear grasp of what is or should be meant by the history of religions (*Religionsgeschichte*, and other equivalents) and/or the science of religion (*Religionswissenschaft* and other equivalents) before considering, or even while considering, the role which this discipline can play in academic life in general and the expectations which it might be required to meet. While not being unduly restrictive (see later) this is the perspective in which "religious studies" should be understood, if the term is not simply to be used as a camouflage for theology. This statement is not to be misunderstood as an *anti*-theological stance; but there are good reasons for maintaining an autonomous, intercultural discipline which in English may as well be called "religious studies," or, when not intended as the designation of a university department, course or degree, simply "the study of religion/s."

The generation of religious studies and discipline identification

Broadly speaking the discipline of religious studies emerged from three major directions, namely, theology, oriental studies (including Far Eastern studies, which should now be called East Asian studies) and the social sciences (anthropology, social psychology and sociology). Many recruits to religious studies programs are trained in one or more of these, and not necessarily in the study of religion as such. Thus from one generation to another the problems of discipline identification pose themselves anew. Some have difficulty with the tension between religious value (assumed in theology) and reductionism (often implied by social-scientific explanation), others with the tension between socio-cultural location (emphasised in social sciences fieldwork) and philology (a *sine qua non* of oriental studies). Needless to say these tensions can be resolved in an autonomous study of religion/s, but this is not always immediately evident to a person trained in one of the above-named directions, where prejudice is not entirely unknown.

In Europe, as in other parts of the world, much of the work which contributes to the study of religion is carried out under other auspices from start to finish. A recently published work on Japanese religion, for example was written by Massimo Raveri, professor of Japanese studies at the Università degli Studi at Venice, who is trained as a Japanologist and a social anthropologist. Yet the title has a non-reductionist implication: *Itinerari nel Sacro, l'Esperienza Religiosa Giapponese*, and the work may be regarded as a fine contribution to the study of religion.[6] Such contributions are found, of course, in other European countries too, as for example in the Netherlands, where the relation between anthropology and oriental studies has always been strong, partly because of the colonial past in Indonesia,[7] or in Finland, where folk-lore studies (akin to what in Germany would be called European ethnology) have contributed mightily to the published output on religion.[8]

---

6 Raveri 1984. In fact the affinity to and probably to some extent the influence of thematic phenomenological studies of religion is quite strong. Thus major themes deal with: space, time, death, power.

7 In an older generation the influence of anthropology on Gerardus Van der Leeuw was not negligible, though it may be said that other aspects predominated in his many-sided interdisciplinary receptivity; but a clear push in the direction of anthropological method and goals was made by his successor van Baaren at the University of Groningen. The influence of van Baaren in this respect was noticeable in the Dutch contributions to an IAHR regional conference devoted to the work of Van der Leeuw (including contemporary implications) held at Groningen in May 1989. The proceedings of this conference will be published under the editorship of Hans Kippenberg [Kippenberg and Luchesi 1991], who, as van Baaren's successor brought a more broadly sociological bearing to the subject. Regrettably van Baaren has died in this same year. Since Kippenberg has now returned to Germany (Bremen) it is momentarily unclear what direction the subject will take in this important Dutch centre of religious studies.

8 One has only to look to the leading Scandinavian journal on religious studies, *Temenos*, or to the publications of the Donner Institute in Åbo to notice this. Leading representatives of this trend are Lauri Honko (Turku / Åbo) and Juha Pentikäinen (Helsinki). Not that religious studies is not restricted to this strand in Finland; Buddhist studies are clearly represented, by René Gothóni (Helsinki), for example, and it is of particular interest that the Scandinavian strand in the psychology of religion associated with the name of Sundén is being carried forward by Nils G. Holm (Åbo), with works such as *Pingströrelsen. En religionsvetenskapelig studie av pingströrelsen*

Equally important is the continued contribution of specialists in classical, ancient, near eastern, ancient Iranian and Egyptian studies, which play a particularly strong role in the history of religions in Italy and France.[9] Leading members of the Société Ernest Renan (the French affiliate of the IAHR, as the highly appropriate name might suggest) specialise in such areas,[10] so that here the philological method is at a premium and comparative work tends to be focused on these interrelated cultural areas rather than bringing in more distant fields, which are left to anthropologists or specialists in East Asia. As a consequence there is a tendency for the social sciences approach to religion to be organised in other ways.

Here the International Conference for the Sociology of Religion, known by the abbreviation CISR from the French title Conférence Internationale de Sociologie des Religions, plays a significant and interesting role. The membership of CISR appears to be largely European and and it is in Europe that its biennial conferences have been held.[11] From some countries (e.g. Britain) it draws participants who do not take much part in "history of religions" activities, being professional sociologists (of religion). From other countries however, especially predominantly Catholic countries, the participants are evidently more religious, both personally and in the orientation of their work, than many historians of religion who have a strong philological or orientalist bias. This is partly because the subject-matter attended to at CISR conferences is largely (though of course not entirely) determined by the present condition of religion in western culture. Thus there is a common interest on the part of non-religious and religiously loyal sociologists to assess the progress of secularisation and to detect shifting features of common re-

---

i Svenskfinland (Holm 1978) and *Mystik och Intensiva Upplevelser* (Holm 1979). A survey may be found in the same writer's *Scandinavian Psychology of Religion* (Holm 1987).

9 For Italy the works of Bianchi and Gnoli (both in Rome) may be mentioned as an obvious starting point. This statement is by no means meant to imply weakness in these studies in other countries. One thinks immediately of Klimkeit and Rudolph in Germany, of Boyce and Hinnells in Britain and of others in the Netherlands and Scandinavia. However names are mentioned in this paper only to give the briefest illustration of leading trends and there can be no question of giving a detailed survey.

10 E.g. Bloch, Caquot, Laperrousaz, Leclant.

11 For example, from 1973 onwards, at The Hague (1973), Lloret de Mar (Spain) (1975), Strasbourg (1977), Venice (1979), Lausanne (1981), London (1983), Louvain (1985), Tübingen (1987), Helsinki (1989); c.f. the published proceedings.

ligiosity. In between these polarised (though friendly) orientations the autonomous study of religion as a focusing discipline in itself is often neglected or regarded as insignificant.

However there seems to be no reason why Christianity, as a religion in the European cultural area, should not be studied in a historical and phenomenological manner just like those religions in Asia and elsewhere which attract more attention in religious studies quarters. This has recently been attempted successfully in a slim volume by Peter Antes entitled *Christentum – eine Einführung* (Antes 1985), which shows a keen awareness of the problems involved in such an enterprise. The larger the scale of the phenomenon taken into view, the greater is the need for conceptual refinement and decision, and the more evident it is whether the work is oriented in a theological or a more autonomous "study of religion/s" direction. The latter is certainly intended in Antes' case. Equally instructive is Xavier de Montclos' *Histoire religieuse de la France* (de Montclos 1988) which thoroughly succeeds in giving a brief history of French religion which is not a "church history." Also illustrative is the empathetic account of Russian Christianity completed by German sociologist Hans von Eckhardt in 1945 [i.e. immediately at the end of the war] under the simple title *Russisches Christentum* (von Eckhardt 1947). When he writes in the preface that the attempt is being made to give an account of the religion of the people which is, though unsystematic, as far as possible unprejudiced by the catechisms and other teaching of the church, then this is entirely in tune with key intentions of the phenomenological tradition in religious studies.[12] These examples are given to show that it is in principle quite possible to conceive of an autonomous[13] study of religion/s which avoids both theological normativeness and sociological reductionism, regardless of whether the particular subject is mainly distant such as (in Europe) Buddhism or mainly proximate such as (in Europe) Christianity.

12 For a restrictive use of the term "phenomenological" in religious studies, avoiding some of its inappropriate meanings, see Pye 1972a, especially 16–17.

13 For exactly what is meant here see also Pye 1982a , "The study of religion as an autonomous discipline", steering between hidden normative interests and a merely philological approach.

Methodological orientations and cultural diversity

It may be questioned whether cultural diversity or national traditions as such have anything to do with the key methodological questions or decisions about our subject. The position taken here is that they may influence the understanding of a discipline in some ways, but that an effort should be made to relativise such diversity in the interests of achieving coherence in the discipline from an intercultural standpoint. Three examples of diversity may be considered in this respect (for Europe): a difference of emphasis between northern and southern Europe, a difference of emphasis between western and eastern Europe, and a partial difference of emphasis between Germany and some other countries such as Britain. These divergences were adumbrated above in the consideration of terminological questions, but will now be considered more directly.

As to the first example, it seems to be clear that the study of religion is clearly and firmly established in Scandinavia, Britain, The Netherlands, Germany and Switzerland, and that representatives of the subject in this northern European area display a wide sense of agreement about the procedures of historical and comparative studies of religion. In the latin countries the situation is less clear. Institutionally the study of religion appears not to exist in Spain [at the time of writing], although it is attended to in publications from the standpoint of various other disciplines. France and Italy both have strong traditions in the philological study of defunct religions and the sociological study of living religions, with a tendency for an autonomous study of religion/s, whether past or present, as a phenomenon in itself, to be left out. This pattern is reinforced by the assumptions of both religious and anti-religious attitudes. The number of French specialists engaged in some way in the study of religions is quite large, and needless to say, the standard established is beyond praise. An integrative view of the discipline is assisted by the previously mentioned Société Ernest Renan and also by the very substantial bibliographical review *Bulletin Signalétique.* If there is a problem it lies in the extent to which there may be said to be a joint methodological discussion in Europe which includes French participation. There was apparently no such participation at the IAHR regional conferences with a methodological emphasis at Turku (Finland) 1973, Warsaw 1979 or Groningen 1989. No doubt this was partly because of a tendency to over-emphasise English (or at Groningen English and German) as conference languages. Of course major intellectual movements such as structuralism emanating from France have been taken up in religious studies in German, British and other northern European contexts, but the more internal, domestic debates on method and theory in religious studies have not been pursued jointly as between France and northern Europe in recent decades.

In the case of Italy the situation is a little different. The subject is institutionally more fragile, but there is a strong tradition of participation in pan-European methodological discussion, associated above all with two names, Raffaele Pettazzoni and Ugo Bianchi, the latter being currently at the University of Rome (La Sapienza). Apart from this individual participation and leadership two most interesting joint projects may be named. The first: a joint Italian-Finnish-Swedish colloquium held in Rome in 1984 on the subject of "transition rites," mentioned here because of the methodological and theoretical interest of its substantial proceedings (Bianchi 1986).[14] These proceedings contain eighteen papers, of which seven are in Italian and eleven in English. The second: a joint colloquium held in Tübingen in 1988 on the subject of the relations between the history of religions in Italy and in Germany (proceedings unfortunately not yet available). These projects show that although there may be an inherent structural fragility for religious studies in Latin countries, as indicated earlier, there is in principle no reason why integrated theoretical discussions cannot take place in conjunction with other interested parties. Nor is there any sign of deep-seated disagreements emerging which go significantly beyond the range of current debate in northern Europe. There is every likelihood that the forthcoming quinquennial IAHR Congress in Rome (September 1990) will lead to further integration of this north-south dialogue.

The difference of emphasis between western and eastern Europe is, needless to say, dominated by the influence of institutionalised Marxism in the east. This does not require to be pursued in detail here. As in countries dominated by catholic culture this means that the dual interest in religion, that of philological orientalism and that of sociology (in this case with the conscious task of hastening secularisation), are not easily brought together into a single discipline for the autonomous study of religion as a phenomenon in its own right. The above-mentioned trends can easily be seen in the Polish religious studies journals *Euhemer* and *Studia Religioznawcze* (with English and Russian summaries). At the

14 Note that [in 1989] neither Sweden nor Finland are members of the European Community and that these countries are really quite distant from Italy.

same time the earlier history of Polish studies of religion in independence from catholic theology, and prior to the establishment of the communist government, is extremely complex. Further east, in the Soviet Union, the study of religion has been coupled, in a sense appropriately, with the study of atheism. There have been signs however that studies pertaining to particular religions, whether ethnological, philological or even archaeological (Buddhist remains in Central Asia) have been pursued without much attention being paid in practice to Marxist theory. A typical example is the work by N.A. Alekseev entitled *Samanizm Tyurkoyazycnych Narodov Sibiri* (Alekseev 1984) recently translated into German as *Schamanismus der Türken Sibiriens* (Alekseev 1987). The foreword and the conclusion contain hard-hitting sentiments about the illusory character of a religious world-view which no longer has any historical or socio-economic function, and the author hopes that the book will assist atheist propagandists in their work. The three hundred pages of contents in between however are just a normal exercise in the study of religion. Conditions seem favourable for a new, more integrated phase in the study of religion to develop in eastern Europe which will no longer be based on the assumption that religion is on the verge of disappearance. Of particular interest in this regard is the recently commenced annual publication *Religii Mira*, published in Moscow, in which the expression *religiovedeniya* is freely used.

Also noted above was a particular emphasis within the field of *Religionswissenschaft* or *Religionsgeschichte* in Germany which is not easily matched in other European countries. This refers to the tendency to pursue questions pertaining to the intellectual history of Germany itself, thus threatening to merge religious studies with philosophy or with ideologically charged sociological or psychological theories of various kinds. Since Germany is large enough, with adjacent German-speaking areas, to sustain such debate within itself, the latter is not easily opened to foreign reaction or stimulus. As a result, interest in the identity of the study of religion/s as an autonomous and internationally identifiable undertaking is sometimes regarded as insignificant compared with attention to some other problem of a more general intellectual kind. Sometimes the relations between religion and the arts or between religion and the natural sciences assume a central importance, so that the specialist in *Religionswissenschaft* becomes an active participant in his own culture, rather like a theologian without a church. It must be said however that the empirical strand in German *Religionswissenschaft* is also quite strong, and that, whether oriented philologically or sociologically, it plays a significant role in various areas of international communication. These reflections on aspects of present-day religious studies in Europe may be completed by brief reference to the extremely lively contributions of various institutions and individuals in the four Scandinavian countries, which, on the basis of more general political and cultural links, cooperate closely with each other in conferences and publications. Here religious studies is quite receptive, as also in the Netherlands and Britain, to stimuli from social anthropology, folk-lore studies, social psychology and other disciplines, mainly in the direction of the fructification of empirical research rather than mere speculative theory.

It is evident from the above sketch that there is certainly some relationship between the general intellectual and cultural background and the methodological and theoretical aspects of religious studies in various countries and regions. At the same time there is a certain coherence in that the idea of a non-partisan, empirical, empathetic study of religion is widely understood and valued, not least by some who are not professionally engaged in carrying it out. Hence the identification of a core discipline along these lines does not appear to be intrinsically difficult in European perspective, even if it is recognised that other questions lead way beyond such an academic activity. Some aspects of the identification of this discipline remain as yet problematical, especially those related to deep-seated academic structures and traditions. In particular the relation between philological studies and field studies, whether sociological or anthropological (in the social sciences sense, not the theological or philosophical sense widely current in some countries) still remains to be resolved. That is to say, there is much informational and educational work to be done in explaining that there is no unbridgeable gulf between these two directions of enquiry. The study of religion must not allow itself to be boxed into one or other of these categories. Equally important is the need to maintain a clear grasp of the relation between the core discipline of the study of religion/s and attention to other, further questions of a philosophical, culture-critical or ideological kind. Confusion here not only threatens the study of religion with loss of identity as an autonomous discipline but also makes it, not easier, but harder to attend to the other questions properly.

Finally, "Europe" is neither small, nor uniform, nor closed, so that the danger of "Eurocentrism" may not be as great as the ethnocentrism of other parts of the world. Nevertheless it should be noted that reflections from other points of view would help to set a wider perspective. Pertinent for quite different reasons, for example, are studies of religion in East Asia and studies of religion in Latin America. The writer is well aware of the importance of this dimension, and it is not further developed here mainly because it will apparently be discussed by other conference participants.[15]

Desiderata for religious studies

It does not seem necessary to look beyond the historical and comparative study of religion in order to establish the fundamental unity of the discipline of religious studies [or the study of religions]. In principle any religion can be studied in this perspective. Moreover any religion can be studied by a person derived from any religious tradition, or none, provided that the attempt is made not to permit the assumption of his own belief system to distort the subject of enquiry. In so far as such assumptions, together with the question of the status of the truth-claims of the religion under study, are provisionally bracketed out, the procedure of the study of religion/s may be described as phenomenological. This term further implies that the religious system under consideration is regarded and characterised in the first instance in its own terms. To say this implies a certain requirement with respect to objectivity. There are those who say that objectivity cannot be achieved. This may, in the last analysis, be so. Nevertheless there is no excuse for willfully applying inappropriate, alien categories to a particular religious system. The attempt should at least be made to understand a given religious system in its own terms. Thereafter the way is open for further theoretical

---

15 For the present writer's own perspective in this regard see Pye 1973a and 1975, and, in press, a full translation of the relevant works of the early eighteenth century Japanese critical analyst of religious traditions, Tominaga Nakamoto [retrospective note: Pye 1990a]. The study of religion in Latin America is finding a strong focus in the work of the Comité Organizador Permanente de las Reuniones Latinoamericanas sobre Religión Popular, Identidad y Etnociencia, based in Mexico, with proceedings published in various places, for example in *La Palabra y el Hombre* (Revista de la Universidad Veracruzana) New Series, Oct.-Dec. 1988. Needless to say, a vast bibliography could be assembled in this field, just as in East Asia, which would no doubt demonstrate special points of view in methodology and theory. At the same time, in spite of vast geographical and cultural distance, a theory of, say, syncretism, should seek to be coherently applicable both in East Asia (in China, for example, with respect to which the word has often been used) and in Latin America, not to mention elsewhere.

elaboration which may go beyond the self-understanding of a particular set of believers. Such theoretical elaboration is a natural intellectual complement to the initial act of understanding. It will take account of the explanatory thrust of the social sciences, and other forms of critically charged investigation including straightforward issues of historical investigation, even to the extent that a tension will be set up with the self-understanding of the believers. This will have little meaning however unless the latter is first reliably established. In this way the study of religion attains a certain coherence without there being any necessity to posit a single type of religious experience which would somehow provide a philosophical base for all specific religions. Here too lies the basis for overcoming the gulf between philological study and fieldwork. Research based on texts which are in principle historical documents, even if recent, must take into consideration, in so far as we are speaking of the study of religion, those persons, at any one time or place, for whom the text is presumed to have had a meaning. Every text has a *Sitz im Leben*, or many. Fieldwork on the other hand has its own philology, even when oral statements or observed rituals take the place of texts.[16]

These rather dry remarks are not meant to imply an underestimation of the hermeneutical process which is involved in the elucidation of anything. The student of religion/s must of course appreciate that there is a subtle relationship between his previous formation and personal state of being and that which he is seeking to observe and understand. However the learnable ability to understand various things should not be so heavily intellectualised that the process of understanding is itself thereby inhibited from taking its course. Understanding a religion is like swimming or riding a bicycle. If one only considers presumed problems one will sink or fall off. At the same time some people can swim or ride a bicycle more effectively and skillfully than others.

This view of the fundamental form of the study of religion/s excludes two alternative models which might seem attractive to some sponsors of religious studies programs. One excluded model is the market stall approach. According to this, representatives of various religions are hired to hawk their wares on the university campus; the students work out their own personal philosophy of religion in order to make their choice. Such an approach does not amount to an academic discipline. At the same time a well balanced program of religious studies can

---

16 Cf. the writer's "Philology and fieldwork in the study of Japanese religion" (Pye 1990b) [re-edited above at 1.4].

allow space for academically sophisticated informants from particular traditions. The other excluded model is the dialogue model. According to this the personal religious standpoint is consciously used as a basis for elucidating the standpoint of another, – who may or may not be present on the campus. Since this elevates into a principle the formulation of questions or interpretative lines or thought which may not arise naturally within the system under consideration, the principles set forth above are clearly compromised.

It was necessary to make the above elementary points before proceeding to a few other desiderata which arise in other ways. If the fundamental unity of religious studies can be institutionally maintained and consolidated in the terms indicated above, and as far as possible in various countries on various continents, then it is certainly desirable to encourage other features on that basis. Here three main strands may be identified which may be thought to be of intellectual and educational importance.

First, it may be argued, where else but in the university context can advanced consideration be given to the truth claims inherent in if not explicitly advanced by various religions? This implies the cultivation of a critical philosophy of religion component in religious studies, broadly conceived, which takes account of the diversity of religion and is not restricted to the theistic traditions. Second, humankind is aware of so many pressing problems in the contemporary world that it would be quite irresponsible not to take some of these under consideration in their relation to religion. Obvious examples are questions of racial discrimination, war and peace and related conflict issues, demographic questions (population control, immigration issues etc.), gender discrimination and, at present of overwhelming importance, the future of the planetary environment. Third, within the range of historical and contemporary religious phenomena, it is culturally desirable to pay particular attention to selected sectors or themes which are particularly prone to being misunderstood in current circumstances Without following any and every popular whim or trend, it is surely reasonable to pay particular attention to Shi'ite Islam, Asian religions in the western world, North American indigenous religion, the position of religion in China or the Soviet Union, or interactions between African traditional religion, Christianity and Islam, to name but a few examples. Such special themes of great contemporary interest should be pursued however in the realisation that at another time other themes may assume prominence. Moreover a balanced overall perspective in the history of religions should always be maintained. This means that non-fashionable areas should not be allowed to lapse into obscurity.

Each of these three strands presupposes the previously mentioned identity of the study of religion/s. Without it, arbitrariness and distortion will rule. If it is maintained the integration of the discipline in European perspective can be further strengthened, while taking natural contemporary interests into account, and partnership throughout the world would seem to be entirely feasible.

APPENDIX

Text agreed by participants at the special IAHR conference organized by the Polish Society for the Study of Religions in 1989:

> "A conference was held at Jablonna, Warsaw (5–9 September 1989) under the sponsorship of the Polish Society for the Study of Religions, the Institute for the Philosophy and Sociology of the Polish Academy of Sciences and the International Association for the History of Religions, with the title 'Studies on Religion in the Context of the Social Sciences: Methodological Relations.' In the conference conclusion it was agreed by the participants that some advance had been made in the discussion of methodological issues in the study of religion. A convergence of opinion became apparent with regard to the nature of 'history' that permits reconceiving the history of religions as a human and cultural science. There was also agreement that such a reconceived study of religion would understand 'religion' as a reality that interconnects social activities both implicitly and explicitly. Of significance in this respect was a shift in attention to the meaning of religion in social interaction. There was general agreement that analyzing social processes which are correlative with religious phenomena would require the evaluation and use of innovative social theories and models as well as those from cognate disciplines. Whether such a methodological orientation will prove fruitful must be judged in the context of future research." (Tyloch 1990: 8)

Bibliographical references

Alekseev, N.A. 1984. *Samanizm Tyurkoyazycnych Narodov Sibiri* .Novosibirsk. German translation 1987. *Schamanismus der Türken Sibiriens. Versuch einer vergleichenden arealen Untersuchung*. Hamburg (Schletzer).

Antes, Peter 1985. *Christentum – eine Einführung*. Stuttgart (Kohlhammer).

Bianchi, Ugo (ed.) 1986. *Transition Rites. Cosmic, Social and Individual Order*. Rome ("L'Erma" di Bretschneider).

De Montclos, Xavier 1988. *Histoire religieuse de la France* (Que sais-je? 2428). Paris (Presses Universitaires de France).

Elsas, Christoph 1988. "Religionskritik und Religionsbegründung; Religionswissenschaftliche Diskussion am Beispiel christlicher Offenbarungstradition und Mystik" in: Zinser 1988: 197–215.

Gaus, Günter 1983. *Wo Deutschland liegt. Eine Ortsbestimmung.* Hamburg (Hoffmann und Campe)

Holm, Nils G. 1978. *Pingströrelsen.En religionsvetenskapelig studie av pingströrelsen i Svenskfinland.* Åbo (Åbo Akademi Foundation 31).

– 1979. *Mystik och_Intensiva Upplevelser.* Åbo (Åbo Akademi Foundation 51).

– 1987. *Scandinavian Psychology of Religion* (Religionsvetenskapliga skrifter 15), Åbo (Åbo Akademi).

Kippenberg, Hans G. and Luchesi, Brigitte (eds.) 1991. *Religionswissenschaft und Kulturkritik.* Marburg (Diagonal-Verlag).

Pye, Michael 1972a. *Comparative Religion. An Introduction through Source Materials.* Newton Abbot, England (David and Charles) and New York (Harper and Row).

– 1973a. "Aufklärung and religion in Europe and Japan" in: *Religious Studies* 9: 201–217.

– 1975. "Japanese studies of religion" in: *Religion* (Special Congress Issue 1975): 55–72.

– 1982a. "The study of religion as an autonomous discipline" in: *Religion* 12: 67–76.

– 1983. "The significance of the Japanese intellectual tradition for the history of religions" in: Slater, Peter and Wiebe Donald. (eds.)*Traditions in Contact and Change, Selected Proceedings of the Fourteenth Congress of the International Association for the History of Religions.* Waterloo Ontario (Wilfrid Laurier): 565–77.

– 1990a. (trans.) *Emerging from Meditation (Tominaga Nakamoto).* London (Duckworth) and Honolulu (University of Hawaii Press).

– 1990b. "Philology and fieldwork in the study of Japanese religion" in: Tyloch 1990: 146–59.

Raveri, Massimo 1984. *Itinerari nel Sacro, l'Esperienza Religiosa Giapponese.*
– Venice (Libreria Editrice Cafoscarina).

Tyloch, Witold (ed.) 1984. *Current Progress in the Methodology of the Science of Religions.* Warsaw (Polish Scientific Publishers/Państwowe Wydawnictwo Naukowe).

– 1990. *Studies on Religions in the Context of Social Sciences. Methodological and Theoretical Relations,* Warsaw (Polish Society for the Study of Religions/ Polskie Towarzystwo Religioznawcze).

Von Eckhardt, Hans 1947. *Russisches Christentum.* München (Piper).

Zinser, Hartmut (ed.) 1988. *Religionswissenschaft: eine Einführung.* Berlin (Dietrich Reimer).

This paper was first published as "Religious studies in Europe: structures and desiderata" in: Klaus K. Klostermaier and Larry W. Hurtado (eds.),

Religious Studies: Issues, Prospects and Proposals, Atlanta, Georgia (Scholars Press) 1991: 39–55.

3.3 Intercultural Strategies and the International Association for the History of Religions

This paper was presented as the introductory address at the regional conference of the International Association for the History of Religions (IAHR) at Harare, Zimbabwe, in 1992, and was first published in 1996.

International and intercultural

The rather long title of this short paper contains the two words "international" and "intercultural", and in short my argument is that the International Association for the History of Religions requires not only an international perspective but also an intercultural one. This may sound simple and easy enough to friendly and open-minded people. Yet it contains an important requirement for the organization of international relationships in scholarship which is not always easy to realize. While thinking about what is happening at the level of practical organization, about which I shall give at least a few details, it is important to reflect also on the assumptions which influence our work, sometimes leading to distortions, sometimes guiding it for the good development of the subject.

The International Association for the History of Religions (usually known as the IAHR) has consisted, since its formal inception in 1950, of a number of affiliated national associations. Having this character, it is also able to be affiliated in turn to the International Council for Philosophy and the Humanities (usually abbreviated as CIPSH, from the French version of the name), which is an agency of UNESCO. This latter body meets once every two years, and the next meeting will be taking place here at Harare in a few days' time. In fact it was as a result of a contact made at the last assembly of CIPSH that the planning of this regional conference of the IAHR was set specifically in motion.[1] When

1 This contact was between Mr. David Kaulem of the University of Zimbabwe and myself. The arrangements were further developed (excellently) by Dr. Mandivenga and Dr. Cox in Harare and by Dr. Platvoet and Prof. Hackett on behalf of the IAHR. Others have of course also contributed, both from Africa and from further

a Zimbabwean also joked in a more general conversation "We treat our whites very well", it was clear that the complexities of such a conference would be both well understood and well managed in this context.

As we all know, this is the first regional conference of the IAHR to be held in the whole of Africa, ever. You will perhaps excuse me for proudly linking this event with the fact that this year has also seen the first regional conference of the IAHR to be held in China, ever; and that was only the second IAHR conference in the whole of Asia, ever. The Beijing conference also owes a great deal to the CIPSH, for without the CIPSH-funded participation of Chinese scholars at the major congresses held at Lancaster (1975), Winnipeg (1980), Sydney (1985) and Rome (1990), it would not have been conceivable. The CIPSH also funded IAHR attendance at a crucial meeting in Mexico in 1990, which created the basis for the proposal to hold the XVII quinquennial congress in Mexico City in 1995. The XVII Congress will be the first IAHR conference to be held in Latin America, ever. These events represent an unprecedented regional diversification of the IAHR. It is here that the difference between "international" and "intercultural" begins to bite. We are seeing developments which mean more than simply that some further countries are added to the list of affiliated associations.

There were in fact several new affiliations at the last General Assembly [Rome 1990] and they were indeed important ones. There will probably be more at the next General Assembly in Mexico. Extension of this kind is of course most welcome, although the effect on the practical management of IAHR business should not be underestimated. Communications become more complex. The International Committee becomes larger. More people would like their conferences to be called IAHR conferences, though at present the limit is normally one per year between the major congresses. The funds for sponsoring those who keep the lines of communication open, already insufficient, become hopelessly overstretched.[2] In spite of the difficulties, however, goodwill breeds more goodwill, and so the positive developments continue. All of this leads to new patterns of interaction between scholars in

afield. Background perspective was also given under the guidance of Dr. Jan Platvoet through the liaison process set in motion by the International Committee of the IAHR at its conference in Marburg, 1988 (cf. Pye 1989a, 16).

2 The secretariat of the IAHR works on the proverbial shoestring, and current secretarial assistance at Lancaster University (England) is gratefully appreciated.

our field. In this way the *international* development may, and probably should, lead to an *intercultural* development in the study of religion.

Intercultural work and methodological independence

The *intercultural* development of the IAHR demands more than a straightforward, incremental accretion of new associations. It demands thought. Above all it demands reflection about the deep assumptions which influence our view of religion. Now we all know that "religion" is a European and consequently a "western" word, and that we should not heedlessly inflict it on cultures where mental and social patterns have run differently for many centuries. People say, for example, that there is no such thing as religion by itself, separated from the rest of life, in the Islamic world, or that Hinduism is not so much a "religion" as a "way of life," or that Buddhism and Confucianism (each very different from each other) are not really religions at all, rather a kind of spiritual path or moral philosophy respectively. I do not want to pursue these arguments here. I would assert however that the term "religions" in the name of the International Association for the History of Religions (IAHR) is certainly not wedded to a limiting view of the nature of religion. The "history of religions" as pursued by specialists from many countries has in fact usually taken a very wide view of the phenomena to be considered.

To take a naive limiting view of the field would simply be bad scholarship. To adopt a limited view of religion intentionally, on the basis of a normative judgment about what is to count as true religion, or as good religion, would be to adopt a confessional standpoint. This however is inimical to good scholarship in the "history of religions," except in so far as it can be temporarily disregarded for the purposes of enquiry. This point has been argued many times before, and indeed there seems to be wide agreement about it in IAHR circles. However here I wish to make the link with organizational strategies, as follows. *The intercultural extension of the work of the IAHR demands not less, but more clarity about its independence from specific religious standpoints.*

Methodological independence from specific religious standpoints, on the other hand, does not require that those who participate in IAHR activities should themselves personally be irreligious in their lives as a whole. We all know that there are excellent specialists in the study of religion who in their personal lives have a sincere faith, whether in the religion which they mainly study or indeed in the religion of their family or community. Nor does methodological independence require that they should normally work in institutional contexts which lack all relation to the contextual religious tradition of their country.

These are subtle matters but they are not insoluble riddles. To give an example, there are in Turkey today ten universities which have faculties of Theology, that is, Muslim Theology. The curriculum and research activities of these ten faculties follow a common pattern, and among the various subjects pursued, which are determined on the basis of Islamic assumptions, there is included the field of comparative religion. Those who work there in the field of comparative religion know that the wider institutional context is defined by Islam, and they also know that the subject-matter into which they research is diverse, and largely non-Islamic. There is no reason why such researchers should not be Muslims, even devout Muslims. The question is simply, can and do they achieve a clear and balanced view of that which they study? My impression is that they do.

In practice this is often easier with regard to religions other than that of one's own dominant tradition; that is, when the attempt is fairly made. The reason for this is obvious. The study of religion within one's own dominant tradition is more likely to lead into the polemical clash of theological viewpoints. This is evident in all the main streams of the theistic tradition, Judaism, Christianity and Islam alike. However it is not intrinsically connected with theism, in spite of the effects of the idea that God is "a jealous God." The phenomenon is not unknown elsewhere, for example in Buddhist studies where confessional allegiance often determines research activity. Yet here too, there is no insuperable problem for Buddhists who wish to study various religions which are not Buddhist. It is simply a question of reflecting clearly on methodological assumptions and intentions.

Thus participants in IAHR activities may be drawn from societies or institutions which are predominantly, for example, Buddhist, Christian or Muslim. There is no question of any kind of "purism" being applied here. Whether the research work which is carried out is good or mediocre, whether it is well balanced, informative and illuminating, or hopelessly biased and distorted, will show up at the conferences. The IAHR itself, not being a religious organization, is in principle neutral in these matters. It is commonly said that neutrality can never be achieved, and this may be so, in organizations as well as in individuals. But it is a question of intention, and this why it may be said that the IAHR is in principle neutral. We appeal to the neutrality of the organization in order to promote the possibility of our cooperative work, both internationally and interculturally.

The neutrality of the IAHR does not mean, on the other hand, that it is inimical to religion. The IAHR may be described accurately as non-religious, but not as irreligious. Nor does it mean that religious bodies may not support it, for example financially, with grants for travel and conference costs, or by giving hospitality to conference participants, especially when they come from countries with economic difficulties. Any such support can and will be most gratefully received. The only proviso is that the procedural neutrality of the IAHR be respected. However there should be no difficulty in reaching an understanding about this with the leading religious and cultural authorities of a country in which a particular conference is held. In this connection the affiliation to CIPSH is also helpful, for it is clear that UNESCO agencies are not supposed to be doing the work of any one religion over against another. This is true even though complex relations are maintained with a wide variety of other organizations from around the world. There is no question of some kind of suicidal "purism" on the part of the IAHR as is sometimes supposed.

There is therefore no intrinsic difficulty about the supportive sponsorship of IAHR conferences by religious bodies. Naturally some care needs to be taken in this regard. It would not be at all desirable for the IAHR to be taken over by a particular religious body. In any particular region of the world, some sympathetic support by the dominant religious community, Islamic, Christian, or other, would seem to be quite appropriate. It will be understood that in another region cordial relations will also be maintained where possible with the representatives of a different tradition. In the case of smaller groups active in inter-religious work it is preferable for funds to be derived from *at least two different religious bodies* in cooperation. This would be the perfect way to show that the procedural neutrality of the IAHR is respected. While full courtesy and respect should be a matter of course, there can be no question of the international, academic cooperation which is encouraged by the IAHR being distorted, not to mention dominated, even in appearance, by the religious program of one particular group. But those who wish well for the work of the IAHR will understand this from the start.

It is well known that some religious bodies themselves like to fund conferences on religious subjects. In this regard it may be pointed out that, as far as my information goes, such conferences have not usually been about the history of religions or the comparative and theoretical study of religion which goes with it. Rather they have addressed questions of interreligious dialogue or directly theological questions such as "God."[3] While these matters are interesting in themselves and of great importance to many people, they may be regarded as providing indirect rather than direct subject-matter for the IAHR. However there is no need for an exaggerated "purism" on the part of the IAHR in this regard. It would surely be appreciated if religious bodies with a sincere interest in the relations between peoples and between religions would cooperate in sponsoring studies in the real history of religions.

There is of course the difficulty, with which researchers are sometimes confronted, that the representatives of religions do not always wish to be informed about the real history of religions. This arises simply because not all religious claims can stand in an equal relationship to the factuality of cultural and social history. This is well known to most of those who participate in the conferences of the IAHR, but not understood by many religious believers. Again, this does not mean that the IAHR is an irreligious body. Moreover most researchers into religion, while being interested in facts, will respect the sensitivities of religious people, which themselves amount to facts of great interest.

It is necessary to be as clear as possible about such matters at an *international*, organizational level in order to create the forum which is needed for the *intercultural* exploration of religion.

The very shape of religion

The study of religion as a historical, cultural and social phenomenon takes on a sharp new interest when we realize, through serious attempts at academic cooperation, that deep assumptions about the very shape of

3 Retrospective note: this is a reference to one of the numerous conferences on religious subjects paid for by the Unification Church during the period when this paper was written, participation at which had become something of an issue among scholars of religion. The writer's own position was (and is) to avoid participation in unilaterally sponsored religious conferences except in so far as an authentic research interest was also at stake.

religion diverge considerably from culture to culture. Thus Chinese, European and Latin American assumptions about what the field of investigation is, and what questions are to be asked about it, are not identical. The present conference in Zimbabwe will surely play an important role both in making explicit and theorizing about African perspectives on these matters.

It is hardly for me to expatiate on what these African perspectives might be, surrounded as I am by African and non-African experts. However I do hope that a mere contrapuntalism between African and Euro-American standpoints can be avoided. For this reason I should like to illustrate the underlying question by looking abroad to China and to Latin America, however briefly. I will then conclude with a few thoughts and questions addressed to the African situation.

In China one of the long-running assumptions about religions is that they are plural and yet somehow related to each other. This assumption has been expressed for many centuries in the phrase "three teachings" (*sān-jiào*). Now in some cases this phrase has been used to express a religious position which might otherwise be called, in European vocabulary, "synthesis." It would also be rather like the assertion of religious "pluralism" as a good thing, which is the way that some people have used the word pluralism lately, though it would be better to keep "pluralism" simply to refer to a situation in which there is more than one religion. To return to China, people have often felt that the "three teachings," namely Confucianism, Daoism and Buddhism, are facets of a single harmonious truth. Hence the further succint expression "the three teachings are one," which has found favour at various times. Note however that there have been different versions of "three teachings" theory, that is, there have been different ways of viewing the relationships between the three major traditions in China, some leaning more to Confucianism as the final meaning, for example. Thus the phrase "three teachings" suggests something more than a religious position as such. Rather it has been used to indicate the very parameters of discussion about religion in China. This may be seen clearly from its use in the title of a short treatise ascribed to the first ruler of the Ming dynasty, namely the "Treatise on the three religions." [For further discussion cf. 2.4 in the present volume.] In fact "three teachings" does not exhaust the parameters of discussion because apart from the three major traditions mentioned, Chinese thinkers and administrators have also attended to the nature and function of state religion on one hand, and of various minority sects on the other hand, the latter usually being regarded as obtrusive and troublesome.

It will be clear from this that the shape of the matters normally taken into account when religion is considered in China is simply not the same as it has been in Europe. In the latter case the main assumptions about religion which have determined theoretical discussion have been set by Christianity in its Catholic and Protestant forms, by the dialectically related critique of and disaffection with religion, i. e. secularism in various forms, and more recently by the renewed activity of alternative religious forms, especially Asian-derived cults and New Age spirituality.

Now of course there has been much interaction in modern times between Chinese and Euro-American theory of religion, notably via the thought not only of Marx but also more recently of Weber. Yet even when western sociologists are adduced, the view of religion as seen within China may still have its own accentuation. Chen Zemin, for example, giving a paper at the recent IAHR regional conference in Beijing [1992], wrote on "The post-denominational unity of the Chinese protestant church". He made use of a typological schema listing ecclesia, denomination, established sect, sect, cult, and new religion, deriving from Weber and Troeltsch via Richard Niebuhr, Howard Becker, Liston Pope and Milton Yinger. At the same time he wrote:

> Religions are like trees. As they grow they bifurcate or trifurcate and branch out into a number of organized groups that bear some resemblance to, and preserve the identity with, the mother trunk, and yet keep on differentiating until at the end they tend to become something mutually exclusive or antagonistic to each other. Attempts at reunion often seem difficult, if not fruitless.[4]

Now this metaphor has its own force. Of course it refers to religious separation and conflict. But it does not speak only of schism and section. It implies firstly organic elaboration, and only later an articulation so profuse that unity can no longer be regained. This is not the place to review the details of church affairs in present-day China, which is

---

4 Chen Zemin (Nanjing Union Theological Seminary): "The post-denominational unity of the Chinese Protestant Church" in: Dai Kangsheng, Zhang Xinying and Pye, Michael (eds) *Religion and Modernisation in China, Proceedings of the Regional Conference of the International Association for the History of Religions held in Beijing, China, April 1992*, Cambridge (Roots and Branches) 1995: 239–45. Here: 239.

Chen Zemin's interest. But note that speaking later of the ideal of church unity in the Chinese context he goes on to say:

> We have learned to move carefully and slowly onward, and guard against hastiness, coercion, artificial uniformity, proselytism, and schismatic division. The cardinal virtue, the essence of Chinese culture, is 'peaceful unity of opposites.' We are endeavoring to achieve church unity by virtue of this virtue.[5]

This is a programmatic view on his part, and not an analytical observation; it follows the description and analysis of the details. However it is quoted here to show that the organic, integrative assumption underlying the tree metaphor, with which he began, is reinforced at the end and regarded as a Chinese way of viewing things.

Turning now to Latin America, we find a situation very different from China in that the dominant languages in which reflection about religious phenomena is largely carried on, are European-derived. The dominant religious tradition, but, as is well known, by no means the only one, is also European-derived. It may be admitted that some significant questions in the sphere of reflection about religion are akin to those familiar in Europe, e.g. the assessment of secularisation as a process of erosion against a dominant Catholic church. The debate over liberation theology, which is a question for inner-church polemics rather than for the external analyst, is less dramatically relevant in Europe but nevertheless easily understood. The religious studies specialist however, as observer and analyst, will notice a different set of parameters which determine the very field of study. Put most broadly, these relate to the political story of the conquest, the imposition of Catholicism, and the attempted subjugation and partial reassertion of previously existing religious life. The indigenous development and the incursion from without of new religions has of course complicated this relationship. For the observer and analyst this has resulted in a fascinating range of materials for research. Moreover, and this is the more important point in the present argument, Latin American investigators have a characteristic view of religion. This is formed partly by the materials: indigenous, catholic, new, and the mutual interactions between these. It is also formed by the two main intellectual approaches which have been brought to bear. One of these is Catholic theology, especially as directed towards missiological and pastoral questions. The other is social anthro-

---

5 Chen 1995: 243.

pology as directed towards both general questions of social change and in particular to study of the numerous minorities of Latin America, whether these be of indigenous, imported or mixed race.

The work of researchers coming from these two directions is interactive in varying degree. Indeed no intellectual anthropologist in Latin America can avoid some awareness of the bearing of Catholicism upon his field of study, and likewise the best Catholic researchers into their fields of interest tend to become anthropologists. The combustion produced by this interaction has led to the production of significant contributions to the study of religion. But what is the shape of the religion which thus becomes the object of study?

A fine case study of religion in the Peruvian Andes may be found in Manuel Marzal's work *La transformación religiosa peruana* (Marzal 1983), in a key chapter of which the formation and the overall characteristics of Andean religion are set out. The three main stages of formation according to Marzal are: the stage of intensive Christianization, the stage of struggle against idolatries, and the stage of the crystallization of Andean religion. For present purposes the dubious characterization of the second stage, doubtless so named by Marzal to capture the point of view of the Christianizing church in post-conquest times, will be overlooked. The main point is that present phenomena are the result of interaction between two systems which were in conflict. The "current Andean religious system" (el sistema religioso andino actual) is viewed under four numbered headings, namely: (1) Andean beliefs, (2) Andean rites, (3) the forms of religious organization, and (4) ethical norms. This in itself amounts to an interesting set of dimensions or aspects of religion; however it would lead too far afield to compare it with other attempts to define such.[6] Rather, I should like to draw attention to the sub-categories which Marzal provides in this case under beliefs and rites, namely, for beliefs, (a) the Andean pantheon, and (b) beliefs and myths, and for rites (a) rites of transition, and (b) festive rites. Even this summary typology of headings and sub-headings is instructive. The fact that "ethical norms" (las normas eticas) is given as one of four major categories is suggestive of the author's Catholic provenance, for it may be suspected that in the Andean religious system other subjective aspects are of comparable importance. By contrast Marzal's anthropological openness to his material is evidenced by the sub-categories adduced for beliefs and rites (see above), which are typical features of primal religion in that

6 Retrospective note: for further discussion see Pye 1994b: 51–75.

they relate specifically to a culturally defined community. Now it should not be overlooked that Marzal's work is immensely detailed and valuable, this particular book being complemented by many other published studies. The interesting point, for the present argument, is that the parameters of his theoretical summary as stated here, in both its diachronic and synchronic aspects, are defined by the historic tussle between a religion with universal claims and considerable power and the religious system of a specifically defined society which, though poor in resources, has turned out to be not without resilience. The resultant picture is not the religion of Europe, and not the religion of China.

The purpose of setting out these examples, however briefly, is to show that in actual studies carried out within a major region or continent, the shape of religion as viewed by perceptive specialists is affected by the major relevant historical determinants. This is a simple point, though it would appear that not all researchers are really aware of it. More often people seem to assume that the model prominent in their own region of the world is the normal state of affairs. This illusion is not necessarily the result of narrow-mindedness. Rather it occurs because the differences are blurred by structural similarities and historical overlaps which are themselves also real. Thus religious pluralism has been and is known in other countries as well as in China. The long-term interaction of intrusive and indigenous religious systems, including the production of new forms, is also known outside Latin America. To fail to recognise this would be to succumb to mere exoticism, sheer desire for difference. But the avoidance of exoticism should not leave our senses paralysed. The Chinese phenomenon is not the Latin American. The same may of course be argued for other parts of the world: Indonesia, India, the Middle East, and indeed Africa with its very significant internal variations. Though recognizable, the shape of religion is not the same everywhere. And the shape of religion in the place where it is frequently perceived has a strong influence on the researcher and subsequent theories.

Thus the intercultural challenge which arises through the increasing activities of the IAHR is that we should reflect with increasing care on those very simple, deep-seated models of religion which we tend to carry with us, influenced as they are by all the historical determinants which continue to exercise their force. They are not necessarily inappropriate, that is, with respect to those phenomena to which they specifically relate. Yet the comparison with neighbouring or even far-distant models may help us in the process of critical refinement. Traditional distortions may be corrected. New dimensions of religion may appear before our very eyes, which had previously been disregarded.

Does this relate also to Africa? Is there, for example, a special three-cornered relationship between Islam, Christianity and traditional religion from which there is no escape, even when we seek to elucidate and explain innovation and a more variegated pluralism? Are possession and prophecy the forms without which, in many regions of Africa, nothing moves? If not these, what is the deep-seated frame of reference, in all its simplicity, which informs the cultural insider's reflection on African religion? Or what are they? For Africa is many!

Bibliographical references

Chen, Zemin 1995. "The post-denominational unity of the Chinese Protestant Church" in: Dai, Zhang and Pye 1995: 239–45.

Dai Kangsheng, Zhang Xinying and Pye, Michael (eds) 1995. *Religion and Modernisation in China, Proceedings of the Regional Conference of the International Association for the History of Religions held in Beijing, China, April 1992.* Cambridge (Roots and Branches).

Marzal, Manuel 1983. *La transformacion religiosa peruana.* Lima: Pontificia Universidad Católica del Peru.

Pye, Michael 1989a. *Marburg Revisited: Institutions and Strategies in the Study of Religion.* Marburg, Marburg (Diagonal-Verlag).

– 1989b "Cultural and organizational perspectives in the study of religion", in Pye 1989b: 11–17.

– 1994b. "Religion: shape and shadow" in: *Numen* 41/1 (1994): 51–75.

This article was first published as "Intercultural strategies and the International Association for the History of Religions" in: Platvoet, Jan, Cox, James and Olupona, Jacob (eds.), *The Study of Religions in Africa. Past, Present and Prospects*, Cambridge (Roots and Branches, distributed by Almqvist and Wiksell International) 1996: 37–45.

3.4 Memories of the Future: Looking Back and Looking Forward in the History of Religions

This article is the text of an opening address held on the occasion of the 18th World Congress of the International Association for the History of Religions (IAHR) in Durban, South Africa, August 2000.

Selecting the past and forming the future

It is well known that different people remember the past in different ways and that they use their selective memory to organise their understanding of the present and their intentions for the future. We have all heard of the invention of tradition and the invention of history. Such a process occurs for individuals and families, for small-scale societies, for organisations within complex societies, for nations, for communities of nations, and for cross-national organisations of many kinds. The concept is also relevant for the International Association for the History of Religions (IAHR), which this year is celebrating its 100th anniversary as a congress tradition and its 50th anniversary as a formal organisation with statutes. While in general there are some common threads to hold on to, such as the sequence of congresses and proceedings, our memories of the past can never be comprehensive. Yet, even though these are difficult to determine with complete accuracy in a manner which commands total assent on all sides, they will always be a significant factor in our understanding and creation of the future.

In recent years various colleagues have been considering the invention of our subject and the invention of our discipline in ever more detail, thereby positioning themselves with regard to an understanding of what they think these should be. While this is a sign of maturity in the history of any academic discipline, it is also, interestingly enough, analogous to the way in which "tradition" may be understood to function in the religious systems which we study. That is, "tradition" is not merely to be understood as an element which lies in the past or which is nostalgic of the past (as implied in some anthropological usage) but rather as synonymous with the very process of *transmission*, which implies the construction of present and future forms. For our discipline, and for the IAHR, the construction of the future requires taking informed, selective decisions about the nature of the past. It is not a question of constructing an artificial past which, in its simplicity, might stand in tension with a historian's critical account of the same events or period. Rather it is a construction of the past which, while historically serious and reliable, at the same time is consciously intended to feed the future. At this congress we are looking back, over one hundred years, but we are also looking forward. Where will the quinquennial congress be held in the year 2020, or 2035? And what will its programme be like? With this in mind I would like to recast our memories of the past as "memories of the future," a phrase intended as a metaphor in the style of science fiction, in which time-travelling is possible.

Let us reflect a little more on the ways in which the past is problematic, and disputed. The anthropologist Raymond Firth discovered this principle in Tikopia, where various different groups would claim descent from the ones who had originally colonised their home, later to be turned into revered ancestors. Or putting it another way, they would declare that the most important ancestors were really *their* ancestors rather than those of other inhabitants of the islands. Moreover we all know that powerful states like to promote an authoritative version of history as part of their state religion, or their civil religion. Such versions of history are "invented" through selection, and may include fictional elements as well. (Incidentally, I am by no means proposing that we include fictional elements in a new history of the IAHR!) The programmatic writing of history has been going on since the composition of the earliest known chronicles in the Ancient Near East and in China. The key elements are origins and legitimations, the glorification of achievements and the explanation of failures, as can be seen so clearly in the most widely known examples, namely the legends and chronicles of the Hebrew Bible. However, clever politicians in modern democratic states are just as interested in weaving their own versions of the past, especially the immediate past. This is the work of so-called "spin-doctors." In Britain for example the current government calls itself "New Labour" thus giving the impression, uncritically conveyed by politically correct media, that the previously existing Labour Party was just "old labour," which it would be folly to revive. It is just the same in religions. The Ahmadiyya movement, for example, claims that a new, secondary prophet enabled them to rediscover the true meaning of Islamic teaching and practice, with the result that Muslims in general do not regard the Ahmadiyyas as being Muslims at all. Everybody present at this congress will easily think of further examples from their own cultural context and specialist field of interest. Where do modern Mexicans come from? Where do today's South Africans come from? And how is the past to be presented to young people and to children? Who writes the history books? In Japan the history books have to be approved by the Ministry of Science and Education (Kagaku-monbushō), and as a result there have been long-running debates between the ministry and the professors who draft the texts, not to mention serious dissatisfaction on the part of Japan's neighbours. One thing that has been learned in post-war Germany is that not only good things have to be remembered, but also bad things, for which responsibility must be taken. This year (2000) has seen a new controversy about what form a Holocaust memorial should take in the reunified capital, Berlin. Since the specific factual documentation is already available at concentration camp locations and elsewhere, the conclusion reached was that the new monument should be a generalised abstract monument. Unfortunately it appears that countries have to lose wars, catastrophically, before they are forced to reflect really critically on their past. Countries which happen to win wars usually obscure their own misdeeds in the glow of victory. Thus, astonishingly for the critical mind, Alexander "the Great" and Julius Caesar, the conqueror who was made into a god, are even today presented in school history books with positive awe. Nor did I ever hear a North American regret the military acquisition of huge areas of Mexican territory. On the other hand even losses can be turned to good account in a nation's story, as with the Niños Heroes of Mexico who are presented as gallant martyrs.

In South Africa, the memory of sufferings in the first modern concentration camp, built by British forces, is kept alive at Die Nasionale Vrouemonument (the National Women's Monument) near Bloemfontein. This episode is not given much prominence in British history writing. Another story about the South African past is displayed in the Voortrekker Monument in Pretoria. This may seem very out-of-date in the new South Africa, especially among liberal whites, not to mention among the majority, and yet it is part of the history of the nation. There must be a serious question about how to preserve it and how to present it. History is full of examples where monuments have been purposely destroyed because they told what came to be regarded as the wrong story. Hundreds if not thousands of Lenin statues have recently been overturned and smashed in Eastern Europe, for example. But is this always the right way forward? I would suggest that the Voortrekker Monument, which is still standing, deserves a different fate. It can provide a new function in the future memory of South Africa, that is, as part of the total story which now has to be retold in new ways.

What has all this got to do with the history of religions? Quite a lot. For one thing most of the examples I have given are intertwined in some way with aspects of religion, religious myth, state religion, civil religion, and so on. But more importantly, they illustrate the dynamics which run through our own professional debates about who we are, where we are, and where we are going. An earlier draft title for this lecture was "disputing the past", but a colleague suggested that it might sound too argumentative. Rather, we should be integrative and holistic, it was suggested. In general, I agree with this, so I changed the title. Nevertheless, the very existence of other organisations for academic activities relating to religion, and of other congress traditions, means that we must, with all due courtesy and accuracy, clearly define the past and thereby dispute it, or (to use an ideologically popular word of our day) "contest" it. My title "memories of the future" may sound paradoxical. It is intended to. Our memories determine our future. What is our future? What is the future of the IAHR? It is up to us, as participants in the academic process which the IAHR represents, to claim the past, with all due dispute, and in so doing to define our present and our future.

Dynamic times for the IAHR

I use the word "process" advisedly, because in recent years the IAHR truly has seen some dynamic developments. This means that the point from which we now define the past, and thereby the future, has itself moved forward dramatically. We are holding our major congress in South Africa just now, in Kwazulu-Natal, though some decades ago this would probably have seemed inconceivable. On the other hand the *idea* has been around for some time, and was probably first advanced by one of our honorary life members, Ninian Smart. The first IAHR meeting of any kind to be held on the continent of Africa was the regional conference staged at Harare in 1992, during which the African

Association for the Study of Religions was founded.[1] Looking at the African presence of the IAHR from today's perspective it is a matter of great satisfaction that the work of this African regional association has developed step by step. For example, a most successful regional conference was also held at Nairobi in 1999. Participation in the IAHR by scholars from Africa has therefore now become normal, in a sense which in earlier decades it was not. The continuing economic difficulties in almost all parts of the continent should of course not be underestimated. However the most recent issue of the bibliographical journal *Science of Religion* shows a good sprinkling of articles by African scholars and by other scholars about African subjects.

To give another example, I remember being told (at that time as General Secretary of the IAHR) that it would be politically impossible to hold a regional conference on religion in the People's Republic of China. But the IAHR managed to achieve just this, in 1992, thanks to the careful cooperation of the Institute for the Study of World Religions with which relations had been nurtured over many years. The select proceedings were published both in Chinese, in China itself, and in an English edition which is still available.[2] Turning elsewhere, people do think *now* that it is possible to hold IAHR conferences in the countries of eastern Europe. However, the IAHR had already held small but significant conferences in Poland in 1979 and again in 1989, when it was still widely held in some quarters to be impossible or at best undesirable. Just recently, in 1999, a special IAHR conference was held in Brno, Czech Republic, at which the effects of the Cold War on the study of religions in both East and West were appraised. Those who read the proceedings, which are due to appear shortly,[3] will discover that the realities behind that extended period of ideological history were rather complex. But even after the end of the Cold War, there is still a question about who writes the history, and from what point of view. In my own contribution to the Brno volume I argue that it is *not* appropriate to write the history of the study of religions during the Cold War period from a point of view which is itself defined by the Cold War. No doubt this observation will be disputed by others.

1 Cf. the proceedings: Platvoet, Cox and Olupona 1996.

2 Cf. the proceedings: Dai, Zhang and Pye 1995. In Chinese translation a number of contributions appeared in the journal *Shijie Zongjiao Ziliao* 世界宗教资料 (1992).

3 Since published in Doležalová, Martin and Papoušek 2001.

However it seems to me that a *post*-cold-war perspective (as in "post-colonialism," to which I will be referring shortly) is required for a correct assessment of that period. That does not mean a point of view which is merely chronologically later than the end of communism in Eastern Europe, but rather one which has advanced *intellectually* beyond the positions of the Cold War which were so dominant on both sides at the time. As a matter of fact, such an intellectual perspective was possible *before* the political end of the Cold War, but this perception was limited to a rather small number of critical spirits.

Post-colonialism and missiology

The currently topical "post-colonial" critique of the study of religions is of course important in principle, and needs to be thought about along similar lines. The term "post-colonial" has arisen on the back of the so-called "orientalism" debate. However, this debate has largely run its course. After all, hardly anybody would nowadays see themselves as "orientalists" in the sense in which "orientalism" is nowadays criticised. (At this point a call for orientalists to "put their hands up" showed that there were none present in the hall.) I regard the somewhat fashionable call for post-colonial studies in the history of religions, or the study of religions, in much the same way. After all, where are the colonialists nowadays? (A call for colonialists to "put their hands up" was answered by just one brave person in the hall, who thereby kindly illustrated the point.) In my own head, though British, I have been a post-colonialist since my adolescence in the nineteen-fifties. And I do not imagine myself to be unique in this respect. However, the idea of "post-colonialism" seems to have arrived rather late in some quarters. The truly "colonialist" contributions to the study of religion were made many decades ago A classic case, which I have used for many years in teaching about the history of our subject, is provided by the detailed descriptions of Tibetan religion which were, at least in part, a by-product of the Anglo-Russian tussle for influence in Central Asia, culminating in the so-called "Younghusband expedition" from Darjeeling to Lhasa in 1904.

The question of "post-colonialism" may well appear differently from the point of view of those whose countries were once colonised by outsiders and which now look back on an increasingly long period of independence. A need may be perceived in this perspective to develop or prove *intellectual* independence to accompany political independence. Indeed, it might seem desirable to seek freedom from the dominance of a perceived, *neo*-colonialist, western intellectualism, and I would like to think that a genuinely international organisation such as the IAHR may be of assistance in this regard, through its varied conference programme which honours difference while maintaining the lines of academic or "scientific" communication between various cultural regions of the world. The real danger is therefore not so much colonialism, to be countered by post-colonialist reflection, but *neo*-colonialism which ought to be countered intellectually by post-neo-colonialism on the part of all concerned.

In this wide picture, complex and fascinating, but too vast to review comprehensively here, the field contributions of missionaries have also played a major role in the development of the history of religions. In some cases, as Eric Sharpe has argued, missionary writers recognised the need for independent reflection on what they observed and therefore sought to do justice to the non-theological criteria of the science of religion. In general however, understandably, a theological or missiological motivation provided the overall orientation. Even today there remains a significant hangover effect in writing which understands itself to be "missiological." Such writing frequently fails, or does not even seek to free itself from programmatic motivations in the analysis, for example, of acculturation processes or the assessment of innovative religious movements. Those who regularly read publications about religious situations in various parts of sub-Saharan Africa will no doubt understand this point clearly. The influence of missiological programmes is still quite strong in this context. Thus, in so far as "missiology" may wish to maintain its own criteria and legitimation, it may be necessary to distinguish it at times from the study of religions as promoted by the IAHR.

The distinctive identity of the IAHR

These are examples of areas where the IAHR, as an organisation and as a process, needs to be clear about its past and its future. Its programmes should of course be open, tolerant, flexible, and responsive to the issues of the times, as I believe the programme here in Durban is, thanks to the vision of Rosalind Hackett and all those who have contributed to it. On the other hand, now and in the future, the programs of the IAHR should not simply be identified or confused with different agendas, whether missiological, dialogical, pastoral or politically topical such as the human rights discussion. I would not like to be misunderstood here. It is of course legitimate to correlate the study of religions with all kinds of other questions, but the IAHR, according to its statutes, stands for and promotes the study of religions as such.

This point was cleared up in principle during the debates at the 10th Congress which was held in Marburg, Germany, in 1960. As is now well-documented, Zwi Werblowsky and others were in debate with Friedrich Heiler about the aims of the IAHR. The latter wished to see it as part of a larger programme of inter-religious understanding in which Christianity would play a dominant role. Just recently I came across an interesting paper in the archives in Marburg, namely the programme of an "ecumenical service" conducted by Heiler himself "on the occasion of the opening of the 10th international congress for the history of religions," with the assistance of Father Thomas of the Syrian Orthodox Church of South India, Professor Ohata of Tokyo and Professor Philippidis of Athens. To give a demonstration of internationality, the closing hymn is printed in German, English and Swedish, which are, it must be said, a rather cosy family of languages. Moreover the contents of the service were exclusively western and Christian. Does it not now seem astonishing that Heiler conceived the idea of celebrating the opening of an IAHR congress with a religious service? Most of those involved in the work of the IAHR nowadays agree that the distinction between studying religions and being religious not only is important, but that it can in fact be maintained. Admittedly this was contested in 1960, and it is not uncommon to hear it disputed by persons not mainly concerned with the study of religions even today. I would like to admit therefore, and indeed I would like to claim, that my version of the history is presented from the independent perspective which is now dominant within the IAHR. I believe that the IAHR should stay with this perspective in the future, and strengthen it. In so doing it has a unique contribution to make by standing for a specific academic discipline in a world-wide context.

Most will be aware that not all academics in the world agree with this approach to the identification of a discipline. Some claim that all such distinctions are fluid and hence superfluous. Whatever may have been the merits of the post-modernist movement, for example, which has now probably almost run its course, one of its most insidious side-effects was to insist that since all positions are negotiable or contestable, all are of more or less equal validity in any context. Now if this really were to be so we might as well close down the IAHR right now. This is because it is quite clear that the IAHR, over the long term, has developed a certain corporate identity. However open and flexible this association rightly is, its identity is defined above all by the intention to study and analyse the religions of the world in their history and in their contemporary forms, without being beholden to any particular religious viewpoint or programme. Though not formulated in exactly these terms, this identity and intention will be found in Article 1 of the IAHR constitution. Thus I am providing a reading of Article 1 in the light of the overall history of the congresses since 1900 and the life of the organisation since 1950. There is no doubt that the main trend in this history, starting with the very first congress in Paris, has been to explore the history of religions *without* taking a religious perspective on it. In this respect the congresses themselves contributed to the gradually continuing emergence of the study of religions as an independent discipline.

Contesting the history of the study of religions

It will be clear by now that I share with various colleagues (Casadio, Despland, Kippenberg, McCutcheon, Michaels, Preus, Rudolph, Sharpe and Waardenburg, to name but a few) a certain interest in the *history* of our discipline. I think these and other colleagues would all agree that this history should be contested, or even disputed. Each one has particular points to make about chosen strands, while some of us are even drawing attention to hitherto unnoticed components, thus demanding that the shape of the past be reconsidered. At the present time, so it seems to me, there is no single satisfactory overall picture of this history.

For the moment I would just like to illustrate the matter very simply by displaying the contents page of a textbook recently published in Germany under the editorship of Axel Michaels, a colleague in Heidelberg. The title is *Klassiker der Religionswissenschaft* (München 1997) and it is indeed an excellent textbook. But who are the "classic" figures who are treated in it? I hasten to say that you have to be dead to qualify. Of course, a textbook with contributions about living pandits would look rather different. Admittedly the list of *authors* alone, that is, those writing about the proposed classical figures, might be thought to give some idea of what our discipline is like today. However, the spectrum of interests is not comprehensive and other multi-authored works would have to bring in interesting new elements such as the harvest of cognitive science. But, returning to the so-called classical figures, is Sigmund Freud really an early *Religionswissenschaftler?* Or Aby Warburg? To face up to the question, in spite of the widespread interest of these figures, I myself would think that they are not. No doubt everybody would make up a different list of those who should be included. For example, I would like to see William James, Ernst Troeltsch and Ernest Renan included. Surely it is not for nothing that the French affiliate to the IAHR is called Société Ernest Renan! And might there not be some candidates from outside Europe and America? While using this textbook recently in a class, I invited my students to consider whether each of the famous intellects treated should be left in, or left out. There was a strong tendency to include those who also count as founding figures of the social sciences such as Durkheim, Van Gennep and Weber. Jung remained, with a question mark, and the clear candidates for exclusion were Freud, Warburg, and last but not least, Rudolf Otto! I hasten to say that while the students were correct in perceiving the strong theological orientation in Otto's writings, which today would be regarded as a severe distortion in the study of religions, I myself would keep him in on historical grounds. Fortunately the essay about him by Gregory Alles puts the record straight with fine clarity. It is interesting to compare Axel Michael's list of "classic" figures with a list of those who receive detailed treatment in Eric Sharpe's well-known *Comparative Religion. A History* (Sharpe 1975). This is not to criticise either of these excellent works as such, but the differences are instructive. In brief, the latter makes no mention at all of Aby Warburg or Victor Turner and only brief mention of Marcel Mauss and Arnold van Gennep, who are all treated by Michaels. On the other hand the following figures not included by the latter receive relatively detailed attention by Sharpe: J. Baillie, S. G. F. Brandon, J. N. Farquhar, E. R. Goodenough, W. James, A. Lang, J. H. Leuba, L. Lévy-Bruhl, J. Lubbock, J. F. M'Lennan, R. Pettazzoni, J. B. Pratt, S. Radhakrishnan, H. Spencer and E. D. Starbuck.

Yet all the time there is much more to this matter than agreeing, or failing to agree, on a collection of founder figures. Are the roots of our discipline to be found in the orientalism, the evolutionism and the armchair anthropology of the nineteenth century? Or are they to be found in the eighteenth century Enlightenment, now unjustly maligned by post-modernists? Or should we look earlier, in the deism of the seventeenth century, or perhaps again later, in romanticism? Is the emergence of our discipline to be seen as a spin-off from Christian theology, leading to some versions of "religious studies" which are indeed still recognisably religious in their own presuppositions? Or are they to be found in the rationalist, atheist counter-tradition? It has certainly been significant that from the earliest days of our discipline, however conceived, historical study and analysis has often conflicted with the religious memory itself, which is part of the object under study. The religious memory does not always wish to know, or remember, that people and events have been characterised by features which do not fit with the religiously effective picture. As the eighteenth century Japanese thinker Tominaga argued, the neo-foundational scriptures of Mahāyāna Buddhism were not uttered by the Buddha himself, in spite of the regular opening line "Thus I have heard" used to suggest legitimacy. "Thus I have heard, indeed!" we can still hear him muttering. That is, we might hear it, if we were even aware that Tominaga, too, is part of the story. Is there not a case for a post-Eurocentric or post-Euro-American history of the history of religions?

Globalizing communications and organizational arangements

While it may be taken as a matter of course that the history of religions, as it has been carried out for quite some time, is and should be "post-colonialist," there is a much greater need to take care of the extreme ambiguity of the recently fashionable idea of "globalization." On one hand certain particular processes may be taking place which can be summed up under this term. When these are specified however, it is not at all easy to agree that these are all new in principle, or even recent. Are the activities of Shell or Toyota really more global than those of the British East India Company or the Dutch United East India Company (Verenigde Oostindische Compagnie) in their day? Or again, while we are now experiencing the revolution of digital communication, the correct historical assessment of this is another matter. It is much too simple to assert that this is the third great qualitative leap forward after the invention of writing and the invention of printing. Looking at it in another way, the enablement of global communication through digital information technology may be seen as an extension of the wireless communication which excited people quite a long time ago. Whether we are old enough or not, we should try to think back to the miracle of those days. Think about the very idea of biological organisms communicating over extremely large distances without messengers, without paper and even without cables and wires!

Of course most of us now enjoy the speed, the informality, even the politics of electronic mail, the rush of new web-sites, and so on. Yet the recent commercialisation of web-sites should warn us once more about the dangers of so-called "globalization" in this regard. In the early days of e-mail communication, though using it myself for most correspondence, I resisted the temptation to shift too much IAHR business into this medium, for this would have led to two different societies within the association. Now the danger has more or less passed, at least in the academic circles which are addressed by the IAHR. However, some caution is needed. The communiqué of a recent meeting of "G8" leaders in Okinawa (2000) called for the spread of internet access to millions of deprived people all over the world. At the same time reports indicated that these powerful leaders, except perhaps President Putin of Russia, do not in fact use e-mail themselves. I do admit that, like the Virgin Mary at Lourdes, they probably have assistants who read their messages for them. My own observations of relative deprivation, remembering a visit to Hammanskraal near Pretoria in 1998, suggest that if all the shanties of Southern Africa are to be provided with world-wide-web connections in the foreseeable future a lot of other things will have to change first. I have commented on this aspect of "globalization," setting our memories into the future, because there is certainly a task here for the IAHR both as an institution and as a process. It is urgently necessary to reappraise the relations between the world-wide communications of the IAHR, taking account of the relationship between the printed word in the form of bulletins, the official journal *Numen* and related publications, and the possibilities of the internet for sending and displaying information.

For the first half of the twentieth century our IAHR tradition existed as a sequence of congresses, of which this is the 18th. But in the second half of the twentieth century it has also existed as an organisation with statutes, committees and officers. Today, people are calling for improvements to organisational systems which, ten or fifteen years ago, were not even in place. Not everybody is equally interested in organisational questions. Some prefer a more bohemian, anarchic view of academic life, and this may be a contribution in its own right. However I believe that these organisational systems are sometimes rather important after all, and that this applies to the IAHR.

Let me briefly draw attention to some of the organisational features. Beginning with 1988 (at Marburg), in 1993 (in Paris) and in 1997 (at Hildesheim) the International Committee of the IAHR has assembled *in between* the world congresses, and on each of these occasions major initiatives were taken which today are influencing the character of our organisation. The International Committee can be seen as the central body of the IAHR, for it is here that all the various national and regional associations are represented. The International Committee on the one hand makes formal recommendations to the General Assembly, for ratification, and on the other hand it elects the much smaller Executive Committee. At the same time the well-being of the national and regional associations is of fundamental importance. It is from them that the members of the International Committee and the Executive Committee are drawn. In recent years there has been a steady series of newly founded national associations seeking affiliation to the IAHR, and this has been a fine development. I would also like specifically to commend the activities of the regional associations, namely, the Asociación Latinoamericana para el Estudio de las Religiones and the African Association for the Study of Religions. The present Executive Committee recommends that these should be joined, as IAHR affiliates, by the recently founded European Association for the Study of Religions (EASR), which is expected to play a significant liaison role in Europe in the coming years. I also personally commend this initiative and request your support for it.[4]

You may wonder why I am talking about such arrangements during a keynote address. The reason is simple. I have learned over the last twenty or thirty years that in very many ways the institutional arrangements for the study of religions, including publication patterns, are extremely important for the way in which the discipline is understood. Of course the intellectual questions are important. Together with the materials which we study it is the intellectual questions which make it all interesting. But institutional contours also shape a discipline, and the IAHR helps to create those institutional contours for the study of religions, both as a historical and a social-scientific enterprise. There is no other international association which has maintained such a steady vision

4 Retrospective note. In the meantime these have been joined by the South and South-East Asian Association for the Study of Religions, and the developmental process of regional networking, at a level between national associations and the IAHR itself, may be regarded as continuing.

in our field, regardless of political pressures from various directions, yet with all due account being taken of intellectual shifts and developments as the times have required.

With these perspectives and developments in mind I am particularly happy to have had the opportunity of giving this keynote address at the opening of this 18th Congress in Durban. Please allow me to end on a personal note. At the end of this congress I will no longer be an office holder in the IAHR. Although the electoral rules would theoretically permit me to be nominated again, I let it be known some time ago that I regard three periods in leading offices (in my case two as General Secretary and one as President) as enough for any one person. It is right to give way, so that others can come forward. The future of the IAHR will be shaped by our common past, to which so many have contributed, and it will also be shaped by the way in which new leaders perceive it. This is not only a matter for the office-holders. Fortunately there are many fine intellectual leaders in our field present at this congress, not to mention numerous absent friends. All of them have a part to play. But my plea is, in particular, for responsible, corporate, *organisational* memory, which in turn will help to structure the way forward. Memories of the IAHR are part of the history of our discipline, and so I conclude by expressing the hope that these memories, selected, contested, and always reflected, will turn out to be not only memories of the past but also constituents of the future.

Bibliographical references

Dai, Kangsheng, Zhang,Xinying and Pye, Michael (eds.) 1995. *Religion and Modernization in China. Proceedings of the International Association for the History of Religions held in Beijing, China, April 1992*. Cambridge (Roots and Branches). A number of contributions appeared in Chinese translation in the journal *Shijie Zongjiao Ziliao* 世界宗教资料 (1992).

Doležalová, Iva, Martin, Luther H. and Papoušek, Dalibor (eds.) 2001. *The Academic Study of Religion during the Cold War: East and West*, Frankfurt, New York (Peter Lang Publishing).

Michaels, Axel (ed.) 1997. *Klassiker der Religionswissenschaft: Von Friedrich Schleiermacher bis Mircea Eliade*. München (Beck).

Platvoet, J. Cox, J. and Olupona, J. (eds.) *The Study of Religions in Africa. Past, Present and Prospects, Proceedings of the IAHR Regional Conference at Harare, Zimbabwe 1992,* Cambridge (Roots and Branches) 1996.

Sharpe, Eric 1975. *Comparative Religion. A History*. London (Duckworth).

This address was first published in: Hackett, Rosalind and Pye, Michael (eds.) 2010. *IAHR Congress Proceedings (Durban 2000). The History of Religions: Origins and Visions*, Cambridge (Roots and Branches): 284–297. Note that this was a limited print-run distributed to major libraries across the world and is not commercially available: enquiries may be made to the serving Publications Officer of the IAHR.

3.5 Political Correctness in the Study of Religions: Is the Cold War Really Over?

This paper was first presented at a special conference of the International Association for the History of Religions (IAHR) in August 1999 in Brno, Czech Republic, organized and sponsored by the Czech Society for the Study of Religions and the North American Association for the Study of Religion. A few passages are included here which were abbreviated for the conference volume.

Introduction

The forms taken by political "correctness" are sometimes very obvious, but sometimes they are subtle and insidious. Public and academic life during the Cold War was influenced on both sides by a confrontational ideology which led to distorted mutual perceptions. In the western world we were often led to believe that religion had almost been abolished in the "godless" Soviet Union and the repressed countries of Eastern Europe. As to the study of religions, only a tiny minority is interested in it anyway, but even among them the study of religions in the above mentioned countries was presumed to be little more than propaganda for the ideological programme of Marxism-Leninism.This makes a reliable reassessment of earlier decades as difficult now as it was at the time. The argument presented here, while not underestimating the difficulties under which specialists in the study of religions laboured in eastern Europe during the communist period, will emphasise first the simple fact that there were indeed such studies, give a brief explanation as to why this fact is frequently repressed, and then plead for those in a position to carry out detailed studies in the relevant intellectual history to do so regardless of new forms of political correctness.

Alternative versions of the history of the study of religions

These reflections on the study of religions during the Cold War are however embedded in wider considerations about the way in which the history of this discipline is conceived. For this, see in particular "Studies of religion in Europe: structures and desiderata" (3.2 above, in this volume). It has often seemed necessary to remind people that the very idea of a reflective, analytic study of religions has natural roots not only in European and American culture but also in Asian culture, particularly in China and Japan (see Part Two of this volume). This is not our theme here, and yet the need to point this out, sometimes against the wishes of scholars from those regions who themselves prefer to see a solely western origin for the study of religions, illustrates how difficult it is to overcome widely prevalent orientations or prejudices. Now the situation is very similar with respect to the history of the study of religions in eastern Europe and the Soviet Union. Even the very idea that there could have been studies of religion which were worth taking seriously was frequently rejected or repressed. I will return to the reasons for this later. First it is necessary to identify that there was in fact a scholarly tradition in the study of religions with related institutions and publications, during most of the communist period and in most of the countries in question.

Some reference points in Poland and the Soviet Union

The historical description of the traditions in the study of religions which can be documented in the countries of Eastern Europe can of course be carried through most effectively by specialists from or related to each specific country. Here a few reference points only will be noted. They are probably sufficient to indicate the complexity of the situation and to validate the remainder of the argument mounted below.

The Polish Society for the Science of Religions, affiliated to the International Association for the History of Religions (IAHR) was founded in 1958. For details see Witold Tyloch's article "Polish Society for the Science of Religion" in the Polish journal *Euhemer* (Tyloch 1979). The same edition of this journal contains a very impressive bibliography of the contents of *Euhemer* itself, both alphabetically and in "systematic order." The outline of the systematic order shows what a clear view was maintained at that time of the possibility of a scientific study of religions which is not itself religious. In that same year of 1979 a regional conference of the IAHR on methodology was held in Warsaw, and the proceedings were published as *Current Progress in the Methodology of the Science of Religions* (Tyloch 1984).[1] During this conference the distinction between studying religions and being religious was almost self-evident for Polish scholars at the time, but still unclear in some western contributions (Peter Slater) and thus still a bone of contention for others (Donald Wiebe). The substantial range of studies known and evaluated in Poland was illustrated in an *International Bibliography of Comparative Religion in Dictionary Order* compiled by Tadeusz Margul (1984) and published in Kraków. This was begun in the fifties and benefited from a stay by the author at the Donner Institute in Åbo, Finland. Both the introduction and the systematic construction of this bibliography are of interest and would repay further examination. The period under consideration concluded with a second methodologicaly oriented IAHR conference in Warsaw in September 1989 (Sept. 5–9), the proceedings of which were also published in Warsaw (Tyloch 1990). The meeting itself took place just at the time when Tadeusz Mazowiecki was cautiously forming the first non-communist government to emerge in Eastern Europe at the end of the Soviet period. Incidentally it is nowadays often overlooked that this took place *before* the East German frontier was opened. This in itself illustrates the way in which history is retrospectively distorted by victorious politicians. In reality Poland was already free, both in consciousness and constitutionally, before significant changes occurred in the German Democratic Republic and the Berlin Wall was dramatically demolished.

It would lead too far afield to debate here in detail the most appropriate way to distinguish different periods in the development of the science of religion, or scientific study of religions, in Poland. In view of the above however, I cannot quite share the analysis proposed by Halina Grzymała-Moszczyńska and Henryk Hoffmann (1988) according to which a first period would run from 1873–1973, while a second period would run from 1974 to the present. This account seems to me to highlight too heavily the foundation of an Institute of the Science of Religion at the Jagellonian University in Kraków. Important though this

1 Note that this publication appeared in Poland itself. Unfortunately I was unable to revisit Poland for this conference because university administrators in Japan failed to grant permission.

was, and however the self-appraisal of those involved may have changed in the meantime, it cannot be gainsaid that the initiative took place right in the middle of the communist period and indeed would not have been possible without the prior existence of studies of religion elsewhere in the country during that time. A more appropriate periodization would be into the pre-war period, the communist period, and the post-communist period, while the connections and affinities between these periods are, as usual in history, as interesting as the differences.

The pre-communist beginnings of the science of religions in Poland have been explored in an article by Zygmunt Poniatowski in another journal specialising in the study of religions, namely *Studia Religioznawcze* (Poniatowski 1979). He dealt with the period 1873–1918 and distinguished even then between a Marxist and a Catholic current. The concluding sentence: "In spite of the difficult circumstances of national captivity, the Polish science of religions in the period under discussion was fruitfully and rapidly developing, though not reaching the status of an autonomous science. It has reached this status only in the Polish People's Republic." Naturally this view does not at all fit in with the prejudices current in the western world! Nevertheless a perusal of the various issues of the journal *Studia Religioznawcze* will easily suffice to demonstrate the impressive spectrum of interests which were covered during the communist period. The imaginativeness and flexibility shown by Polish scholars in this and other fields was matched by the maintenance of a relatively high degree of freedom in other domains such as the publication of literature (extensively translated from French for example) and in the field of religion itself.[2]

Turning now to the Soviet Union, particular attention may be drawn to the periodical publication *Religii Mira*, of which six issues were published between 1982 and, theoretically, 1987. The last issue appeared late however, in 1989, and with the end of the Cold War the publication seems to have been discontinued altogether. According to a Russian source the publication was a "series" rather than a "journal" in a strict sense. Nevertheless the range of contents was very wide; it mixed articles with a clearly political orientation with others

2 For personal observations and reflections on the admittedly extremely complex and difficult history of the churches in Eastern Europe under communism, see Pye 1994d (also in 7.3 below) This account, like the present article is intended as a corrective to some of the more blinkered presentations which are themselves a product of the Cold War.

of mainly historical or contemporary social interest, for example dealing with the role of religion in the political conflict in Northern Ireland.

As is well known, one set of institutions which dealt in some sense with religion were the Institutes of Scientific Atheism, in which the official ideological orientation was strongly represented. This was based on the Marxist view that religion is an essentially undesirable phenomenon which will, with the increase of communism, ultimately and inevitably pass away. In this perspective it is not surprising that churches are mainly attended by old ladies (outliving their husbands), although it is a little surprising that the supply of old ladies seems to continue from decade to decade. A regular subject for research was therefore (as also in other countries under communist rule) the rate of change and the secondary factors which slow down or accelerate change.

Scientific atheism was also the guiding principle behind the Museum of Religion and Atheism (Musey Religii i Ateizma) for many years housed on the Nevskiy Prospekt in Leningrad. This museum was in effect a museum of religions, for it did not really have any exhibits illustrating "atheism" as such. The main floor contained shamanic objects, including a fine example of a Siberian shaman's attire (probably Yakutian, and similar to others elsewhere such as that on display in more general museums in Irkutsk and Khabarovsk). It also contained items from the Orthodox Church including icons, before which some visitors stood with reverent and misty eyes. In an underground floor was an extensive series of reliefs, apparently modelled in wax, which illustrated the ways in which a clerical hierarchy oppressed the masses.[3] It is not clear what has happened to these since the end of the communist period, but if they could be identified they ought to be re-exhibited on historical grounds.[4] From my own observations in 1973 it was evident that groups visiting Leningrad from other parts of the Soviet Union were led to the museum. This was no doubt a "correct" place to visit and was understood to be a contribution to political education. At the same time it is extremely interesting that this museum existed at all, for the number

3 Personal observations from 1973. For further information on this museum see especially James Thrower's "The study of religion in the USSR" (Thrower 1983). This article was a notable exception to the general western trend of the time, which was simply to ignore the possibility that there might be any scholarly study of religions at all in the Soviet Union. Its author and the present writer were at one in resisting this trend. Cf. also on Mark Batunsky below.

4 The museum as a whole was rehoused and redeveloped some years after the fall of the Soviet Union, and no longer includes the word "atheism" in its name.

of museums devoted specifically to religion is very small indeed.[5] The concept presupposes not only the possibility of considered, systematic reflection upon religion but also the recognition that religion has a practical, plastic aspect which finds expression in artefacts.

Alongside the official channels, many contributions were made by Russian scholars during the Soviet period in the context of a variety of other disciplines such as ethnology and archaeology, both in the form of independent publications and as contributions to works published elsewhere. It is arguable that such contributions were more significant than studies undertaken under the heading of scientific atheism. To some extent these were known in the west, though unfortunately not sufficiently honoured. Contributions by Russian scholars to the IAHR conference in Warsaw 1979 remained untranslated into western languages and have therefore not been taken up later by others who were at the same conference. Moreover, not enough attention has been paid even to the simple fact that a number of valuable contributions were in fact available in western languages. Consider for example the extensive contributions on shamanism by Soviet specialists which, in collaboration with the Hungarian scholar Vilmos Diószegi, appeared in English under the title *Popular Beliefs and Folklore Tradition in Siberia* (Diószegi 1968). This work, published in the Netherlands, is not only valuable as a contribution to the study of shamanism in particular, but also as an element in the overall pattern of the study of religions.[6]

Another example is the article by Mark Batunsky on trends in Soviet studies on Islam, published in the journal *Religion* in 1982. Fascinatingly, this article argued in favour of a trend in Soviet studies of Islam which sought to go beyond the politically correct sociological analysis and ex-

5 The oldest and most well-known collection of religious artefacts is presumably the Religionskundliche Sammlung of the University of Marburg, Germany, originally established by Rudolf Otto in 1927. In recent years a museum of religions with an accent on religious art was opened in Glasgow, Scotland. Another in Taiwan was being planned by a religious foundation at the time of writing. [This has since been opened, is presentationally ambitious, and seeks to promote a sense of religious experience.]

6 The book was printed in Hungary and published in the Netherlands: It was also included as Volume 57 of the "Uralic and Altaic Series" of Indiana University, Bloomington, thus being in all a remarkable piece of international collaboration. Of the thirty-two contribuors, sixteen were from the Soviet Union (Moscow, Leningrad, Kazan, Novosibirsk and Tomsk), twelve from Hungary, one from the German Democratic Republic (East Berlin) and one from Sweden (Stockholm). For an overall account of Diószegi's work see Hoppál 1975.

planation of its time and to seek an understanding of Islam in its own terms as a religious system.[7] By highlighting the intentionality of the believers, the article in effect makes a methodological shift in the direction of the phenomenological study of religions. Naturally, the legitimation for taking an interest in Islam during the Soviet period lay in the potential political problems which might be caused by self-conscious Muslim populations within the borders of the Soviet Union. Politically, this was also the main reason for the military engagement in Afghanistan. That is, the motive was to defeat Islamic fundamentalism *outside* the southern borders, rather than to wait to deal with it as an internal threat. Naturally, the western view did not seek to understand the actual Soviet intentions but simply depicted the action as blatant, aggressive expansionism. At the time some commentators even adduced the very fanciful idea that "the Russians" hoped thereby to get hold of a "warm water port," a favourite theme in British history books. Such commentators clearly had access to maps which were drawn to a rather large scale! However that may be, the point to be noted here is that there is a need, in understanding the history of studies of religion, to take account of the way in which studies of Islam have been legitimated, whether from a Soviet point of view or from a western point of view. In the latter case it appears that an interest in Middle Eastern oilfields has been the main criterion for distinguishing between politically acceptable and unacceptable forms of Islam. It is only against this dual background that consideration can be given to the extent to which the studies of Islam in various quarters have been worthwhile as a component in the study of religions. It was not and is not correct to assume, one-sidedly, that there could not possibly have been any worthwhile studies of Islam in the Soviet Union.

Buddhism was also a field of interest to a number of scholars during the Soviet period. Theoretically, it was possible years ago to obtain articles by Russian writers on archaeological studies in central Asia pertaining to the history of Buddhism, or works on "Lamaism" in Buryatia such as the extensive and highly scholarly writings of Kseniya Maksimovna Gerasimova. But, given the language barrier and the number of primary languages required in the study of Buddhism, how many specialists in western countries went to the trouble of doing it? More well-known is the tradition of studies in Buddhist thought, pursued notably by Fedor Shcherbatskoi (also transcribed as Stcherbatsky) in Len-

7 Batunsky 1982. The present writer was involved in the editorial process, not without its complications, leading to the publication of this article.

ingrad and later in Tartu, Estonia, where it was continued notwithstanding the emigration of Alexsandr Moiseyevich Pyatigorskiy (also transcribed Piatigorsky) to London in 1972.[8] Moreover there had been a continuing relationship to the Mongolian-Buryat tradition of Mahāyāna Buddhism in Leningrad, where a Tibetan-style Buddhist temple stood, and in Moscow where a museum of Asian art housed an impressive collection of Buryat religious paintings. However, in the early 1970 s, specialists in Buddhist studies became even more closely entangled with the religious and political life of Buryatia, and this led to events which in themselves demand more detailed consideration (see below on the case of Bidiya D. Dandaron) but which are only indirectly related to academic studies of religion.

More widely, studies of religion carried out in oriental and anthropological institutes, and in the context of the various academies for the social sciences, often appeared under titles which did not specifically refer to religion. A typical example would be the collective work *Mirovozzrenie Finno-ugorskich Narodov* ("World-views of Finno-Ugrian peoples") (Gemuyev 1990).[9] In this work several contributions are more or less closely related to religion, a clear example being the analysis of the concept of calendar among the Komi people offered by Nikolay Dmitriyevich Konakov. The concept of time or calendar is of course a fundamental feature of all primal religious systems. It should not be thought however that the word "religion" necesssarily had to be avoided. To take an example more or less at random, The Soviet Academy of Sciences published a work by Arkadiy Fedorovich Anisimov in 1958 on the "religiya evenkov (the religion of the Evenks) (Anisimov 1958) Finally, for the Russian speaking world reference must also be made to the work of Sergey Aleksandrovich Tokarev, which became at least somewhat known outside the Soviet Union thanks to the publication by Progress Publishers in Moscow of his comprehensive work *Istoriya Religii* in English translation as *History of Religion* (Tokarev 1986,1989). The thematic structure and the general orientation of this work are of considerable interest.

---

8 Retrospective note. Interesting sidelights on the Tartu school were reported by Linnart Mäll in his "Semiotics as a possibility for the study of religious texts under the conditions of communism" at the IAHR conference in Brno (Doležalová, Martin and Papoušek 2001).

9 Though published in 1990, this of course reflected work done before and up to the date of publication (undertaken by the Soviet Academy of Sciences in Novosibirsk).

Excursus: Why did Dandaron have to go to prison?

In this section a brief excursus is offered concerning the imprisonment of the Buryat Buddhist teacher Bidiya D. Dandaron, who also wrote scholarly papers. It might be argued that this case is not of central relevance to our subject, for there is no evidence that Dandaron was in any way interested in the scientific study of religion. He taught and wrote within and for a religious tradition. Nevertheless the matter will be considered briefly here for two reasons. First it will illustrate that the question as to what happened to the religious traditions themselves cannot be ignored (and has not been ignored by this writer) as a background element in the history of the academic study of religions. Second, as will be seen, the problem which arose lay in an unfortunate and perhaps irresponsible construal of the relations between religious activity and the activity of studying religions. This in itself is instructive and continues to be relevant as a moral tale. Historically, the life and work of Dandaron have been studied in detail by the Czech researcher Luboš Bělka (see Bělka 2001), whose extremely valuable thesis on the wider subject of Buryat Buddhism in the western world (in this case European Russia) is available in Czech.

Unfortunately, as it may be said in retrospect, there was an entanglement during the Soviet period between the scholarly tradition of Buddhist studies based on texts and an interest in the living practice of Buddhism as represented by Buryat teachers. This came to a head with Dandaron's trial, leading to imprisonment, at which the previously mentioned scholar Gerasimova played a role as an expert witness. In the course of the conference in Brno the question was posed more than once, and with some bewilderment, as to why the Soviet state should have been so antagonistic to the re-emergence of Buryat Buddhism as a cultural force. Without attempting to offer a detailed history, I would like to suggest four main reasons for this. This argument may also be read as a comment on the tradition of Buddhist studies in the Soviet Union.

First, it should be remembered that Buddhist texts studied philologically were not necessarily perceived to represent a challenge to the Soviet system. Shcherbatskoi's (Stcherbatsky's) researches carried out in Leningrad continued for quite a long time after the revolution and his writings, published in English, were rather influential on Buddhist studies in other countries. A key example is his work *The Conception of Buddhist Nirvana.* This was originally published in 1927 by the Academy of

Sciences of the USSR in Leningrad and only reprinted in the Netherlands in 1965, following the growing popularity of Buddhism in the western world.[10] In the 1950 s Constantin Regamey referred to the Leningrad school as one of three main orientations in Buddhist studies outside Asia, the others being the Anglo-German and the Franco-Belgian (Regamey 1950 and cf. Pye 1973b). (This was before the massive development of Buddhist studies in North America, as a result of which Regamey's story now requires rewriting.) However Buddhism as a system of ideas eventually came to be seen as problematic in the Soviet Union because it was at one and the same time religious and atheistic, while not being religion-critical like scientific atheism. In other words Buddhism did not fit the "correct" distinction between religion on the one hand and scientific atheism on the other hand. Thus, personal interest or even enthusiasm for Buddhism on the part of those for whom it was not a quaint and disappearing folk-tradition inevitably came to be regarded as a sign of political incorrectness.

Second, the laws of the Soviet Union permitted religion to be practised but not to be propagated. This point has often been misunderstood or wilfully overlooked by outsiders crusading for "religious freedom," by which is meant, for example, freedom to give away Bibles on street corners. There is no doubt that religion was repressed in various ways during the Soviet period and there have been hot and cold periods in this regard.[11] The Russian Orthodox Church has suffered great variations in this regard, though its existence as such has never been seriously under threat since its patriotic mobilisation during the Second World War. For an accurate understanding of any historical situation during the Soviet period, however, it is necessary to distinguish carefully between freedom to exist with a specific religious identity and freedom to distribute propaganda to spread a system which might be considered to be inimical to the state. Buddhism in Buryatia was a local tradition

10 Once again the publishers were, commendably, Mouton. However Shcherbatskoy also published elsewhere in western languages. For example, he waged acerbic argument with Berriedale Keith about the essential nature of Buddhist teaching in the *Bulletin of the School of Oriental and African Studies* 6 (1933), 867–96.

11 For a brief survey see Owen Chadwick 1992. This book, by the well-known church historian, is cautiously politically correct from a western point of view. It appeared when not a few church observers and historians in western Europe suddenly realized how little they knew about the complex situation which the churches in eastern Europe had experienced.

which suffered considerable repression, such as the closure of most lamaseries (*datsan*), the socially useful reemployment of lamas, and so on, and even so the tradition continued in some form. But the critical point in the developments surrounding Dandaron, who stood ethnically as well as religiously in a tradition of authoritative teachers of Buddhism, arose when he was perceived to have become involved in the *propagation* of Buddhism.

Third, the Soviet system inherited in some respects the problems, and the solutions, of Czarist Russia. The conquest and colonisation of Siberia had found an early stabilisation with the establishment of the city of Irkutsk as a trading outpost and at the same time an outpost of Russian civilisation. At least during the later Soviet period (but personally last observed in 1979) the prominent Russian Orthodox Church in Irkutsk had an external mural painting exhibiting "the conversion of the Buryats". This shows that, from a Russian point of view, the Buryats are not supposed to be different, or at any rate not very different. They are supposed to be converted. An alien, possibly competitive religious tradition was not desired. In his regard the Russian view informed the Soviet view. Whatever may have been said, and even meant, about the cultural diversity of the peoples of the Soviet Union, the Russian component continued to play a dominant role, as illustrated by the successful imposition of the Russian language as a lingua franca and indeed by the display of "Moscow time" on the clocks of all the stations of the Trans-Siberian railway! Hypothetically, therefore, I suggest that the challenge of russification symbolised by the celebration of the "conversion" of the Buryats was carried forward into the mind-set of those responsible for geo-cultural engineering in Siberia, Transbaikalia and the Soviet Far East in general. Yet at the same time the cultural situation was fragile for the Soviet Union precisely because of the weakening of the authority of the Orthodox Church. Even in the seventies, Russians in Irkutsk were interested in "yoga." Moreover it cannot be overlooked that the political tensions with China during the seventies made the whole region east of Irkutsk extremely sensitive, and that the Trans-Siberian railway, also inherited from Czarist times, runs through Ulan-Ude, the capital of Buryatia. It turns southwards from Irkutsk to dip below Lake Baikal through what is (for the perspective of that region) a very narrow strip of land north of the Mongolian frontier. (The new line bypassing Lake Baikal to the north had not yet been built.) I can personally recall conversations with Russian military personnel on the train in that region in 1973 who were very nervous indeed about relations with China.

Fourth, this whole situation was greatly exacerbated because in the early seventies "western," that is, Estonian and Russian scholars were linking themselves with an oriental Buddhist tradition which had at the same the potential to be a social tradition with separatist political characteristics. Admittedly, life was not easy in any case for those wishing to study religious systems such as Buddhism in the Soviet Union. But the scholars west of Moscow had an interest in Buddhism which was not just textual and philological, or even semiotic, but in principle also mystical and exoticist. They were keen to be associated with a guru from an eastern Buddhist tradition, a role fulfilled for them by Dandaron. Unfortunately, by drawing attention to him, they naively drew him out into a position of prominence, a position which for him also had a quite different dimension, namely that of continuing ethnic identity. Moreover the specific form of Buddhism in Buryatia was, traditionally, the Tibeto-Mongolian form usually referred to in Russian as "Lamaism", which always implies a close identification of religious and political leadership, as is well known from the case of Tibet. This aspect was not of any significance for the neo-Buddhist scholarship of the western Soviet Union, but it was an ineradicable part of the tradition for Buryats themselves.

So, in sum, what happened? On the one hand, ethnic identity and folklore traditions were held to have a certain validity in the Soviet Union. The double page on ethnic groups in the official atlas of the Soviet Union was impressive indeed. A kind of cultural pluralism was celebrated through ethnicity within the framework of the state, provided that this overall framework was not threatened. In the case of Buryat Buddhism however, the traditional concept of the relation between religion and society led inevitably to the question of potential separatism, and the matter therefore took on a political dimension which led to the tragedy of Dandaron's arrest and imprisonment. Astonishingly, according to Luboš Bělko, Dandaron was still able to have things published in Estonia from within his internment in the Gulag (Bělko 2001).

Further commentary on the study of religions in Eastern Europe under communism

The above brief references to the situation in Poland and the Soviet Union are only intended to illustrate the fact there was indeed a serious tradition in the study of religions during the communist period. The story for other countries, especially Czechoslovakia and Hungary, is evidently also both complex and interesting, but the writer is not able to pursue this in detail. Let it be noted however that in the latter case the close interest in Hungarian origins led to a special concentration on the world views and religious traditions of related peoples in Siberia and in particular on the study of shamanism. The energetic development of studies in shamanistic culture since the end of the Soviet period, in Hungary, was possible not least because of the *existing* scholarly tradition, as can easily be documented from the works of Mihály Hoppál, who wrote both before and after the political changes. Ethnographic and folkloristic studies also provided an avenue for contemporary studies with at least some relevance to the study of the religions, and an opportunity for younger researchers to do fieldwork without ideological strain or political difficulties. Indeed, the celebration of folkloristic difference was politically correct.

Naturally there are conflicting views on the history relating to any one country. And it should not be forgotten that the historical changes swinging between relative openness and relative tightness in ideological control ran at a different pace in the various countries involved. In particular there is, understandably, a considerable divergence of interpretation between those who left their country of origin for some western refuge and those who remained through changing circumstances and tried to make the best of a sometimes difficult situation. This can even be followed in the course of individual careers, as in the case of Kurt Rudolph, professor of the history of religions at the Karl Marx University of Leipzig in the German Democratic Republic (GDR).[12] While the subject could not be unfolded as a major program for students at the university, the subject nevertheless existed at research level and Rudolph was able to build up an international reputation in Mandaean and Gnostic studies. There was, evidently, a considerable amount of scientific literature available from all parts of the world, partly as a result of research time being available for extensive reviewing in the East German *Theologische Literaturzeitung*. There were also possibilities for international travel. Two essays by Rudolph are of particular interest for the understanding of his work during the GDR period (before he left for California, and then for the Federal Republic of Germany (Western Germany), and still before German reunification). His article "Grund-

12 Deutsche Demokratische Republik (DDR).

positionen der Religionswissenschaft" shows the close affinity to historically conceived, philologically based, but at the same time comparatively oriented studies of religion in many countries, east or west.[13] "Religionswissenschaft und Ideologiekritik", on the other hand, shows how the discipline was able to be correlated with the political orientation required by communist governments, while at the same time remaining an intellectual perspective open to anyone, anywhere, who finds himself or herself to be in the tradition of the Enlightenment (*Aufklärung*).[14]

This raises the question, for all the countries with communist governments, as to how individuals who operated successfully over many years managed to do this. What mechanisms were developed for this? One obvious method was to work more or less neutrally and normally, just getting on with scientific research, and then at the end of a report or article to make some reference to the speed with which the religious phenomena in question were thought to be dying out, to reflect briefly on what might be hindering such a process, or to note the unexpected persistence of religion among particular groups of people. Quotations from Marx, Engels or even Lenin also conveyed an impression of political correctness. Since these were in some cases counted to see if there were enough, Zygmunt Poniatowski brilliantly turned this procedure itself into a mode of scientific research and counted quotations of other authors in other writings to provide alternative images of the subject matter. Articles written in this vein may seem odd in some eyes, but in the Polish situation under communism they illustrated, with wonderful irony, the flexibility and freedom of science. Another manoeuvre practised in Poland was to make use of western publications by re-quoting them from Soviet publications, thus establishing political correctness but drawing further attention to them. Poland itself provided a major

13 Rudolph 1981. This paper was presented at the 14th Congress of the International Association for the History of Religions held in Winnipeg, Canada in 1980 and the English translation was prepared by and at the suggestion of the present writer.

14 First published while Rudolph resided in Leipzig, this article was republished in extended form in his valuable collected essays *Historical Fundamentals and the Study of Religions* (Rudolph 1992), some years after he had emigrated to the West. His own presentation of the tradition of the history of religions in Leipzig may be found in the first chapter, but the GDR/DDR period is only commented on briefly, and negatively. This was perhaps to be expected in the context of lectures held in the USA (Chicago 1983–4), shortly before his removal to California.

service by allowing room for much more substantial translation programs in the seventies and eighties than were possible for example in Czechoslovakia.

Finally, during the whole communist period subsequent to the Second World War, the role of interaction with Nordic and, in particular, Finnish scholars should not be underestimated. Both Finland and Sweden, in their different ways, maintained their neutral status, being members neither of NATO nor of the Warsaw Pact. Trade could therefore be developed on a quite different basis and was particularly important for Finland, which consequently went into recession after the end of the Cold War. With trade came accompanying cultural exchanges, conferences, publications, even extended research visits. To some extent the modelling of the discipline ran along similar lines, with a strong interest and advanced skills in the study of folk traditions (Lauri Honko) and shamanism (Juha Pentikäinen) providing a focus for scientific exchanges. In addition, there were some affinities in the language used to analyse religious change from a social scientific point of view, with equivalents to "world-view" or "religious world" playing a prominent role both in the Slavic languages and in Finnish (*maailmankuva, uskomusmaailma*) especially in the seventies and early eighties (Harva, Helve, Pentikäinen and others). Of course the term has a wider and more complex history, being also used by social scientists in North America. A social scientist such as Helena Helve could therefore use it without any particular political implications (Helve 1993).[15] Nils G. Holm of Åbo Akademi University directed a research project entitled "Humanitas et Vita" but this was generally referred to as the "World View Project."(see Holm and Björkqvist 1996). In the Polish context, however, the same term permitted a conceptual *differentiation*, and hence when necessary a *correlation* between a "world-view", which could be religious, and an "ideology", which could be politically correct (cf. Pye 1994d, also at 7.3 below). In other words, one could be politically correct by furthering the right ideology (Marxism-Leninism) while being free to maintain, for example, a theistic world-view. In studies emanating from Finland this function was in itself unimportant since, contrary to cold war discourse on the western side, there was no stronger communist ideological pressure on Finnish intellectual life than there was in western countries. However the widespread use of "world-view" and related terms such as "reli-

15 The opening discussion and the bibliography of this work were particularly instructive for the present argument.

gious world" in research undoubtedly facilitated correlations with researchers in various countries of eastern Europe by establishing a common reference point in scientific discourse. Thus Juha Pentikäinen, sensitive to the nuances of political and scientific discourse, was able to make field visits to Karelia and elsewhere in the Soviet Union for his studies of Old Believers and of shamanism. In the other direction, an essay by the Hungarian Mihály Hoppál, for example, was published in Finnish under the title "Shamanismi ja uralilaisten kansojen uskomusmaailma" (Shamanism and the World-view of the Uralic Peoples (Hoppál 1975). The Finnish connection was definitely important for the facilitation of contacts between eastern Europe and the International Association for the History of Religions (IAHR). The IAHR conference on methodology held in Turku in 1973, for example, established personal relationships which had a forward influence right up to the end of the Cold War. In 1979 and 1989 there were related meetings in Warsaw, the latter, as mentioned previously, being contemporaneous with the formation of the first post-communist government in eastern Europe. Although the political changes were already in progress, the participation list in an IAHR regional conference in Helsinki in 1990 (presided over by Juha Pentikäinen) was a striking demonstration of Finland's special facilitatory role, with considerable numbers coming from Estonia (still within the Soviet Union), Hungary (still in the Warsaw Pact), northern Russia (from the University of Siktivkar in the Komi region) and Siberia (researchers from Novosibirsk) and cultural representatives of the Khanti and Mansi peoples. At the same time it may be observed that Finnish scholars themselves were not only oriented towards the east but had plenty of contacts with other countries too, especially sunny ones such as Italy and Greece!

Parallelism with the western view of religions under communism

Returning to the main theme, the question has to be posed as to why studies of religion carried out in countries under communist rule were widely ignored in western countries. The forms taken by political "correctness" are sometimes very obvious, but sometimes more subtle. Both public and academic life was influenced during the Cold War, in both directions, by a confrontational ideology which led to distorted mutual perceptions. In the western world the idea was widely current and energetically propagated that religion had been more or less abolished in the Soviet Union and the countries of Eastern Europe. Accordingly the study of religions in these countries, in so far as it was recognised to take place at all, was *presumed* to be little more than propaganda for the ideological programme of Marxist-Leninist communism. There is therefore an important parallel here between the western perception of religion under communist rule and the (much more restricted) perception of the study of religions, which was generally prejudged to be impossible.

This relationship can be seen in another way in the subsequent developments, following on the end of the Cold War. While there has been room for religious revivals of various kinds, there has accordingly also been room for more wide-ranging studies of religion. But what has happened with these more wide-ranging studies of religion? It would appear that increasingly they are themselves nowadays religiously or theologically oriented. That is, the Marxist ideological perspective to which deference was previously paid, at least formally, seems to have been replaced by the view, even in non-theological schools, that religion is probably, in general, "a good thing". This change can be observed even in the contents of the Polish journal *Studia Religioznawcze*, when the issues which appeared before and after 1989 are compared. Before 1989 the work was more secular, while thereafter it became more religious in orientation. Ironically, religion itself in the form of organized Catholicism, while gaining ground in some legal and institutional respects, has been losing some of its importance for the Polish population in general during the 1990's (as I used to predict in the late 1980's).

Conclusion: fighting the trends of political correctness

Like a very small number of others[16] the author of this paper made his own discovery in the course of many years, through personal meetings, observations and reading, that the reality both of religion and the study of religions in Eastern Europe and the Soviet Union was far more complex than commonly supposed in the western world. But references to

16 These include James Thrower of the University of Aberdeen, with whom I was in correspondence about these matters shortly before his untimely death.

this complexity were met in the western world with suspicion. They simply were not politically correct. Now that the Cold War is supposedly finished, political correctness makes a new demand, namely that the "victory" of the western world over "communism" be indefinitely celebrated, thus making a reliable reassessment of earlier decades as difficult now as it was at the time. Those who left for the west in earlier times became devoted to their new homelands, while also finding much to surprise them. In some cases one can even speak of a kind of culture shock being experienced. Additionally, their memory of an eastern European situation was irrevocably marked by one particular country in one particular period. Their recollections and biographies are of considerable importance, but so too are those of colleagues who continued within the system. All providers of information (informants, in the fieldwork sense) have to be treated as such and understood in the context of their own biography and motivations. Longitudinal studies could be important here.

There is of course a strong temptation for the younger generation in what used to be the communist world, although they are no longer obliged to take account of communist ideology, to adopt in its place the political correctness of the capitalist world. I call upon them, however, to resist this trend and to use their knowledge of the relevant languages to document in detail the real history of the study of religions in the countries of eastern Europe. This history is not related solely to the period of the "Cold War" but also to the time before and the time after. Only with reference to the before and after can the activities during the Cold War themselves be adequately appraised.

As to colleagues in western countries, with few exceptions their interest in the matter has only really begun to develop since about 1989, when the feeling grew that one could personally visit a country in eastern Europe, just out of interest, without running the risk of being regarded as politically incorrect in their own countries.[17] But now that more people are beginning to get to know each other, perhaps a more balanced view can be developed on the western side as well. Then the Cold War could really come to an end. Unfortunately it is still being fought out with China. Thus the Tibetan connection runs wild in the western media. Dissenting sects such as Falun Gong are en-

17 Mention of my own journeys from to Czechoslovakia, Poland and the Soviet Union at various times between 1961 and 1990 was frequently met with scorn and/or suspicion by colleagues in western countries.

couraged from outside China while, fascinatingly, they meet with the same kind of oppressive response within China which they met with in pre-Communist times (cf. 5.5 below). The usual entanglements between political correctness, notions of religious freedom, religious propaganda, and the academic study of religions are still current. Even so, it proved possible to hold an IAHR conference in Beijing in 1992 and to protect it successfully from both religious and political pressures (cf. Dai, Zhang and Pye 1995). Could perceptive views of the history in eastern Europe be of assistance in the further development of academic interactions with China relating to the study of religions?

The study of religions is supposed to be neither religious, nor ideological, nor politically correct. Yet it has to be pursued patiently in ever-changing political and cultural circumstances. And in a small way, might it not help to free and preserve humankind from one or two of its worse follies? At the very least, it may be said that studies of religion in the countries of eastern Europe, during the extended difficulties created by the Cold War, contributed to the creation of areas of human sensitivity and respect for difference. The study of religions undoubtedly has a certain educational value and indeed a critical function, the implications of which are by no means critically pre-programmed. In this sense it shares in the best overall inheritance of the Enlightenment. Thus the study of religions draws on intellectual traditions which are older and broader than the categories of both sides of the Cold War, and this in turn is important for the future.

Bibliographical references

Anisimov, A.F. 1958. *Religiya evenkov v istoriko-geneticheskom izuchenii i problemy proiskhozhdeniya pervobytnykh verovanii.* Moscow (Izdatel'stvo Akademii Nauk SSSR).

Batunsky, Mark 1982. "Recent Soviet Islamology" in: *Religion* 12: 365–389.

Bělka, Luboš 2001. "Bidiya D. Dandaron: the case of Buryat Buddhist and Buddhologist during the Soviet Period" in: Doležalová et al. 2001: 171–182.

Chadwick, Owen 1992. The Christian Church in the Cold War. London (Allen Lane).

Dai Kangsheng, Zhang Xinying and Pye, Michael (eds.) 1995. *Religion and Modernization in China. Proceedings of the International Association for the History of Religions held in Beijing, China, April 1992.* Cambridge (Roots and Branches).

Diószegi, Vilmos 1968. *Popular Beliefs and Folklore Tradition in Siberia.* The Hague (Mouton).

Doležalová, Iva, Martin, Luther H. and Papoušek, Dalibor (eds) 2001. *The Academic Study of Religion during the Cold War: East and West.* Frankfurt and New York (Peter Lang).

Gemuyev, I. N. (ed.) 1990 *Mirovozzrenie Finno-ugorskich Narodov* ("Worldviews of Finno-Ugrian peoples"). Novosibirsk (Soviet Academy of Sciences).

Grzymała-Moszczyńska, Halina and Hoffmann, Henryk 1988. "The science of religion in Poland: past and present" in: *Method and Theory in the Study of Religion* 10: 352–72.

Helve, Helena 1993. *The World View of Young People: A Longitudinal Study of Finnish Youth Living in a Suburb of Metropolitan Helsinki.* Helsinki (Suomalainen Tiedeakatemia).

Holm, Nils G. and Björkqvist, Kaj (eds.) 1996. *World Views in Modern Society: Empirical Studies on the Relationship between World View, Culture, Personality and Upbringing.* Åbo (Åbo Akademi University).

Hoppál, Mihály 1975. "Šamanismi ja uralilaisten kansojen uskomusmaailma" [Shamanism and the worldview of the Uralic peoples] in: Hadjú, P. (ed.) *Suomalais-ugrilaiset.* Pieksämäki (Suomalaisen Kirjallisuuden Seura): 189–219.

– 1998. "Vilmos Diószegi: Life and Works" in: *Shaman* 6: 117–149.

Mäll, Linnart 2001. "Semiotics as a possibility for the study of religious texts under the conditions of communism" in Doležalová et al. 2001: 163–170.

Margul, Tadeusz (ed.) 1984. *International Bibliography of Comparative Religion in Dictionary Order.* Kraków (Uniwersytet Jagiellońska).

Poniatowski, Zygmunt 1979. "The beginnings of the Science of Religions in Poland (1873–1918)" in: *Studia Religioznawcze* 14, Series B: "Teoria i Metodologia Religioznawstwa": 11–51.

– 1990. "Studia Religiologica (1977–1988) – próba analizy edytometrycznej" in: Euhemer 1 (2): 143–49.

Pye, Michael 1973b. "Comparative Hermeneutics in Religion" in: Pye and Morgan 1973: 1–58.

– 1991b. "Religious studies in Europe: structures and desiderata" in: Klaus K. Klostermaier and Larry W. Hurtado (eds.), *Religious Studies: Issues, Prospects, and Proposals* (University of Manitoba Studies in Religion2). Atlanta (Scholars Press): 39–55.

– 1992a. "An Asian starting point for the study of religion" in: Nowaczyk M. and Stachowski, Z. (eds.) *Language,Religion, Culture: In Memory of Professor Witold Tyloch.* Warsaw (Polish Society for the Study of Religion) 27–35.

– 1994a. "What is 'religion' in East Asia?" in: Bianchi, Ugo, Mora Fabio and Bianchi Lorenzo (eds.) *The Notion of "Religion" in Comparative Research: Selected Proceedings of the XVIth Congress of the International Association for the History of Religions, Rome, 3rd-8th September, 1990.* Rome ("L'Erma" di Bretschneider): 115–22.

– 1994d. Christian churches and political change in Eastern Europe" in: Gill, S. D'Costa G. and King, U. (eds.) *Religion in Europe, Contemporary Pespectives.* Kampen (Pharaos): 188–200.
– 1995b. "Three teachings (sanjiao) theory and modern reflection on religion" in: Dai, K., Zhang, X. and Pye, M. (eds.) 1995. *Religion and Modernisation in China, Proceedings of the Regional Conference of the International Association for the History of Religions held in Beijing, China, April 1992.* Cambridge(Roots and Branches): 111–16.
Pye, Michael and Morgan, Robert (eds.) 1973. *The Cardinal Meaning. Essays in Comparative Hermeneutics: Buddhism and Christianity* (Religion and Reason 6). The Hague (Mouton).
Regamey, Constantin 1950. *Buddhistische Philosophie.* Bern (Francke).
Rudolph, Kurt 1978. "Die 'ideologie-kritische' Funktion der Religionswissenschaft" in: *Numen* 25: 17–39.
– 1981. "Basic positions of Religionswissenschaft" in: *Religion* 11: 97–107.
– 1985. *Historical Fundamentals and the Study of Religions,* New York (MacMillan).
– 1992. *Geschichte und Probleme der Religionswissenschaft.* Leiden (Brill).
Shcherbatskoy, Fedor I. [Stcherbatsky, Theodor] 1993 "The doctrine of the Buddha" in: *Bulletin of the School of Oriental and African Studies* 6: 867–96.
– 1927. *The Conception of Buddhist Nirvana.* Leningrad (Academy of Sciences of the USSR). Reprint: 1965 The Hague (Mouton).
Stcherbatsky, Theodor: see Shcherbatskoy, Fedor I.
Thrower, James 1983. "The study of religion in the USSR" in: *Religion* 13: 113–126.
Tokarev, Sergey Aleksandrovich 1986/1989. *History of Religion.* Moscow (Progress Publishers). (Translation of *Istoria Religii.*)
Tyloch, Witold 1979. "Polish Society for the Science of Religion" in: *Euhemer* 3 (113): 3–8.
Tyloch, Witold (ed.) 1984. *Current Progress in the Methodology of the Science of Religions.* Warsaw (Polish Scientific Publishers).
– 1990. *Studies on Religions in the Context of the Social Sciences: Methodological and Theoretical Relations.* Warsaw (Polskie Towarzystwo Religioznawcze).

In a slightly shorter form, this paper was first published in: Doležalová, Iva, Martin, Luther H. and Papoušek, Dalibor (eds.) 2001. *The Academic Study of Religion during the Cold War: East and West.* Frankfurt and New York (Peter Lang): 313–333. The redactional details vary slightly.

3.6 Difference and Coherence in the World-wide Study of Religions

This article is based on a contribution to a conference at Boston, Massachusetts, USA, in September 2000. This conference carried the title "Congress 2000: The Future of the Study of Religion" and was co-sponsored by Boston and Harvard Universities and the Ernst-Troeltsch-Gesellschaft. (It should not be confused with the 2000 Congress of the International Association for the History of Religions (IAHR) held in Durban, South Africa.)

Language and cultural identity in the study of religions

It is doubtful, and for this very reason interesting, whether any single person today could present an evenly balanced account of the study of religions in a truly global perspective. This is not only because of the huge quantity of relevant materials. In spite of vastly increased communication and the political and economic pressure for globalization, the major cultural and linguistic regions of the world in many ways remain stubbornly independent and different. Rather than trying to give a country-by-country tour, therefore, and an unfairly abbreviated list of specialists in the study of religions to be found in them, I intend to emphasize the significance of the diversity of models of religion which are deeply lodged in some of the cultural regions of the world. At the same time I will argue that in spite of their difference these are related, or could be related, to a contemporary study of religions that is internationally coherent. That is to say, while cultural difference is interesting, and important, this does not mean that the study of religions can or should be just arbitrary. If it is to be *scientific*, though the word sits uneasily in an English sentence about the humanities, then the study of religions must display certain features which themselves are not subject to cultural difference to a significant degree. It is the interplay between the perceived differences and the sought coherence of reflections upon them which gives the study of religions much of its fascination.

It will be well to begin by considering the relative independence of the various linguistic worlds in their relation to the study of religions. Even for North America, with its massive scholarly output, it is true to say that not only studies in particular religions but even meta-studies on the history and theory of the subject are often locked into one language world. This is not to deny the excellence of the works themselves, nor to deny that there are exceptions, but simply to state an overwhelming cultural fact. It is not surprising therefore that, over against this, Quebecers often feel the need to assert the value of francophone presentations. The very choice of language to some extent affects the discourse. It is for this very reason that the electronic discussion list Yggdrasill was set up to facilitate exchanges on the study of religions in German.[1] In general, the larger a particular cultural region is, the more self-sufficient it can be, and the less urgent it is for the majority of scholars in a given academic field to be open to the osmosis of influences from without.

The dominant language foci in Europe are of course English, French and German. There is a tendency for those in the Nordic countries and the Netherlands to make regular use of English in scholarly writing, though without neglecting their own languages, for those in East European countries to make additional use of German and English, and for those in Italy and Spain to prefer French. Of course there are innumerable other interactions, as when a Polish scholar reads and speaks Italian fluently, or when an Estonian is familiar with Finnish. The point made here however is that a self-sufficient language area, even within multilingual Europe, tends to restrict the scholarly discourse or at least to recycle it around the linguistic expectations found within it. Thus the quotation of "foreign" works in the original is often regarded in Britain as being somewhat distasteful. In Germany it is much more acceptable to cite works in English or other languages, but works in German are in fact more likely to be read than works in English, not to speak of those in less widely known languages.

But this is only the beginning. There is much more to the study of religions, in global perspective, than that which can be found in North America and Europe alone. Attention should be directed for example to

1 Since the time of writing, the European Association for the Study of Religions has provided a network of six cross-border electronic discussion lists to provide a service for the multi-lingual continent which it represents. Details of these lists: Candide, Dolmen, Most, Synkron, Tonantzin and Yggdrasill, may be found on www.easr.de.

East Asia, that is in particular, to China, Korea and Japan, where a long and complex intellectual history still needs to be taken fully into consideration in identifying the emergence of the contemporary study of religions. Here the importance of the language frame is evident. Is it indeed *religion* (or *religions*) which *studies of religions* in these countries study? In passing, it may be noted that there is in none of these languages a regular distinction between a singular and plural form of nouns, although, before the reader gets too excited about this, there are various ways of indicating that reference is being made to things, or events, in their plurality. Moreover, the recognition that religions, or *teachings*, occur in plurality, is not only one of the prime requirements for the emergence of advanced reflection about them, but also one which has been present in East Asia for centuries.[2]

Various studies taking these matters into account have focused on the term *religion* and its equivalents, or its alternatives, or its distant relatives, in a variety of cultures. Thus Arabic *din*, Sanskrit *dharma*, and so on, are adduced. Usually the argument is that these do not really correspond to western *religion*, and that the western concept leads to a distorted or inappropriately constructed view of non-western cultural systems. There is some truth in this. However, the fault, like beauty, lies in the eye of the beholder. As has already been argued, for example, by Peter Antes (Antes 1994), we may recognize that the particular terms have all had their history in the particular cultures and yet still require that the term selected to refer to the field under study be defined accordingly for the purpose.[3] Thus studies of religion today, even in the western world, are not beholden to a specific view of religion which would necessarily reflect, for example, the specific characteristics or supposed characteristics of the Christian religion. It is evident to most specialists in the discipline that it is the structures of the systems under study which are determinative, at least as far as the preliminary steps of elucidation and

2 I have argued this in various places since 1973 with increasingly detailed documentation. Cf. in particular the introduction to my translations of the eighteenth century Japanese writer Tominaga Nakamoto (Pye 1990a), and Part Two in the present volume.

3 Essentially, Kurt Rudolph comes to the same conclusion in his paper "Inwieweit ist der Begriff 'Religion' eurozentrisch?" (Rudolph 1994). It is quite impossible here to go into all the studies which have attended to this problem, but attention may be drawn to *The Notion of "Religion" in Comparative Research*, being the selected proceedings of the 16th IAHR Congress (Rome 1990) which were largely devoted to the question (Bianchi, Mora and Bianchi 1994).

characterization[4] are concerned. It is not necessary, indeed it is well known that is undesirable, to insert a preemptive, normative view of *religion* into that which is under study. Training oneself to avoid this pitfall is an elementary feature of the discipline of the study of religions (that is, *Religionswissenschaft*).

The question of the terminology therefore, though interesting, has really lost its drama. Indeed, in so far as people continue to assert, erroneously and/or misleadingly, that East Asian terms for religion such as the Japanese *shūkyō* are loaded with western meanings, they are guilty of a kind of inverted orientalism, which I call *westernism* (Pye 2000) The problem arises partly because of the continuing ethnocentricity of many of those who normally write in English, which is indeed the dominant language of globalization processes, and partly, on the other hand, by the very understandable, continuing need to prove identity on the part of articulate representatives of those who are mainly using *other* important languages, especially Asian ones. The latter seek to establish their own *distance* by discriminating against selected terminology in their own language, arguing that it is western-derived, or that it bears inappropriate "western" meanings. The standard commentary on the Japanese term *shūkyō* is a classic case of this deplorable syndrome. It may be agreed that, for a particular period in the nineteenth century, it addressed that which, at that time, at least in the minds of politically alert and active Japanese, demanding westerners supposed *religion* to be. However, the term has both a pre-history and a post-history. I will not go into the older history of it here (see Pye 1994a) As to recent years, it has come to mean hardly more and hardly less than either *religion* or *religions*, depending on the context, without necessarily implying a pre-eminence of scripture and dogma, or of definite personal faith, such as was highlighted in the nineteenth century.

All of this does not mean that just any terms in any languages may be regarded as equivalents to *religion*, or for that matter to other apparently satisfactory words such as the Finnish *uskonto*, or again to the Dutch term *godsdienst.* The latter, incidentally, might be regarded as unsatisfactory because of the evident highlighting of particular aspects of religion. Interestingly the Afrikaans equivalent *godsdiens* was at some point complemented by *religie* which has more general connotations. Clearly some words in some languages refer to matters which do not precisely match

4 The overall methodological sequence should be: elucidation, characterization, structural analysis and correlational explanation (cf. papers 1.2 and 1.6 above).

the area which is addressed by modern studies of religions. *Dharma* is a good example. But this is no reason for general despair. If we turn to Indonesia, to take another case, we find the word *agama*. This is of Indian derivation, but it is used also as in the Indonesian plural *agama agama*, to refer to religions in their plurality. It is used also in compound terms to refer to psychology of religion, sociology of religion, and so on. This usage of *agama* is not really significantly different from the usage of *religion* when we speak in English of the study of religions. I conclude at this point therefore that the discussion of this admittedly central terminology, though interesting and indeed necessary, is intrinsically no more important than the poly-linguistic discussion of much other theoretical terminology in the study of religions, which by now has become more urgent. Not only have people become unduly worked up about it, the trend of the discussion has usually been faulty.

Nevertheless, there is cultural difference between the major regions of the world, and this difference has important effects on the ways in which religions, religious systems and religious processes are perceived. Partly it is connected to the vocabulary available in diverse languages, which cannot always immediately be related to internationally recognizable terminology. But it is not only a question of diversity of language. The dominant languages of Latin America, Spanish and Portuguese, have a more or less seamless openness to the traditional intellectual discourses of Europe, and yet the widely presupposed model of religion is not the same as that which is current in Europe, as I will argue in more detail below. On the continent of Africa south of the Sahara, the dominant educational and scholarly languages are French and English, but here too a recognizable *model* of religion is widely presupposed which has common and distinctive contours. Before taking up these models in detail a few words need to be said about the coherence of the study of religions as a scientific enterprise.

A certain understanding of the study of religions

The approach taken here does presuppose a certain understanding of the *study of religions*, whatever cultural region they are most at home in, which may not be shared by all. There is no way around this. I am speaking here of the study of religions as a coherent discipline in its own right. This does not mean that a single autonomous religious principle is presupposed, as by Schleiermacher, Otto, and others. What it does mean is that there is a perceivable field of historical, cultural and social data which can be studied, which is not the same as just any other field, which can conveniently be denoted by the very general term *religion* and which requires a particular clustering of otherwise known methods for its elucidation, characterization, analysis and explanation (Pye 1999a, and as 1.2 above). In this sense, without privileging any particular religious or metaphysical assumptions or assertions, and without excluding the usual interdisciplinary interaction between the social and cultural sciences, the study of religions takes its place as an autonomous discipline among others.

Broadly speaking, this perspective is consistent with the center of gravity shared by those who participate in the work of the International Association for the History of Religions (IAHR), and its numerous affiliate associations world-wide.[5] Not that this widely based association prescribes a specific scientific orthodoxy. My own understanding of *study of religions*, for example, is more tightly formulated than that of some others who have been involved in it in various ways, as may be seen in Ursula King's review of the proceedings of a small IAHR conference in 1988 entitled *Marburg Revisited*.[6] In general, however, there has been a widespread perception that the work of the IAHR can at any rate be distinguished from that of not a few other associations which are somehow devoted to *religion*, especially those with a strongly and religiously programmatic profile, such as the recently revived World's Parliament of Religions. It is also instructive that the IAHR

5 A recent account of the work of the IAHR, with special reference to methodological perspectives, may be found in a special issue of *Method and Theory in the Study of Religion* (Geertz and McCutcheon 2000) and in the journal editors' own introductory paper. This is not the place to list all the affiliate associations of the IAHR, which may be found on the appropriate website. Suffice it to note, for example, that the journal just mentioned is the official journal of the North American Association for the Study of Religion, and that the various national associations in the European context have recently found a new, regional coordinatory focus in the European Association for the Study of Religions (cf. www.easr.de). There are national associations of the IAHR all over the world, that is, in various countries such as China, Indonesia, Japan, Korea, Mexico, South Africa, and two other important regional associations should be noted, namely those for Latin America and for Africa.

6 The review is in *Method and Theory in the Study of Religions* 3 (1). The conference itself was a concerted attempt by specialists from various countries to consider "institutions and strategies in the study of religion," taking cultural and indeed political diversity into account (see Pye 1989a).

has had its own internal, clarificatory debates. There was an important moment in 1960 when Friedrich Heiler's religiously idealistic approach was differentiated from the mainstream within the IAHR of the day, which emphasized the importance of distinguishing historical and comparative studies of religions from theological interactions. That debate also took place in Marburg, and the title *Marburg Revisited*, mentioned above, was chosen to reflect the fact that a number of senior persons were present on both occasions.[7] This is not just gossip; it indicates longitudinal coherence within a recognizable community of international scholarship. Over the last quarter of a century there has been, in IAHR events, an increasing recognition of the importance of the social scientific perspective, leading to the debate, between 1990 and 1995, over a possible change of name which would have replaced the word *history* by *study*. This debate ended when the General Assembly in Mexico City voted not to make the change, largely in order to maintain the brand value of the well-known acronym. However the interest aroused demonstrated that the corporate perception of all concerned balanced historical and social-scientific perspectives rather evenly. It is true to say that both of these aspects complement each other to this day in congress programs, as has recently been seen at the 18th world congress in Durban (2000). On the other hand, it remains as clear as ever that the IAHR, while permitting very varied participation in its activities, does not itself stand for or promote any particular religious ideas or programs.

In sum, the position taken here is that such an approach to the study of religions, tolerantly and inclusively conceived, and typified by the world-wide membership and programs of the IAHR yet intellectually, of course, by no means restricted to these, is a legitimate and desirable contribution within the academic community. It is characterized by the interaction of historical-philological methods and social-scientific methods. It is the correlation between the field of study, the relevant sources and the appropriate methods which together form the character of this discipline, just as in other cases such as social anthropology or archaeology. Moreover this understanding of the discipline has become increasingly recognized throughout the world in recent decades, even though

7 Ugo Bianchi, Lauri Honko, Kurt Rudolph, Annemarie Schimmel, Heinrich von Stietencron, Noriyoshi Tamaru, R. J. Zwi Werblowsky, as well as the two Marburg colleagues Hans-Jürgen Greschat and Martin Kraatz. The 1960 debate was documented in the IAHR journal *Numen* 7 (1960), 215–39, by Zwi Werblowsky, Annemarie Schimmel and C. J. Bleeker.

the political and social acceptability of the discipline varies from place to place because it is, not surprisingly, affected by the dominant ideological and/or religious culture.

While the fundamental motivation is that of scientific enquiry, the study of religions may or may not be regarded as having socially or religiously useful applications, for example by contributing to religious education, to inter-communal relations in pluralist societies, or to the stabilization of activities in the realm of inter-religious dialogue. In these contexts, although the topic is very well worn, it still seems to be necessary to distinguish between scientific and religious activities. The scientific motivation is not in itself religious. This does not mean, on the other hand, that it is necessary to be irreligious in order to study religions. A religious person may wish to undertake a scientifically conceived enquiry into religions. But an exercise in the study of religions is not in itself a religious enquiry. Religious persons may even conclude that the study of religions is in some way helpful for them. Any such functions however *presuppose* the independent viability of the discipline as such. Without this, the value of any wider educational contributions within society will be lost.

There are all kinds of reasons why people may not wish to share this view of the study of religions. At its simplest, the common denominator is that they are mainly interested in, or seeking to carry out research into something else. Carrying out research into other fields is of course entirely legitimate. People may be interested in philosophical and cultural questions raised by thinkers like Nietzsche, Freud, Bloch or Habermas. Or they may be Buddhists, Muslims, Christians, Jews or Sikhs, etc., who wish to work primarily, as academics, on the textual and intellectual sources of their own particular religion. For such specialized clerics the field of study is not *religions* but rather a circumscribed collection of data which are presumed to bear high religious significance for their own particular religious community. Others may have a programmatic interest in religious or religiously related issues, for example in attempts to define a *world ethic*, in correlations with ecological questions, human rights, and so on. Or they may be social scientists whose main interest is in the analysis of society in general. For these investigators, religion or religions are one factor in the overall development of hypotheses, but not themselves the main object of study. It may seem attractive to think of all these as 'options' or 'approaches,' and even to collect them up under general phrases such as 'religious studies' or even 'theology and religious studies.' But then we should ask, 'options' or 'approaches' about or towards what? We will quickly find that people are looking and running in quite diverse directions, and that a focused academic discipline cannot be identified. Perversely, this situation may then be taken as indicative of an 'identity crisis' in the study of religions, when it really has nothing to do with it, being no more than a collective muddle created by various people who themselves, primarily, have no intention of carrying out *study of religions* to begin with.

There are relatively few settings in which the study of religions is clearly established institutionally as a discipline in its own right. At the same time the number of academics who in some sense study religions is very great. Many of them have a primary loyalty to another discipline such as anthropology, sociology, classics, medieval history, a particular branch of oriental studies, and so on. This inevitably means that the clarity of the discipline is often obscured, though with the advantage that interdisciplinarity is often attained through osmosis. This situation may therefore be regarded quite positively. But it should also be seen clearly. The importance of contributions from all these disciplines and others not mentioned here may be seen in the extent to which they figure in bibliographical publications such as *Science of Religion.*[8]

Cultural diversity and divergent models of religion

If it is possible to see some convergence regarding the academic study of religions as an enterprise which is itself scientifically and not religiously motivated, where are we left with regard to the diversity of the major cultural regions whose difference was emphasized in the first section of this paper? Typically, studies of religion in different parts of the globe, while sharing some assumptions about the independent, reflective and analytical character of our discipline, address above all the situation of religions in those specific parts of the globe, taking account of which religions are particularly important there and whatever social and political questions are current at any one time. It is interesting therefore that there are in fact different underlying models of *religion* current in the major cultural areas of the world. In this regard, as already argued, it is not of crucial importance to debate the Latin-derived term *religion* and its intercultural viability or lack of it. Rather, we should get to

8 Published in English since 1976, following a Dutch prototype. By the end of the year 2000 some 16,660 articles had been summarized and indexed.

know the historically conditioned parameters, in any one region, for the perception of the possible subject of study, and the key features of the social and political debate which surround it. Let us briefly consider therefore how the fundamental features of the religious scene are perceived in diverse regions of the world. These perceptions have a tremendous effect on what people regard as the field of study and even on the way in which it is studied. It should be emphasized that such models are themselves sub-scientific. Indeed, they have a more or less unshakeable, memetic quality.[9]

In Latin America we have an evident juxtaposition of Catholicism on the one hand and pre-conquest religious systems and elements thereof on the other hand. The interaction between these two has provided a classic model for studies of religion in Latin America, whether they have been approached from a religious, i. e., in most cases Catholic point of view, or an 'anthropological' point of view. Sometimes these two run together, a fine example of the genre being Manuel Marzal's *La transformación religiosa peruana* (1983). At the same time, pre-conquest religions and their continuing remnants, especially in the smaller ethnic groups which were not at first affected greatly by the invasion, have also been the subject of many independent historical and field studies which do not have to be adduced in detail here. Latin American Catholicism, on the other hand, has not been studied very much as a phenomenon in its own right until recently. Particularly important cults such as that of the Virgin of Guadalupe in Mexico have of course attracted attention, but the main reason for this has been the strength of its non-Catholic functions, as may be seen in a recent study edited by sociologists Paolo Giuriati and Elio Masferrer Kan (1998).[10] This model of two main elements, in interaction, has gradually been complemented by two additional factors. First, new religions of varied provenance such as the frequently studied Brazilian Candomblé and Umbanda have rightly attracted attention. Second, and more recently, the picture has been redrawn by the wave of Pentecostalism throughout the continent,

9 The relation, indeed the tension, between common, memetic models and scientifically differentiated theories of religion is the subject of a related paper (Pye 2002a) delivered at a meeting of the European Association for the Study of Religions in Messina (March 2001) (for proceedings see Gasparro 2002). The term *memetic* was devised by Richard Dawkins (Dawkins 1976) and unfortunately is easily confused with *mimetic*.

10 For a substantial historical and phenomenological study of the cult see Nebel 1995, but note the interesting name “”Santa María Tonantzin” in the title.

which is drowning out the relatively weak impact of earlier protestant missions. This in turn has attracted the interest of sociologists interested in the big picture. Recently, the complete spectrum of the complex religious life of the continent has been establishing itself as the object of study, from a scientific point of view, as in seen in the conferences of the Asociación Latinoamericana para el Estudio de las Religiones.[11] Nevertheless it continues to be widely assumed by most researchers, other intellectuals, and significantly also by politicians, that the field of study is constituted by the dominant elements which I have just named, and their interactions. Hinduism and Buddhism, by contrast, are not commonly regarded as part of the Latin American story, even though they are not unknown on that continent. In Europe and in North America, on the other hand, they have come to be a part of the publicly perceived pattern of religious pluralism.

Now consider the main parameters in Europe, for they are different. Three main traditions set the basic scene. In the more western countries and regions these are Catholicism and anti-Catholic secularism on the one hand, and Protestantism and post-Protestant secularism on the other hand. In the east the major backdrop is provided by Orthodoxy. Set on this background of three major Christian traditions is a web of significant religious pluralism including very diverse forms of Christianity at least in the larger urban areas, a strong presence of Islam and a regular sprinkling of smaller groups such as Sikhs, Hindus and others, depending on the country or region. Recently an increased range of post-industrial options is perceived to have been provided by New Age culture and by religions newly adopted from Asia or America. These are the main elements of which 'religion' is perceived to consist by those who reflect on it in a European context. Works on religion by sociologists in post-communist times are simply full of these themes.[12] This may all seem very obvious to most Europeans, and even somehow "right". Yet it is remarkable that other religious worlds are almost completely ignored in this picture, for example the world of Latin America, which we have just been thinking about. Also ignored, except by specialists, are the pre-Christian religions. After all, these are supposed to have been displaced long ago. Their reappearance in New Age culture

11 See, for example, the fascinating range of themes treated at a conference of the association held in Columbia in 1996 (see Ferro Medina 1997).

12 See, for example, Irena Borowik and Jabłoński 1995 and Borowik and Babinski 1997.

is very grudgingly perceived. The religions of antiquity are a matter for classicists and archaeologists, and do not form part of the standard model. In educational contexts we may note in some countries the continued study of major religious cultures such as India and Egypt, and of major religions such as Buddhism, Islam and Judaism, because they are regarded as "world religions." But this is based on contributions by professional teachers with specialized knowledge. More theoretical categories such as civil religion, or the idea that nationalisms or monarchies can be analyzed as religions, are not regarded in the popular mind as really belonging to the main pattern of religion. Such thoughts lead away again into a different level of reflection.

I hesitate to attempt a similar delineation for the United States and Canada, where I have had much less opportunity for first-hand observation either of the field itself or of what scholars do with it. Superficially at least it seems to have more affinity to the pattern seen in Europe than that of Latin America. However, some special features are prominent. First, there is a profound recognition of the respect-worthiness of religious voluntarism and dissent, which can only partly be matched in European countries. Second, there is a stronger concept of civil religion as an immediate ingredient in the foundation of the nation, at least in the USA if less in Canada. The development of the concept of civil religion by Robert N. Bellah, especially in *The Broken Covenant* (1975,1992), seems to have been in part an expression of a publicly recognized need, against the background of freedom for religious diversity, for a continuing, if watered-down religious and moral motivation on the part of the general populace. That it also became a transferable, analytic concept, is important, but was perhaps secondary. The continued strength of various evangelical denominations is also striking. The only real parallel in Europe might be found in the life of the so-called "free churches" in Britain, but these have weakened radically since the Second World War. The U.S.A. has also seen a greater propensity to religious innovation than Europe, though nowadays there may not be so much difference in this respect as there used to be. The relative acceptability of innovative movements in the popular model may have been due first to the wider areas available for social and cultural expansion, as for example in Utah, and second, to even more extensive and complex demographic movements caused by immigration. The recognition of significant religious pluralism as a result of the distinctive ethnic minorities from Europe, Asia and elsewhere is also important. These minorities benefited from the established public recognition of religious diversity, even though the religions in question themselves do not necessarily display dissent or voluntarism as a religious orientation. It is only hesitantly that the at once traditional and innovatory religious culture of North American Indians has seriously been allowed to impinge on the wider consciousness. What does all this add up to, when stated simply? I would suggest that the dominant model in North America is of religious diversity within a dominant Christian and post-Christian culture. However the details are or might be negotiated, it is also not the same as the Latin American model.

Turning now to Africa, the time when it was presumed that "Africans" were simply "without religion" altogether is now but dimly remembered. Nowadays a four-fold pattern is widely presupposed consisting firstly of indigenous religions, commonly referred to as *African traditional religion*; secondly, Christianity in its Roman Catholic and World Council of Churches forms; thirdly, Islam; and fourthly, African independent churches and other religious movements which have arisen since the impact of the colonial and missionary period. These are the ever-recurring elements among the subjects chosen for study not only by Africanists in general, but more importantly by specialists on religion working within Africa, by Africans and non-Africans alike. Of course, there are also scholars here and there who study specific examples of religion which do not fall within these categories, such as the various forms of Hinduism found in Kwazulu-Natal (Diesel and Maxwell 1993), or who lean towards Buddhist studies, such as Jacobus Krüger who translated the *Sutta Nipata* into Afrikaans under the title *Skep die skip leeg* (1999) But these are the contributions of scholars who see *beyond* the edges of the dominant model.[13] It remains to be seen how far new programs of religious education, for example, those under development right now in South Africa, will be influenced by the underlying fourfold model of what is important in the field of religion in Africa, and how far concepts such as 'world religions' will conspire to introduce and highlight new elements.

In each of the continents mentioned so far the continuing presence of Christian theological education and research means that the history of religions preceding and surrounding the Christian tradition continues to receive attention. There is a certain tension between the relative importance of the Jewish and Christian trajectory in the history of religions

13 For a valiant attempt to turn these edges, see J. S. Krüger's inspiring title *Along Edges. Religion in South Africa: Bushman, Christian, Buddhist* (1995).

and the sense that consideration must be given to the study of religions in general. However, even though Islam may be added to the Abrahamic family, especially in Europe because of the demographic pressures, the main religions of Asia still tend to be regarded as "other religions," with which Christianity might or might not have relations. Amazingly, the phrases "other religions," and in German *fremde Religionen*, are still in widespread use, in spite of efforts by a small minority to get rid of them.[14]

In order to escape this syndrome let us therefore finally consider the East Asian model or models. A very instructive starting point in this case is the view of religion advanced by the first emperor of the Ming Dynasty in China, who (like Constantine and Aśoka) decided that it would be politically expedient to have a policy on religion. Not only that, he composed a short treatise on the subject. Beginning with the already well-established idea of the *three teachings,* that is, Confucianism, Buddhism and Daoism, he also took account of three further elements in the total pattern. These were the rites of the state, the general belief in a network of gods and spirits providing support for the teachings of Buddhism and Daoism, and lastly, teachings which lead people astray and which are therefore to be forbidden.[15]

In various forms this model has persisted in the East Asian states influenced by the Chinese literary, intellectual and political tradition. One of the main features of the model is that political registration and to a considerable extent control of religions have an established history. This seems to most people in the countries concerned to be quite natural, and may be contrasted, for example, with Brazil, where religious organizations are unregulated. The political importance of this underlying Chinese model has, in turn, an effect on what many scholars in those countries think they are studying. In Japan, for example, most specialists in religion are familiar with the yearbook of statistics and other registration material (*Shūkyō Nenkan*) published by the Ministry of Science and Education (*Kagaku-Monbushō*). It contributes to the determination of

14 In view of the fact that the conference at which this paper was delivered was a meeting of the Ernst Troeltsch Society, I draw attention here to my article "Ernst Troeltsch and the end of the problem about 'other religions'" (Pye 1976) which appeared in a multi-authored book of Troeltsch studies edited by John Powell Clayton.

15 For an English translation of this short but fascinating treatise see Taylor 1983, and for a discussion of the implications see, for example, my above mentioned paper "What is 'religion' in East Asia?" (1994a).

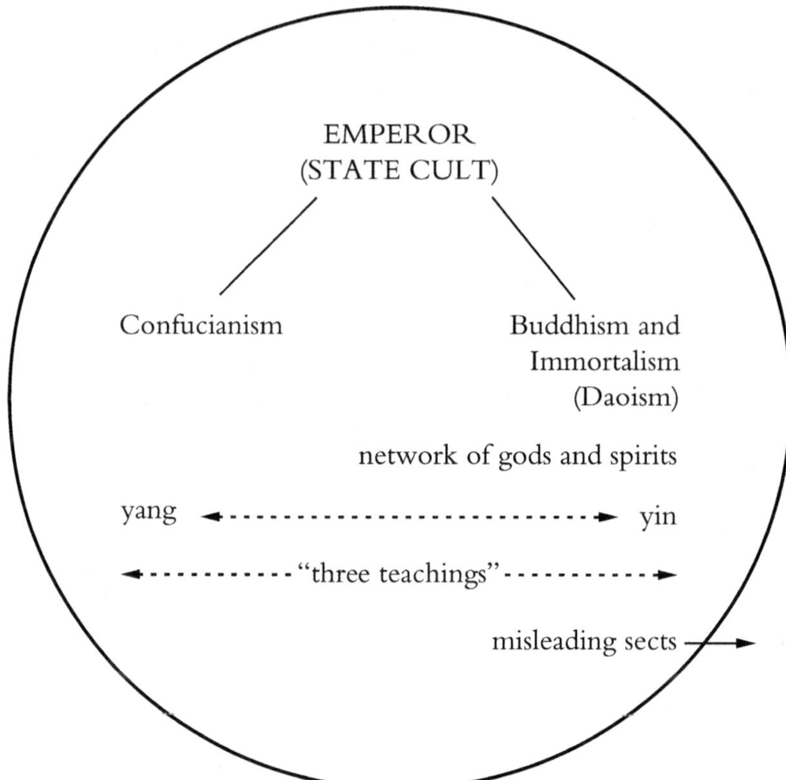

Fig. 1. Religions of China as perceived by the founder of the Ming Dynasty.

their field of study. This is not to deny that their perspective is also influenced by various other considerations of a theoretical kind and by interaction with scholars from other continents.

The suspicion with which innovatory sects have been and are viewed in the countries of East Asia arises because of this dominant model. Recent problems relating to Aum Shinrikyō in Japan and to Falungong in China must be understood in this light. In the first case the authorities were slow to investigate Aum Shinrikyō and to check its activities, for fear of contravening the post-war law on religious freedom. Liberal though that law is, it nevertheless envisages the registration of religious bodies as "religious juridical persons" (to use the older literal translation), or "religious corporations" (to use a recently favoured term).[16] In the af-

16 For a general account of the legal arrangements concerning religion in Japan see Pye 2001a.

termath of the criminal acts committed by the leadership of Aum Shinrikyō, the law has been tightened and there are greater possibilities of controlling religious movements which might be publicly regarded as leading people astray. In the case of Falungong, the official Chinese position that it leads the people astray arises less from Communist doctrine, which theoretically regards all religions as a drug for the masses, but rather from the older idea that some religions are relatively acceptable in society while others are disturbing, unpredictable, and probably dangerous for the state. Since Falungong members are led from outside the country (the meditation guru resides in New York), and its members are called upon to meditate, somewhat provocatively, in the Tiananmen Square which in many minds has become a symbol of political dissent, it is not surprising that the Chinese government has defined it as a superstition which leads the people astray. Other religions, by contrast, have found acceptance in modern China, in an admittedly very strictly regulated system. Currently there are five officially recognized religions, namely Buddhism, Daoism, Islam, Christianity and Catholicism. Fascinating, at least for outsiders, is the long history of religious innovation in the countries of East Asia. While new movements and organizations have often been regarded with suspicion by the authorities (think also for example of the political trajectory of Cao Dai in Vietnam), there is a widespread assumption that it is natural for new teachers to announce new revelations or spiritual methods. So there has always been a question in the minds of leaders about how such initiatives can be seen to fit in with the current stable pattern, if at all.

Apart from the sheer interest of particular cases, the general point being made here is that there are certain firm parameters in those widely shared models which influence and indeed largely determine the studies of religion in particular cultural regions of the world. The details are, of course, another question altogether. The models not only do not exhaust the details, they may not even have room for them. For example, reflecting on my own observations in Mexico, I recently ran up the following list of elements in contemporary Mexican religion: pre-conquest elements, assimilated pre-conquest elements, resurgent pre-conquest elements, reinvented pre-conquest elements, evangelizing Catholicism, architecturally dominant Catholicism, catholic polytheism, Guadalupenismo as a vehicle of pre-conquest elements, Guadalupenismo as Catholic inculturation, Guadalupenismo as Mexican identity (Criollos), Guadalupenismo in fusion with civil religion, secularism (anti-Catholicism), civil religion (including some of the above), amuletism, New Age themes, Charismatic movement (cf. Pye 2000b, also as paper 1.5 above). Naturally, there might be considerable discussion about these. On the other hand, the really determinative elements of the various models I have set out above are fewer and simpler. They are rarely up for discussion. They are just there. If they do get to be altered through a shift in relations between the main elements, or by the intrusion of a newcomer element, then it is a matter of considerable social and political interest with possibly far-reaching implications. In other words, new elements threaten to produce a paradigm shift in the dominant perception within the region itself. An example of such a shift has been the recent recognition, in Europe, of the social reality of a plurality of religions from without the Christian tradition.

I hope that I have shown that, in taking seriously the cultural diversity of various regions of the world, we are compelled to take account of divergent models of what counts as the field, when people engage in the study of religions. However, this does not mean that the study of religions cannot be and should not be a coherent undertaking in a world-wide perspective, allowing for the collaboration of scholars from within the various cultural regions. Precisely this is desirable to achieve the stabilization both of descriptive terminology and of theoretical analyses. Over against the deep-seated, extremely simple models, which for significant historical reasons are culturally diverse, are to be set two important considerations. The first is the unity of the scientific approach to the study of religions, which was set out in the first part of the paper. The second is the differentiated theoretical analysis of the field, in all its variety, which comes about when specialists begin to attend to it in detail. The elaboration of these perceptions, in all their variegated interest, is part of the shared work of those who are seriously engaged in the study of religions, so that theoretical coherence is to be expected in the long term.

Bibliographical references

Antes, Peter 1994. "Religion, *din* et *dharma* dans la perspective d'une recherche comparative" in: Bianchi, Mora and Bianchi 1994: 641–44.

Bellah, Robert N. 1975 (1992). *The Broken Covenant. American Civil Religion in the Time of Trial.* Chicago (Chicago University Press)

Bianchi, Ugo, Mora Fabio and Bianchi Lorenzo (eds.) 1994. *The Notion of "Religion" in Comparative Research: Selected Proceedings of the XVIth Congress* *of the International Association for the History of Religions, Rome, 3rd-8th September, 1990.* Rome ("L'Erma" di Bretschneider):

Borowik, Irena, and Przemysław Jabłoński (eds.) 1995. *The Future of Religion. East and West.* Kraków (Nomos).

Borowik, Irena and Babinski, Grzegorz (eds.) 1997. *New Religious Phenomena in Central and Eastern Europe.* Kraków (Nomos)

Clayton, John P. (ed.) 1976. *Ernst Troeltsch and the Future of Theology.* Cambridge (Cambridge University Press).

Dawkins, Richard 1976. *The Selfish Gene.* Oxford (Oxford University Press).

Diesel, Alleyn, and Maxwell, Patrick 1993. *Hinduism in Natal. A Brief Guide.* Pietermaritzburg (University of Natal Press).

Ferro Medina, Germán (ed.) 1997. *Religión y Etnicidad en América Latina.* 3 vols. Santafé de Bogotà (Instituto Colombiano de Antropología).

Gasparro, Giulia Sfameni 2002. *Themes and Problems of the History of Religions in Contemporary Europe (Proceedings of the International Seminar Messina, March 30–31 2001).* Cosenza (Edizioni Lionello Giordano).

Geertz, Armin W. and McCutcheon, Russell T. 2000. "The role of method and theory in the IAHR" in: *Method and Theory in the Study of Religion* 12 (1/2), 3–37.

Giuriati, Paolo and Kan, Elio Masferrer (eds.) 1998. *No temas...yo soy tu madre. Un Estudio Socioantropológico de los Peregrinos a la Basílica de Guadalupe.* Mexico City (Plaza y Valdés Editores).

González Torres, Yolotl. 1985. *El Sacrificio Humano entre los Mexicas.* Mexico City (Fondo de Cultura Económica).

Holm, Nils. G. et al. (eds.) 2000. *Ethnography is a Heavy Rite. Studies of Comparative Religion in Honor of Juha Pentikäinen* (Religionsvetenskapliga skrifter 47). Åbo (Åbo Akademis Tryckeri).

Krüger, Jakobus S. 1995. *Along Edges. Religion in South Africa: Bushman, Christian, Buddhist.* Pretoria (University of South Africa)

1999. *Skep die Skip Leeg, en ander vroeë Boeddhistiese gedigte in vertaling, uit Pali, van die Sutta Nipata.* Pretoria (University of South Africa).

Marzal, Manuel. 1983. *La Transformación Religiosa Peruana.* Lima (Pontificia Universidad Católica del Peru).

Nebel, Richard. 1995. *Santa María Tonantzin Virgen de Guadalupe. Continuidad y Transformación Religiosa en México.* Mexico City (Fondo de Cultura Economica).

Pye, Michael. 1976. "The end of the problem about 'other' religions" in Clayton 1976: 172–195.

– 1989a (ed.). *Marburg Revisited. Institutions and Strategies in the Study of Religion.* Marburg (Diagonal-Verlag).

– 1990a. (trans.) *Emerging from Meditation (Tominaga Nakamoto).* London (Duckworth) and Honolulu (University of Hawaii Press).

– 1994a. "What is 'religion' in East Asia?" in: Bianchi, Mora and Bianchi Lorenzo 1994: 115–22.

– 1999a. "Methodological Integration in the Study of Religions" in: Tore Ahlbäck (ed.) *Approaching Religion, Scripta Instituti Donneriani Aboensis XVII*

(1), Åbo/Turku, Finland (Donner Institute for Research in Religious and Cultural History): 188–205.
– 2000a. “Westernism unmasked” in: Jensen, Tim and Rothstein, Mikael (eds.) *Secular Theories on Religion. Current Perspectives*. Copenhagen (Museum Tusculanum Press): 211–230.
– 2000b. “Participation, observation and reflection: an endless method” in: Holm et al. 2000: 64–79.
– 2001a. “Religion und Recht in Japan: Pluralismus, Toleranz und Konkurrenz” in: *Marburg Journal of Religion* 6 (1): http://www.uni-marburg.de/religionswissenschaft/journal/mjr/pye.html
– 2002a. “Memes and models in the study of religions” in: Gasparro 2002: 245–59.

Rudolph, Kurt 1994. “Inwieweit ist der Begriff ‘Religion’ eurozentrisch? “ In Bianchi, Mora and Bianchi Lorenzo 1994: 131–39.

Taylor, Romeyn 1983. “An imperial endorsement of syncretism. Ming T’ai Tsu’s Essay on Three Teachings: translation and commentary” in: *Ming Studies* 16: 31–38.

Tominaga, Nakamoto: see Pye 1990.

This paper was first published as “Difference and coherence in the worldwide study of religions” in: Jakelic, Slavica and Pearson, Lori (eds), *The Future of the Study of Religion*, Boston and Leiden (Brill) 2006: 77–95.

Author's Publications Cited in the Present Work

This integrated overview lists publications by the author which are cited in one or both volumes of the present work. The lettered sequences found here (a, b, c, etc.) are adopted within the bibliographies of particular articles. A more detailed list including writings not cited in these volumes, going up as far as 2003, was kindly compiled by Renate Stegerhoff-Raab and included in Kleine, Christoph, Schrimpf, Monika and Triplett, Katja (eds.) 2003: *Unterwegs. Neue Pfade in der Religionswissenschaft (Festschrift…)*, München (Biblion Verlag):17–28. Multi-authored or multi-edited works which include the present writer are listed in a separate section below, following the alphabetical sequence of the first person to be named.

1969

"The transplantation of religions" in: *Numen, International Review for the History of Religions* 16 (3): 234–9. (N.B. published under the name E.M.Pye.)

1971a

"Syncretism and Ambiguity" in: *Numen. International Review for the History of Religions* 18 (2): 83–93.

1971b

"Assimilation and skilful means" in: *Religion* 1 (2): 152–8.

1972a

Comparative Religion: An Introduction through Source Materials. Newton Abbot (David and Charles) and New York (Harper and Row).

1972b

"A Buddhist approach to comparative religion in schools" in: *British Journal of Educational Studies* 20 (3): 270–81.

1973a

"Aufklärung and religion in Europe and Japan" in: *Religious Studies* 9: 201–217.

1973b

"Comparative hermeneutics in religion" in: Pye and Morgan 1973: 1–58.

1974

"Problems of method in the interpretation of religion" in: *Japanese Journal of Religious Studies* 1 (2–3): 107–123.

1975

"Japanese studies of religion" in: *Religion* (Special Congress Issue): 55–72.

1976

"The end of the problem about 'other' religions" in: Clayton, John P. (ed.), *Ernst Troeltsch and the Future of Theology*. Cambridge (Cambridge University Press): 172–95.

1977

"Troeltsch and the science of religion" in: Morgan and Pye 1977: 234–252.

1978a

Skilful Means. A Concept in Mahāyāna Buddhism. London (Duckworth) and (Routledge – 2nd edition 2003).

1978b

"Diversions in the interpretation of Shintō" in: Anthony, D.W. (ed.), *Proceedings of the British Association for Japanese Studies 1977 (Volume Two, Part Two: Social Sciences)*, Sheffield (University of Sheffield: Centre of Japanese Studies): 77–92. (Republished Pye 1981.)

1979a

The Buddha. London and Dallas (Duckworth).

1979b

Theologie im Kontext des religiösen Pluralismus, in: Kremkau, Klaus (ed.), *Christus allein – allein das Christentum? (Vorträge der vierten theologischen Konferenz zwischen Vertretern der Evangelischen Kirche in Deutschland und der Kirche von England).* Frankfurt am Main (Verlag Otto Lembeck): 11–25.

1980a

"On comparing Buddhism and Christianity" in: *Studies (Tsukuba Daigaku Tetsugakushisōgakkei Ronshū)* 5 (1979 issue): 1–20.

1980b

"Comparative hermeneutics: a brief statement" in: *Japanese Journal of Religious Studies* 7/1 (1980) 25–33.

1981

"Diversions in the interpretation of Shintō" in: *Religion.* 11: 61–74. (Republication of 1978b).

1982a
"The study of religion as an autonomous discipline" in: *Religion* 12: 67–76.

1982b
"Diversions in the interpretation of Shintō" in: *Religion*. 11: 61–74. (Republication of Pye 1978).

1982c
"Religion and reason in the Japanese experience" in: *King's Theological Review* 5 (1): 14–17.

1983
"The significance of the Japanese intellectual tradition for the history of religions" in: Slater, Peter and Wiebe, Donald (eds.) *Traditions in Contact and Change, Selected Proceedings of the Fourteenth Congress of the International Association for the History of Religions.* Waterloo Ontario (Wilfrid Laurier): 565–77.

1984
"Tominaga Nakamoto (1715–1746) and Religious Pluralism" in: Daniels, Gordon (ed.) *Europe Interprets Japan* (select proceedings of the den Haag conference of the European Association for Japanese Studies 1982). Tenterden (Paul Norbury): 191–7.

1986
"National and international identity in a Japanese religion: Byakkōshinkōkai" in: Hayes, Victor. C. (ed.) *Identity Issues and World Religions, Selected Proceedings of the International Association for the History of Religions*, Netley Australia (The Australian Association for the Study of Religions): 234–241.

1987a
O-meguri, Pilgerfahrt in Japan. Katalog einer Ausstellung. Marburg (Universitätsbibliothek der Philipps-Universität Marburg).

1987b
"A common language of minimal religiosity" in: *The Journal of Oriental Studies* 26 (1): 21–7.

1988
"Nationale und internationale Identität in einer japanischen Religion" (Byakkō Shinkōkai) " in: Zinser, Hartmut (ed.) *Religionswissenschaft. Eine Einführung.* Berlin (Dietrich Reimer): 239–251. (German translation of Pye 1986.)

1989a
(ed.) *Marburg Revisited. Institutions and Strategies in the Study of Religion.* Marburg (Diagonal-Verlag).

1989b
"Cultural and organizational perspectives in the study of religion" in: Pye, Michael (ed.) *Marburg Revisited. Institutions and Strategies in the Study of Religion.* Marburg (Diagonal-Verlag): 11–17.

1989c
"Shintō and the typo1ogy of religion" in: *Method & Theory in the Study of Religion* 1/2: 186–95. (Summary version 1984 as "The place of Shintō in the typology of religion" in: Yamamoto, Y. (ed.) *Proceedings of the Thirty-first International Congress of Human Sciences in Asia and North Africa.* Tokyo) Institute of Eastern Culture): 1055–6.)

1990a
(trans.) *Emerging from Meditation (Tominaga Nakamoto).* London (Duckworth) and Honolulu (University of Hawaii Press).

1990b
"Philology and fieldwork in the study of Japanese religion" in: Tyloch, W. (ed.) *Studies on Religions in the Context of Social Sciences. Methodological and Theoretical Relations*, Warsaw (Polish Society for the Study of Religions/Polskie Towarzystwo Religioznawcze): 146–59.

1990c
"Skilful means and the interpretation of Christianity" in: *Buddhist-Christian Studies* 10: 17–22.

1991a
"Religious tradition and the student of religion" in: Geertz, A. W. and Jensen, J. S. (eds.) *Religion, Tradition and Renewal.* Aarhus (Aarhus University Press): 29–36.

1991b
"Religious studies in Europe: structures and desiderata" in: Klaus K. Klostermaier and Larry W. Hurtado (eds.), *Religious Studies: Issues, Prospects, and Proposals* (University of Manitoba Studies in Religion, 2). Atlanta (Scholars Press): 39–55.

1991c
"Reflections on the treatment of tradition in comparative perspective, with special reference to Ernst Troeltsch and Gerardus van der Leeuw" in Kippenberg, Hans G. and Luchesi, Brigitte (eds.) *Religionswissenschaft und Kulturkritik.* Marburg (Diagonal-Verlag):101–111.

1992a
"An Asian starting point for the study of religion" in: Nowaczyk M.

and Stachowski, Z. (eds.) *Language,Religion, Culture: In Memory of Professor Witold Tyloch.* Warsaw (Polish Society for the Study of Religion) 27–35.

1992b

"An Asian starting point for the study of religion" in: Despland, Michel and Vallée, Gérard 1992. *Religion in History. The Word, the Idea, the Reality / La religion dans l'histoire. Le mot, l'idée, la réalité:* 101–9.

1993

Syncretism versus Synthesis. (*Occasional papers of the British Association for the Study of Religion No. 8*). Cardiff (BASR). Republished in: *Method &Theory in the Study of Religion*, 6 (3) (1994): 217–29.

1994a

"What is 'religion' in East Asia?" in: Bianchi, Ugo, Mora Fabio and Bianchi Lorenzo (eds.) *The Notion of "Religion" in Comparative Research: Selected Proceedings of the XVIth Congress of the International Association for the History of Religions, Rome, 3rd-8th September, 1990.* Rome ("L'Erma" di Bretschneider): 115–22.

1994b

"Religion: shape and shadow" in: *Numen. International Review for the History of Religions* 41 (1): 51–75.

1994c

"Syncretism versus synthesis" in: *Method & Theory in the Study of Religion*, 6 (3): 217–29. (Previously published in *Occasional papers of the British Association for the Study of Religion*, Cardiff 1993.)

1994d

Christian churches and political change in Eastern Europe" in: Gill, Sean, D'Costa Gavin and King, Ursula (eds.) *Religion in Europe, Contemporary Perspectives.* Kampen (Pharaos): 188–200.

1994e

(ed.) *The Macmillan Dictionary of Religion.* London (Macmillan) and as *The Continuum Dictionary of Religion*, New York (Continuum).

1995a

"Religion and identity: clues and threads" in: de Gruchy, J. W. and Martin, S. (eds.), *Religion and the Reconstruction of Civil Society (Papers from the founding congress of the South African Academy of Religion, January 1994).* Pretoria (University of South Africa): 3–17.

1995b

"Three teachings (*sanjiao*) theory and modern reflection on religion" in: Dai Kangsheng, Zhang Xinying and Pye, Michael (eds.) 1995. *Religion and Modernisation in China, Proceedings of the Regional*

Conference of the International Association for the History of Religions held in Beijing, China, April 1992. Cambridge (Roots and Branches): 111–16. (Chinese translation as "Sanjiaolilun yu duizongjiaode xiandai fansi" in *Shijie Zongjiao Ziliao* (ISSN 1000–4505) (1992/4): 1–3.)

1996a

"Intercultural strategies and the International Association for the History of Religions" in: Platvoet, J. Cox, J. and Olupona, J. (eds.) *The Study of Religions in Africa. Past, Present and Prospects, Proceedings of the IAHR Regional Conference at Harare, Zimbabwe 1992.* Cambridge (Roots and Branches): 37–45.

1996b

"Aum Shinrikyō. Can Religious Studies cope?" in: *Religion* 26 (3): 261–73.

1996c

"Syncretism: Buddhism and Shintō on one island" in: Doležalová, Iva, Horyna, Břetislav and Papoušek, Dalibor (eds.) *Religions in Contact. Selected Proceedings of the Special IAHR Conference held in Brno, August 23–26, 1994*, Brno (Czech Society for the Study of Religions): 159–62.

1996d

"Reflecting on the plurality of religions" in: *World Faiths Encounter* 14: 3–11.

1996e

"Shintō, primal religion and international identity" in: *Marburg Journal of Religion* 1/1.: <http://www.uni-marburg.de/fb03/ivk/mjr/pdfs/1996/articles/shinto1996>.

1997a

"Reflecting on the plurality of religions (full text)" in: *Marburg Journal of Religion* 2: (virtual pages). (Also published in abbreviated form in *World Faiths Encounter* 14 (1996): 3–11.

1997b

"East Asian rationality in the exploration of religion" in: Martin, Luther J. and Jensen, Jeppe Sinding (eds.) *Rationality and the Study of Religion.* Aarhus (Aarhus University): 65–77.

1997c

"Perceptions of the body in Japanese religion" in: Coakley, Sarah (ed.) *Religion and the Body.* Cambridge (Cambridge University Press): 248–261.

1997d
"Friedrich Heiler (1892–1967)" in: Michaels, A. (ed.) *Klassiker der Religionswissenschaft. Von Friedrich Schleiermacher bis Mircea Eliade.* München (Beck): 277–289 and (footnotes) 399–400.

1998a
"Die 'geschickten Mittel'. Zur Dialektik der Ausdrucksformen in Buddhismus und Christentum" in: Viertel, Matthias (ed.) *Buddhismus und Christentum.* Hofgeismar (Evangelische Akademie Hofgeismar): 41–64.

1998b
"Innovation und Modernität im Won-Buddhismus" in: Keil, S., Jetzkowitz, J. and König, M. (eds.) 1998. *Modernisierung und Religion in Südkorea*, Köln (Weltforum Verlag):183–94.

1999a
"Methodological Integration in the Study of Religions" in: Tore Ahlbäck (ed.) *Approaching Religion, Scripta Instituti Donneriani Aboensis XVII (1)*, Åbo/Turku, Finland (Donner Institute for Research in Religious and Cultural History): 188–205.

1999b
"Soteriological orientations in religion" in: Tenri Organizing Committee of Tenrikyo- Christian Dialogue (eds), *Tenrikyo-Christian Dialogue*, Tenri City (Tenri University Press): 99–113.

2000a
"Westernism unmasked" in: Jensen,Tim and Rothstein, Mikael (eds.) *Secular Theories on Religion. Current Perspectives.* Copenhagen (Museum Tusculanum Press), 211–230.

2000b
"Participation, observation and reflection: an endless method" in: Holm, Nils G. et al. eds. *Ethnography is a Heavy Rite. Studies of Comparative Religion in Honor of Juha Pentikäinen* (Religionsvetenskapliga skrifter 47). Åbo (Åbo Akademis Tryckeri) 2000: 64–79.

2001a
"Religion und Recht in Japan: Pluralismus, Toleranz und Konkurrenz" in: *Marburg Journal of Religion Vol. 6 No.1* (2001): <http://www.uni-marburg.de/religionswissenschaft/journal/mjr/pye.html>

2001b
"The study of religions and the dialogue of religions (Shūkyōgaku to shūkyōtaiwa)" in: *Marburg Journal of Religion* 6 (2): < http://web.uni-marburg.de/religionswissenschaft/journal/mjr>

2001c

"Political correctness in the study of religions: Is the Cold War really over?" in: Doležalová, Iva, Martin, Luther H. and Papoušek, Dalibor (eds.) 2001. *The Academic Study of Religion during the Cold War: East and West.* Frankfurt and New York (Peter Lang): 313–33.

2002a

"Memes and models in the study of religions" in: Giulia Sfameni Gasparro (ed.) *Themes and Problems in the History of Religions in Contemporary Europe. Proceedings of the International Seminar, Messina, March 30–3, 2001.* Cosenza (Edizioni Lionello Giordano), 245–59.

2002b

"Traces of Shinran Shōnin" in: Thierfelder, Constanze and Eibach, Dietrich Hannes (eds.), *Resonanzen. Schwingungsräume Praktischer Theologie (Gerhard Marcel Martin zum 60. Geburtstag)*, Stuttgart (Kohlhammer): 215–24.

2002c

"Won Buddhism as a Korean new religion" in: *Numen. International Review for the History of Religions* 49 (2): 113–41.

2002d

"Religion et conflit au Japon. Concernant surtout le Shinto et le Sanctuaire de Yasukuni" in: *Diogène* 199: 52–70.

2002e

" Modern Japan and the science of religions" in: Wiegers, Gerard A. and Platvoet, Jan G. (eds.) *Modern Societies and the Study of Religions. Studies in Honour of Lammert Leertouwer.* Leiden (Brill): 350–376.

2003a

"Religion and conflict in Japan, with special reference to Shinto and Yasukuni Shrine" in: Diogenes 50 (3): 45–59. (English version of Pye 2002.)

2003b

"Overcoming westernism: the end of orientalism and occidentalism" in: Schalk, Peter et al. (eds.) *Religion im Spiegelkabinett. Asiatische Religionsgeschichte im Spannungsfeld zwischen Orientalismus und Okzidentalismus (Acta Universitatis Upsaliensis. Historia Religionum 22).* Uppsala (Uppsala Universitet): 91–114.

2003c

Rationality, ritual and life-shaping decisions in modern Japan (Occasional Papers 29). Marburg (Centre for Japanese Studies). Republished in Raud, Rein (ed.) 2007. *Japan and Asian Modernities*, London (Kegan Paul): 1–27.

2003d
"Modern Japan and the science of religions" in: *Method and Theory in the Study of Religions* 15/1 (2003): 1–27. (Previously agreed publication of 2002e.)

2004a
The structure of religious systems in contemporary Japan: Shintō variations on Buddhist pilgrimage. (Occasional Papers 30). Marburg (Centre for Japanese Studies).

2004b
"Zur Legitimation, Struktur und Durchführung von interreligiösem Dialog" in: Barth et al. 2004: 13–20.

2004c
"Shinran als mystischer religiöser Denker" in: Schönemann, Friederike and Maaßen, Thorsten (eds) *Prüft Alles, und das Gute behaltet! Zum Wechselspiel von Kirchen, Religionen und säkularer Welt. Festschrift für Hans-Martin Barth zum 65. Geburtstag.* Frankfurt am Main (Otto Lembeck): 309–35. (Translated from the English of 2001 by Gerhard Marcel Martin.)

2006a
"Models of religious diversity: simplicities and complexities" in: Franke, Edith, Mas'ud, Abdurrahman, Pye, Michael and Wasim, Alef Theria (eds.) *Religious Harmony: Problems, Practice and Education. Proceedings of the Regional Conference of the International Association for the History of Religions, Yogyakarta and Semarang, Indonesia, September 27th – October 3rd, 2004.* Berlin (de Gruyter): 23–33.

2006b
"Die 'Drei Lehren' und das Tauziehen der Religionen in chinesischen Tempeln Südostasiens" in: Franke, Edith and Pye, Michael (eds.) *Religionen Nebeneinander. Modelle religiöser Vielfalt in Ost- und Südostasien.* Münster (Lit-Verlag): 41–60.

2006c
"Difference and coherence in the worldwide study of religions" in: Jakelic, Slavica and Pearson, Lori (eds), *The Future of the Study of Religion,* Boston and Leiden (Brill) 2006: 77–95.

2007
"Research on prayer in the contemporary study of religions" in: Hashimoto, Taketo (ed.) *Prayer as Interaction. (Tenri University and Marburg University Joint Research Project September 2006).* Tenri (Tenri University Press) 2007, 3–28.

2009a
"Nossa Senhora Aparecida and Solo Sagrado: creating sacred space in Brazil" in: Court, Jürgen and Klöcker, Michael (eds.) *Wege und Welten der Religionen. Forschungen und Vermittlungen. Festschrift für Udo Tworuschka* .Frankfurt am Main (Lembeck): 457–62.

2009b
"Ephemera in Japanese religion with special reference to Buddhist pilgrimage" in: Baskind, James (ed.) *Scholars of Buddhism in Japan: Buddhist Studies in the 21st Century. The Ninth Annual Symposium for Scholars Resident in Japan*, Kyōto (International Research Center for Japanese Studies) 2009: 67–78.

2009c
"Leading patterns in everyday Japanese religion" in: *Sphinx, Yearbook 2008–9* (Societas Scientiarum Fennica): 45–53.

2010
"'Polytheism' and 'monotheism' as a problem in the typology of religions" in: Charles Guittard (ed), *Le Monothéisme: Diversité, Exclusivisme ou Dialogue. (Actes de l'Association Européenne pur l'Étude des Religions (EASR) Congrès de Paris, 11–14 Septembre 2002)* Paris (Editions Non Lieu): 25–32.

2011a
"O Estudo das Religiões: novos tempos, tarefas e opções" in: da Cruz, Eduardo and De Mori, Geraldo (eds.) 2011. Teologia e Ciências da Religião. A Caminho da Maioridade Acadêmica. São Paulo (Ed. Paulinas): 15–24.

2011b (ed.)
Beyond Meditation. Expressions of Shin Buddhist Spirituality (Eastern Buddhist Voices 1). London (Equinox Publications).

2011c
"Refletindo sobre Primos Distantes. Distância cultural na transplantação de religiões japonesas em países distantes," *Rever* 11/2 July/ December : 11–31.

2012 (ed.)
Listening to Shin Buddhism. Starting Points of Modern Dialogue (Eastern Buddhist Voices 2). London (Equinox Publications).

Jointly Authored or Edited Writings (Alphabetical Order of the First Name Recorded)

Barth, Minoura and Pye 2000a:
Barth, Hans-Martin, Minoura, Eryō, and Pye, Michael (eds.) *Buddhismus und Christentum. Jōdo Shinshū und Evangelische Theologie. III. Internationales Rudolf-Otto Symposion am Fachbereich Evangelische Theologie der Philipps-Universität Marburg in Zusammenarbeit mit der Ōtani-Universität Kyōto.* Hamburg (EB-Verlag).

Barth, Minoura and Pye 2000b:
Bukkyō to kirisutokyō no taiwa. Jōdo Shinshū to fukuinshugishingaku. Kyōto (Hōzōkan). (Japanese edition of 2000a, Barth et al.)

Barth, Kadowaki, Minoura and Pye 2004a:
Barth, Hans-Martin, Kadowaki Ken, Minoura Eryō and Michael Pye (eds.). *Buddhismus und Christentum vor der Herausforderung der Säkularisierung.* Hamburg (EB-Verlag).

Barth, Kadowaki, Minoura and Pye 2004b:
Barth, Hans-Martin, Kadowaki Ken, Minoura Eryō and Michael Pye (eds.). *Bukkyō to kirisutokyō no taiwa III: Sezokuka kara no chōsen ni shokumen suru bukkyō to kirisutokyō.* Kyōto (Hōzōkan). Japanese edition of Barth et al. 2004a.)

Dai, Zhang and Pye 1995:
Dai, Kangsheng, Zhang,Xinying and Pye, Michael (eds.) *Religion and Modernization in China. Proceedings of the International Association for the History of Religions held in Beijing, China, April 1992.* Cambridge (Roots and Branches). A number of contributions appeared in Chinese translation in the journal *Shijie Zongjiao Ziliao* 世界宗教资料 (1992).

Franke, Mas'ud, Pye and Wasim 2005a:
Franke, Edith, Mas'ud, Abdurrahman, Pye, Michael and Wasim, Alef Theria. *Religious Harmony: Problems, Practice and Education. Proceedings of the Regional Conference of the International Association for the History of Religions, Yogyakarta and Semarang, Indonesia, September 27th – October 3rd, 2004.* Yogyakarta (Oasis Publisher).

Franke, Mas'ud, Pye and Wasim 2005b:
Franke, Edith, Mas'ud, Abdurrahman, Pye, Michael and Wasim, Alef Theria. *Harmoni Kehidupan Beragama: Problem, Praktik dan Pendidikan. Proceeding Konferensi Regional International Association for the History of Religions, Yogyakarta dan Semarang, Indonesia, 27 September*

– *03 October, 2004*. Yogyakarta (Oasis Publisher). (Indonesian version of Franke et al. 2005a.)

Franke, Mas'ud, Pye and Wasim 2006:

Franke, Edith, Mas'ud, Abdurrahman, Pye, Michael and Wasim, Alef Theria (eds.) *Religious Harmony: Problems, Practice and Education. Proceedings of the Regional Conference of the International Association for the History of Religions, Yogyakarta and Semarang, Indonesia, September 27th – October 3rd, 2004*. (Religion and Reason 45). Berlin (de Gruyter). (Revised English edition of Franke et al. 2005.)

Franke and Pye 2004:

Franke, Edith and Pye, Michael. "Ilmu agama dan kontribusinya terhadap penyelesaian masalah dalam dunia yang plural / The study of religions and its contribution to problem solving in a plural world" in: *Marburg Journal of Religion* in 2004:http://www.uni-marburg.de/fb03/ivk/mjr/pdfs/2004/articles/franke-2004.pdf

Franke and Pye 2006:

Franke, Edith and Pye, Michael (eds.). *Religionen Nebeneinander. Modelle religiöser Vielfalt in Ost- und Südostasien*. Berlin and Münster (Lit-Verlag).

Hackett and Pye 2010:

Hackett, Rosalind and Pye, Michael (eds.) 2010. *IAHR Congress Proceedings (Durban 2000). The History of Religions: Origins and Visions*, Cambridge (Roots and Branches): 284–297. Note that this was a limited print-run distributed to major libraries across the world and is not commercially available: enquiries may be made to the serving Publications Officer of the IAHR.

Helve and Pye 2003:

Helve, Helena and Pye Michael 2003. "Theoretical correlations between world- view, civil religion, institutional religion and informal spiritualities" in: *Temenos* 37–8 (2001–2): 87–106.

Morgan and Pye 1977:

Morgan, Robert and Pye, Michael (eds. trans.) *Ernst Troeltsch: Writings on Theology and Religion* London (Duckworth) and Louisville Kentucky (Westminster/John Knox).

Pye, Miyashita and Minoura 2003:

Pye, Michael, Miyashita, Seishi and Minoura, Eryō 2003. *Bukkyō to kirisutokyō no taiwa II: Jōdo shinshū to fukuinshugi no shinkō. Hans-Martin Barth kyōju Gerhard Marcel Martin kyōju wo mukaete (Dialog zwischen Buddhismus und Christentum II, Jōdo Shinshū und Evangelischer*

Glaube: Mit Hans-Martin Barth und Gerhard Marcel Martin im Gespräch). Kyōto (Hōzōkan).

Pye and Morgan 1973:
Pye, Michael and Morgan, Robert (eds.) 1973. *The Cardinal Meaning. Essays in Comparative Hermeneutics: Buddhism and Christianity* (Religion and Reason 6). The Hague (Mouton).

Pye and Triplett 2007:
Pye, Michael and Triplett, Katja. *Streben nach Glück. Schicksalsdeutung und Lebensgestaltung in japanischen Religionen* (Mit Beiträgen von Monika Schrimpf) Berlin (LIT-Verlag).

Pye and Triplett 2011:
Pye, Michael and Triplett, Katja. *Pilgerfahrt visuell. Hängerollen in der religiösen Alltagspraxis Japans* (Veröffentlichungen der Religionskundlichen Sammlung 5), Marburg (Diagonal Verlag) 2011.

Wasim, Mas'ud, Franke and Pye 2005:
Wasim, Alef Theria, Mas'ud, Abdurrahman , Franke Edith and Pye, Michael (eds.) *Harmoni Kehidupan Beragama: Problem, Praktik dan Pendidikan. Proceeding Konferensi Regional International Association for the History of Religions, Yogyakarta dan Semarang, Indonesia, September 27th – Oktober 3rd, 2004*. Yogyakarta (Oasis Publishers). (Indonesian version of Franke et al. 2005.)

Consolidated Index to Volumes I and II

To reduce the scale of this index the following are not included: contents pages and other pre-pages, items in the list of author's publications cited, names of editors of composite works, publishers and places of publication, elements of duplicated bibliographical references, and so on. All such references will be found at the relevant bibliographical positions. Also omitted are a number of terms or names appearing incidentally, e.g. in quotations, but not in themselves germane to the wider argument; and on the other hand general words which occur very frequently indeed such as: culture, history, society, sociology, tradition and some of their cognates. Some general entries point to compact sections of text where specific cases will be found. Foreign words with obvious English equivalents are often indexed under the latter, e.g. fenomenologia under phenomenology, Modernität under modernity. Diacritical marks are not used in this index if, for any reason, they do not occur in the main text; the index should therefore *not* be regarded as a conclusive guide to diacritical marks.

www.ingramcontent.com/pod-product-compliance
Lightning Source LLC
LaVergne TN
LVHW020505100826
845148LV00003B/701